Shitty Breaks

Also by Ben Aitken

Dear Bill Bryson: Footnotes from a Small Island
A Chip Shop in Poznan: My Unlikely Year in Poland
The Gran Tour: Travels with My Elders
The Marmalade Diaries: The True Story of an Odd Couple
Here Comes the Fun: A Journey into the Serious Business of Having a Laugh

Shitty Breaks

A CELEBRATION OF UNSUNG CITIES

BEN AITKEN

Published in the UK and USA in 2025 by
Icon Books Ltd, Omnibus Business Centre,
39–41 North Road, London N7 9DP
email: info@iconbooks.com
www.iconbooks.com

ISBN: 978-183773-046-9
eBook: 978-183773-047-6

Text copyright © 2025 Ben Aitken

The author has asserted his moral rights.

This is a work of nonfiction, but the names and some identifying details of characters
have been changed throughout to respect the privacy of the individuals concerned.

Every effort has been made to contact the copyright holders of the material reproduced in this book. If any have been inadvertently overlooked, the publisher will be
pleased to make acknowledgement on future editions if notified.

No part of this book may be reproduced in any form, or by any
means, without prior permission in writing from the publisher.

Typeset in Baskerville MT by SJmagic DESIGN SERVICES, India.

Printed in the UK.

Appointed GPSR EU Representative:
Easy Access System Europe Oü, 16879218
Address: Mustamäe tee 50, 10621, Tallinn, Estonia
Contact Details: gpsr.requests@easproject.com, +358 40 500 3575

For all things unsung. (Including Leslie from Norwich.)

Contents

	Preamble	ix
1	Sunderland: I could have been in LA	1
2	Chelmsford: Three pies, three mash, and lots of chilli vinegar	29
3	Preston: Nothing is either good or bad but thinking makes it so	49
4	Wolverhampton: The best thing since avocado	71
5	Wrexham: Too much love can kill a place	93
6	Limerick: A chicken fillet roll from the SPAR near his mammie's house	113
7	Newry: The kind of landscape that makes you think twice	135
8	Milton Keynes: Radical Optimism	153
9	Bradford: A pair of alpacas called Blur and Oasis	175
10	Newport: You knows it	199
11	Gibraltar: Very strange but very nice	225
12	Dunfermline: The somewhat loveliness of anything and anywhere	249
	Acknowledgements	275

Preamble

From a young age I've always done two things – barked up the wrong tree and backed the underdog. As a kid, I demanded to be bathed in the kitchen sink. I insisted on odd socks and preferred the company of pensioners to the company of my classmates, the latter seeming to me – and I had a good view – to be a few sandwiches short of a picnic. I got into S Club 7 when they were going out of fashion; moved to Poland when the reverse journey was trending; and subscribed to *The Oldie* at the age of 32. In light of the above, becoming a cheerleader for the likes of Wolverhampton and Preston was perhaps always on the cards.

But what prompted such behaviour? The contrary streak? The wrong trees? The underdogs? It wasn't an intellectual stance, that's for sure. Nor was it a moral position. And I didn't think it made me cool either. Then why? At risk of sounding dramatic, I got bullied a fair bit at school. I was never in a headlock for more than five minutes, and it was never about my race or my faith or where I grew up. Instead it was about my weight, the fact that I got free school dinners, and the fact that I wore corduroy flares on a mufti day once. In any case, all the while this bullying was happening, I remained fairly confident that it wasn't entirely deserved. For at the same time as I was getting it in the neck, I was also clocking an assortment of wallies and plonkers winning all the attention and esteem and plaudits and prizes and status and popularity and so on. While you couldn't have called me especially insightful back then, it was nonetheless clear to me that life wasn't straightforwardly meritocratic. I'm not saying I was an absolute legend and the popular kids were all scumbags and worthless. Not at all. We were all just kids growing up, with braces or glasses or acne or whatnot, and yet, by some peculiar matrix, some were being vaunted and admired and gushed over and fawned upon, while others were being punched and ignored and disregarded and sat upon. That's what got me. That's what interested me. That's what *stayed with me.* That's what made me, twenty years later, head to Sunderland for a holiday in October.

I don't bring up my experience of being on the wrong end of the status quo to win sympathy or curry favour. I bring it up simply because it was *telling.* It told me that not everything that glitters is gold, that cream isn't alone in being able to rise to the top (crap can manage it too), and that popularity is by no means a reliable indicator of quality. All of these lessons, incidentally, were later confirmed when, in 2003, *Love Actually* was a massive hit at the box office. From that day on, I knew for certain that the system couldn't be trusted. And from that day on, I had an irresistible soft spot for the wrong direction, for the film that tanked, for the actor getting no work, for all the stuff I wasn't being asked to look at or listen to or value or patronise – like Milton Keynes, for example.

It's worth saying at this juncture that a thing being unfavoured or unsung or entirely ignored is no guarantee that it will issue a pleasant or meaningful encounter. The biggest lemon I've ever met was an historically overlooked fisherman from Grimsby. Nonetheless, it seems to me that there's something inherently pleasing and important about heading in the wrong direction, about heading outside the box, about looking beyond the pale, in search of joy and beauty and fascination and so on. The world we live in is forever trying to sell us dummies or pull the wool over our eyes, and so doing to render us blind and insensitive to all sorts of wonderful things. More fool us if we keep adoring the emperor's new clothes – and busting a gut to do so – when there's so much low-hanging fruit elsewhere, going unpicked, unsampled, unloved. It's too early for banging drums so I'll just say this: things in the shade are often most brilliant.

It'll be clear by now that the aim of this book was to visit (and hopefully celebrate) less popular cities. But how did I decide where to go? Well, I didn't follow a hunch. Instead, my route was driven by data. In a burst of professionalism that was frankly out of character, I contacted some tourism boards and got hold of some stats, which told me where people were willingly going for a weekend away. When I got hold of that league table, and saw Edinburgh near the top and Leeds in midtable and Portsmouth flirting with danger just above the drop zone, I turned it upside down and went from there. The twelve cities that feature in the pages to come are some of the least visited in the UK and Ireland (or were in 2019 at least).[1] I visited them in good faith, with an open mind, and on my own dime. My goal wasn't to take the piss or stick the boot in, but rather to seek out their assets and virtues. In those instances when neither asset nor virtue were

---

[1] This isn't necessarily true of Gibraltar, but I went there anyway. Author's prerogative.

forthcoming, I just sat on a bench, ate two sausage rolls from Greggs, and daydreamed about Rome and Vienna.

I don't mind offering a gentle spoiler here. *I had a flipping good time.* I may well be easily pleased (my idea of a peak experience is finding out you've got ten minutes more than you thought you did), but still, every single one of the trips I took proved nourishing and enjoyable and full of surprises. Grayson Perry popped up in Chelmsford. I ran into Hockney in Bradford. Beyoncé made an appearance in Sunderland. Epic history reared its head in Preston. Limerick proved the match of Dublin, while the Northern Irish city of Newry delivered a five-star treehouse. Every city left its mark, made its case, put a decent foot forward. And by doing so each city made a slight mockery of the league table, which has them down as more or less pointless. Don't get me wrong, the destinations weren't faultless. Some of the places I visited were definitely easier to enjoy than others, and posed tricky social, cultural and political questions that couldn't, in good conscience, be shied away from. But on the whole, and for the most part, and with the caveat that one person's cup of tea is another's idea of hell, my shitty breaks were nothing of the sort. Off we go.

1

Sunderland

I could have been in LA

I didn't so much arrive in Sunderland as wake up in it. My train got in late, you see, and when I emerged from the station it was raining old ladies and sticks (as they say in Welsh), so I blew a fiver getting cabbed the three miles along the coast up to my digs, The Seaburn Inn, where I fell asleep cradling a cup of tea and watching the first episode of *Dinnerladies*, which I had wrongly supposed to be set hereabouts.

It wasn't until the next morning, when I drew the curtains and stepped out onto the balcony, that I got what I was looking for – an eyeful of Sunderland. I was confronted with a massive outdoor swimming pool (known as the North Sea) and a sizable stretch of sandy coastline. People were jogging, lots of them, and one couple was even rollerblading while holding hands. I could have been in LA. I confess it came as a bit of a shock. A gob-smacking beach wasn't something I associated with Sunderland. I took a deep breath – the prelude to action – and it smelt of bacon, umpteen rashers of said, their collective waft having escaped a beachside kiosk and drifted invitingly towards me.

Ah, Sunderland. Queen of Northumbria, cradle of Alice in Wonderland, former shipbuilding heavyweight ... but also routinely denigrated, reflexively shunned, automatically pooh-poohed – and not only by Geordies, that well-meaning tribe who reside ten miles up the coast in a big village called Newcastle. Although by no means a perfect metric, a recent International Passenger Survey revealed that Sunderland was just about the least likely place a passenger arriving in the UK would be heading to. The only places less likely were Douglas and Ayr. In the 850-page Lonely Planet guide to England, meanwhile, Sunderland isn't mentioned at all – ouch. When I told the lady running the café on the train that I was going on holiday to Sunderland, she stopped what she was doing and asked me two things: 1) was I right in the head, and 2) would I pop into the bookies on Station Street to make sure her mother wasn't in there? I think it's fair to deduce that, at the time of my visit, Sunderland wasn't at the top of many bucket lists.

Nonetheless, up on my balcony, surveying the scene, weighing up the sea, I felt unreasonably excited. It felt good to be abroad, and unmoored, and carefree, and clueless, with nothing more pressing ahead than a stroll and a butcher's, my ordinary responsibilities hundreds of miles away, minding their own business. Item number one on my agenda: a clueless mooch.

My hotel was enwrapped by Lowry Road. This didn't take me by surprise – I knew that the painter was fond of this spot. He would come across from Lancashire, from the other side of the Pennines, for a change of scene, for a new shade of grey. Sunderland became a bit of a bolthole for L.S. Lowry; a place where he could escape the pressures of his escalating success. Lowry saw something in Sunderland, something that others didn't, something worth capturing, something worth getting down. He stayed in the same room at the same hotel on each of his visits, and according to the bloke that served him dinner each evening, Lowry never deviated from a menu of cold roast beef, chips, gravy, orange juice, sliced banana, fresh cream, and coffee. The artist clearly knew a good thing when he saw one.

To work up an appetite for such a feast, Lowry would walk south along the promenade, down to the river and the shipyards (of which there were hundreds), where he'd watch all the workers spilling out, heading for home, dashing for the tram or the bus, pulling their collars up against a crisp northeasterly and thanking their lucky stars it was that time of day again. My dad used to work in the shipyard at Portsmouth. He said that come knocking-off time, thousands of men could be seen streaming out of the shipyard's gate on bicycles. My dad didn't think anything of it – it was too normal to be interesting – but Lowry obviously did. As chance would have it, Lowry spotted a young girl sketching the workers once, as they spilled and headed, and dashed and pulled, and he made a point of saying: 'Nee lass, that's not how you do it; that's not how you do men in a hurry; give it 'ere.'

To my mind, Lowry distinguished himself as a painter by shining light where it wasn't customarily shone; by highlighting shady spots and overshadowed slices of life and showing them to be beautiful – if only in a quiet way, a humble way, an accidental way. As I stood on the promenade, facing the sea, polishing off my morning bap (or is it a cob around here?), it wasn't hard to see why Lowry held this bit of the world in such high regard. I'm not much of an aesthete, but it seemed to me that the palette was a winner: the steely sea and sky above roughly golden sand. Lowry's 1966 painting *The North Sea* – a large seascape that captures exactly this palette – went for a million quid not long ago. Just think how much sliced banana and cream he could've got for that. Interestingly, I'm told there's one of Lowry's paintings

Sunderland

in the Morrisons supermarket just along from my hotel, hanging proudly, and mostly ignored, above the hot sausage rolls. There's something fitting, and lovely, and very Sunderland about that. At least I think there is.

Also lovely was the pair of chaps in front of me now, who were painting the railing that runs the length of the promenade, rolling black over green. On the face of it, one was getting paid by the hour and the other by the job. The former was being fabulously creative in finding ways not to crack on. They had one of those industrial-sized radios, the type that could survive a nuclear disaster. It was playing The Beautiful South.

Just along from the painters, a woman was walking her dog on the beach. She was on the phone and playing fetch at once – you know, getting things done, being proactive – but then somehow got her wires crossed and instead of chucking the tennis ball threw her phone. I enjoyed the woman's reaction to her mistake, which was dramatic and panicked and instinctive at first, but then muted and measured, as if trying to give the impression that she did this sort of thing all the time. Saving face, I guess. I had a good view of the balls up, for the land had climbed by this point, up to Roker Cliff Park, which offers a decent vantage point. The elevation belittled the beach, squashed the sea, conjured a new frame entirely, as contours are wont to do. It suits me fine when the lie of the land is all over the show.

The park is dominated by a lighthouse. I gleaned from an info panel that said lighthouse had recently upped sticks; that it used to be down there by the harbour, rather than up here not by the harbour. I like the idea that lighthouses can move, that their lanterns can shift, that the focus and scope of their light can alter. It bodes well for places in the dark. They call this coastal stretch the Roker Riviera, I'm told, with Roker being this part of Sunderland, and Riviera being something else entirely. It's a tongue-in-cheek appellation, but it holds up under scrutiny (just). The three-mile stretch is no one-trick pony: it's got flat stretches, rocky outcrops, sheer drops, idiosyncratic geology. The pier down at this end of things, Roker Pier, is an accidental beauty. Its graceful brick curve was, of course, a purposeful construction – to enclose, to shelter – but there's no doubt that beauty was a byproduct of its overarching intent. A beauty in the making, if you will.

The pier was finished in 1903, having been designed by Henry Hay Wake, who oversaw its construction from a nice semi-detached gaff up on the cliff. I fancy Henry headed down periodically, to say to some bricky or another, 'Nee lad, that's not how you build a pier in a hurry!' There's a little plaque outside Henry's old house, giving away his deed. I love such plaques, such small displays of public affection, such quiet calls for attention, for an engineer or a poet, or a pair of local sisters who smuggled 29 Jewish families out of Germany and Austria in the 1930s (that one's on Croft Avenue, near a pub called Chesters), though I do fancy that such plaques could be a bit more down-to-earth sometimes, remembering an Alan who stubbed his toe on this spot in an otherwise unremarkable decade, or a Shelia who had eleven children at this address, not one of them thanking her for it. If only for a giggle, you understand, to lighten the mood of those going about town, and to show that all sorts go into the making of a place. I reckon plenty of local treasure would be uncovered. Tall orders and small miracles, feats of courage and genius and kindness by everyday folk, to complement the do-gooding of the illustrious.

One thing that could be remembered hereabouts is the time the current captain of Sunderland AFC saved a labrador from drowning. I was told the story by a fella turning an old tram shelter into a café, just along from the pier. I asked him for the time initially, as a way into some chitchat, but he said he didn't know because his phone was in the van. Then I told him I was on holiday, and in thanks he told me that the Sunderland captain saved a labrador from drowning just over there, saw it struggling in the surf then stripped off and did a proper *Baywatch* job. Apparently the Sunderland supporters now sing about the episode when they concede a goal and have nothing else to be happy about. There's a lighthouse at the end of Henry's pier, for the record, and unlike the one up the road, this one is wearing a Sunderland strip – red and white stripes. There must have been a few times when, short of bright ideas, and losing 3–1 at home, the Mackem fans would have happily seen the lighthouse relocated and stuck up front.[2]

At this end of the promenade, down by the mouth of the Wear, the railing's fresh black paint, I couldn't help but notice, was starting to flake. The green was already coming through again. Which means that as soon as that duo in the overalls were finished up at the northern end, they'd be back down here to start all over again. They had a job for life. I'd love to see a Lowry painting of those two, eternally applying a fresh lick of paint, for no better reason than to make the experience of walking Sunderland's prom that little bit nicer. A proper pair of Mackems.[3]

I continued past the North Dock and picked up the north bank of the river. It was fairly quiet, tranquil even, but that's a new thing, because for hundreds of years this part of Sunderland

---

[2] The locals are called Mackems, by the way, because, historically speaking, they were in the habit of making stuff – ships, principally. I'm also told that not everyone approves of the demonym, preferring 'Wearsider', so I'll use both interchangeably going forward, in order to aggravate everyone equally.

[3] I later learned that both of these men were from Leicester.

would have been hectic with effort and toil, enterprise and endeavour. Shipbuilding was Sunderland's *thing* – from wood through iron to steel – and its associated industries – rope, masts, blocks, sails – added further ballast to the local economy. By the early twentieth century, Sunderland's shipbuilding was second to none, with scores of yards knocking out hulls and decking and rigging and rivets, left, right and centre. But, as sure as eggs is eggs, things changed. The inter-war depression, plus foreign competition, sent the UK's shipbuilding industry into a gradual decline, which had a devastating social impact in Sunderland. And it wasn't just shipbuilding that was floundering. The local coal trade was going up in smoke, too, with Sunderland's last pit closing in 1993. If the Japanese car manufacturer Nissan hadn't pitched up in the 1980s, and enlisted thousands to start putting together Bluebirds, the mood locally might have soured to the point of rebellion, and a march on London – like the one from Jarrow in 1926 – would have been a distinct possibility. Make no mistake, Lowry would have had much to sketch down on the banks of the Wear, not all of it bonny.

Another of Sunderland's old industries that waxed and waned and eventually disappeared was glass. The city was well placed to knock out windows. Trading ships, having dumped their loads in Europe, would return carrying the perfect sand as ballast, which, along with local limestone and coal, facilitated the glassmaking industry. I came to the National Glass Centre now. Opened in 1998, the centre is dedicated to promoting glass in all its forms. As diverting as trying to absorb hundreds of years of industrial history can be, it was the glassblowing demonstration that truly got me going. For about half an hour, I enjoyed the spectacle of a young blower (one of the uni students, though presumably not a fresher) turning a portion of molten glass into a vessel fit for tulips or pasta.

First the student (let's call them Tim) fished out a dollop of molten glass from a furnace that had been burning for years at over a thousand degrees. He then rolled this red-hot dollop across a bed of metal oxide crystals, as if dipping whipped ice-cream into crushed nuts (it is these crystals that give the glass colour). Tim then returned the nutty blob to the furnace until the crystals had been incorporated and the glass was once again malleable, at which point he injected some volume into his budding bowl or vase with a few puffs on his blower. He repeated this process a few times, the vivid orange balloon growing with each fresh bellow.

As impressive as all that was, it wasn't until Tim began shaping the scorching glass with his hand that I was persuaded of the man's brilliance. As his left hand spun the glass, his right hand, covered with a damp mitten made of the *Daily Telegraph*, shaped it. Now and again he would blow into his pipe or get up and start swinging the whole thing about like a lanky sabre (don't try this at home). Taken together – the blowing, the swinging, the spinning, the shaping – it was a somehow-musical thing of ambidextrous beauty. When the vase was reckoned done – its bottom sealed, its top curved just so – it was left to cool in the oven, which hardly sounds right but there you go.

It was a beguiling half-hour. Not just the sight of the glass-blowing, but the very fact of it also. I marvelled at what this one demonstration pointed to, what it contained, what it depended on. The millennia of gradual advance. The centuries of accumulated knack. The amount of trial and error. The volume of brilliance and endeavour required to push the technology on, to improve the gizmos, to refine the science – until it was at a point where a wee slip of a lad, with a bandaged arm and eyes that hinted at too many pints in The Peacock, could turn a cup of sand into a vase of flowers, in front of an audience of four and in a matter of minutes, by recourse to a range of ancient paddles and tweezers, jacks and puffers, and with the help of a steaming mitten made out of yesterday's news, as though there were truly nothing to it. I'll never look through a window the same way again. I raise my glass.

Around the corner from the National Glass Centre was St Peter's Church, which used to be an Anglo-Saxon monastery and seat of learning, and a rather important one, too. Said seat was sat on by none other than the Venerable Bede – who was a monk-scholar from the age of seven, if you'll credit that. Back in the late 600s, and while resident at St Peter's, Bede completed the pithily titled *Historia ecclesiastica gentis Anglorum* (The Ecclesiastical History of the English People), a feat which earned him the title 'The Father of English History', and made him, technically, somewhat responsible for such things as corned beef, Nigel Farage, and Gareth Southgate's penalty miss against Germany. Bede wasn't just into history, though. When he wasn't bowling around Monkwearmouth (as this part of Sunderland was then known), he was swatting up on this, that and the other. His scholarship covered a wide range of subjects, including astronomy, theology, science, music and language. If the Venerable Bede was on *Mastermind*, his specialist subject would have to be his own flipping brilliance.

'Venerable Bede. How clever are you?'

'Exceptionally.'

'Incorrect.'

'Uniquely?'

'Wrong.'

'Unconscionably?'

'Afraid not.'

'Fuck it, I pass.'

'You're off the chart clever.'

'Ah, yeah. That's right. Silly me.'

I spent a happy ten minutes exploring the church and its grounds. I was pleased to learn that bits of the original monastery remain intact, notably most of the west wall and the porch. The guy who had the church erected in the first place – one Benedict Biscop, a Northumbrian nobleman – spared no expense. He even had cutting-edge glassmakers over from France to do the windows. Sounds like the sort of bloke who'd want you to take your shoes off when you come in. Which isn't what the Vikings did, I'm afraid to report, when that mob shipped up a couple of hundred years later, full of goodwill and *hygge*. They didn't think much of St Peter's. Didn't care for the fancy illustrated bibles, or the nice windows. Torched the lot.

Arguably, though, it's less the building itself that is of interest here, and more what that building stood for – learning, knowledge, enlightenment. Along with the affiliated monastery at Jarrow, this place was essentially Oxford and Cambridge plus Harvard under one roof and on steroids. In short, what was done here was groundbreaking, was genuinely world-leading, and for the second time in an hour, I was forced to reckon with some big questions, about knowledge and existence and how slight and puny and pathetic my contribution to the human race is destined to be when compared to the pioneering people who rolled this whole circus forward; to reckon with the fact that, next to the likes of that lot, whose brain and brawn and bravery contributed to the betterment of mankind, I'm the sort that just watches them do it and scratches their head, or weighs up the fruits of their brilliance and toil and cunning and graft – a simple bowl, say – and can do nothing better in the face of it than pour in some Shreddies.

I came to Wearmouth Bridge, a good-looking green sweep, its appeal heightened by its purpose and point – to join, to connect, to overcome. When it was first built, back in 1796, it connected the two halves of the emerging town, and helped forge a shared identity, a kilometre zero from which Sunderland spoked and sprawled and sparked. Halfway across the bridge, I paused to read an embellished section of the railing. 'NIL DESPERANDUM AUSPICE DEO' was spelt out in wrought iron – none will be desperate under the guidance of God. Try sharing that sentiment with the umpteen who have called it a day here. Pinned to the D of 'DEO' was a handwritten note: 'You are worth more than you think.' Hear, hear.

It was about time I ate something, so I popped into Dickson's on the high street.

'Cheesy chips pie, please,' I said.

'Cheesy chips pie?'

'Yeah, someone told me about it.'

'Someone's having you on. You not from round here?'

'No, I'm on holiday.'

'I've just got back from holiday.'

'Oh yeah?'

'Went to Greece. Husband got arrested for driving a moped into a supermarket.'

'Crikey.'

'It's the ouzo.'

'I see.'

'No, I'm only kidding.'

'Ah.'

'He was as sober as a judge. Have you tried pease pudding?'

I hadn't, and then I had, and then I wished I hadn't. Yellow split peas, water, salt, spices – a soup that is left to cool and harden, then slapped into a bap as though it were the most natural thing in the world. Soup in a roll! When the lady asked if I'd ever had a saveloy dip, I said I wasn't that way inclined and scrammed.

Sunderland

I wandered around the centre for half an hour and reached the conclusion that you couldn't, with a straight face, call it conventionally good-looking. The city has known too much grief and strife for that to be the case; it's done too many days' hard work, and copped too many bombs, for it to be winning any beauty pageants. But a city is more than how it appears – much more. Just because a place is 90% neoclassical, doesn't mean you're going to have a laugh there, doesn't mean it's going to put a spring in your step. Besides, if it's buildings that get you going, then Sunderland's got the lot. Baroque. Gothic. Arts and Crafts. Modern. More Modern. Even More Modern. Detached piles, towering flats, terraces of one-storey redbrick cottages. And besides, value comes with scarcity, meaning the flashes of architectural splendour in Sunderland are better for being seldom.

I'd like to introduce you, at this stage, to something rather odd. The stottie. It's essentially a bread roll on an industrial scale – you'd need a tectonic plate to serve one on. I got my first look of a stottie in the window of a bakery in The Bridges shopping centre, and it held my attention for at least a minute. The lady working in the bakery spotted me eyeing up her massive baps and rightly called me in to discuss the matter. I shared my opinion that one of the reasons the local football team hasn't won a trophy since 1973 might be these rolls. She said I ought to invest in a pair.

'I'm a bit intimidated by their girth, to be honest.'

'Eeeeeee, you'll be fine.'

'You could ferry coal on these things down the Wear.'

'You can only get 'em round 'ere.'

'Yeah. I'm not surprised.'

'You not from round 'ere?'

'No, I'm on holiday.'

'Then take some home with yer. Yer family will be proud.'[4]

I know what you're thinking – it's about time he went skiing. And you're right. It was about time. So I took the 33 bus out to the big Sainsbury's in Silksworth, a couple of miles west of the city centre, then cut through the carpark and made my way towards the North East's premier ski facility – 160 metres of potential catastrophe.

The first thing that occurred to me on seeing the slope at close quarters was that there wasn't a flake of snow on the thing. They're taking the piste, I thought. The slope, I quickly learned, is basically an old slag heap that's been covered in a very abrasive material. There are some that lament the demise of British industry but if skiing is the result of post-industrialisation, then count me in. I paid my fifteen quid, got kitted out with boots and poles and gloves and helmet, proceeded to the foot of the slope in a fashion that couldn't be described as elegant, then returned to the main building because I'd forgotten my skis.

Finally good to go, I went nowhere at all – preferring to tarry at the bottom considering the task ahead of me. No matter which way I looked at it, the task was anything but appealing: the quality of some things can't be altered by perspective. It was the prospect of getting the button lift up to the top that bothered me most. I've been skiing half a dozen times, mostly when I lived in Poland where it was affordable, and I've always found getting up the slope more parlous than getting down it. Over the years, I've been able to refine my approach. I grab the pole, stick it between my legs, close my eyes and then hope for the best. The routine has only failed on two occasions, and I've come to believe that 'grab, stick, close and hope' is a mantra that can be profitably applied to other areas of life. On this occasion, things went

---

[4] I did and they weren't.

Sunderland

quite well, until the pole yanked of a sudden and the button all but disappeared up my arse, causing my composure to plummet and my skis to squirt off in opposing directions, one towards Durham and the other towards Glasgow.

I hesitated at the top – but only because of the view, you understand. I could see a fair bit: the tall towers of downtown Sunderland, the long, winding Wear, the nascent ascent of a supermoon, and the outline of Hilton Castle, which is said to be haunted by the ghost of a lad who was murdered after trying it on with Baron Hilton's daughter. Whether this was last year or many moons ago, I can't say.

Another thing I could see from the summit was the Penshaw Monument, a Victorian folly based on a Greek temple that sits proud and daft atop Penshaw Hill. The folly is topless and listed and cut from a type of sandstone that started bright but has darkened with time, a progression many of us can relate to. At the bottom of Penshaw Hill – if I looked very hard and fantasised wildly – I could just about make out the fabled Lambton Worm. That's a local legend and a half. In short, a lad goes fishing, catches a worm, tosses it in a well, and then sods off on a crusade. In the lad's absence, the worm grows to a monstrous extent and then starts eating the local sheep and children. When the lad comes home from the crusade, and sees the havoc being wreaked by the giant worm, he does what all heroes would do in the same situation, which is to consult a woman from Durham, who says that the lad must 1) kill the worm in the River Wear, and then 2) kill the first living thing he encounters after doing the deed. If he doesn't do the second bit (the woman from Durham is at pains to stress), the lad's family will be forever cursed.

The lad and his dad hatch a plan: when the lad has killed the worm he will sound his horn, at which point the dad will release the family pet, Bruno, a French Bulldog who presumably consented to playing the role of sacrificial lamb. On paper it's the perfect plan, but unfortunately something goes wrong during its execution, i.e. upon hearing the horn, instead of releasing the dog, the dad legs it down to the river to congratulate his son, who's like, 'Fuck's sake, Dad'. The dad says, 'Ah, shit', runs back to get the dog, but of course it's too late and the family is cursed. And that's pretty much it. There are other versions of the story, but to be honest they're a bit far-fetched by comparison. I'm pleased (and amazed) to report that an opera was written about the legend. *The Lambton Worm* (1978) was conceived by the composer Robert Sherlaw Johnson, with a libretto by the poet Anne Ridler.

When I finally took the plunge and began my descent down the bristly honeycomb, I skied like a wobbly, foulmouthed snail. So gradual was my descent, it must have appeared that I was trying to return to the top. I was well and truly out of my comfort zone – supposedly a good place to be, though I can't say I thought much of it. The anticipated endorphins didn't turn up, and the adrenaline that comes with panic failed to have a positive effect. When I bumped into an instructor halfway down, I was grateful for the respite. When she enquired what I was up to and I said I was on holiday, she wasn't having any of it and radioed through to reception to do a background check. It was only when I started banging on about Roker Pier and the Lowry in the Morrisons that she accepted I was legit. When I asked whether she liked living in Sunderland, she said that she did, very much. When I asked why, she cited the city's proximity to Newcastle and Durham, which is a bit like saying that you like England because it's close to Wales. I managed three descents in my allotted two hours, then called it a day.

I took the bus back into town. After resisting The Blandford on Maritime Street (£2.80 a pint, bingo daily, free shot if you sing a song), and Speedy Turkish Barber on Holmeside (I'd rather my barber wasn't in a rush), I proceeded to Mexico 70 on High Street West for some much-needed hand-pressed experimental tacos, having been tipped off by the driver of the 33 bus. The menu at Mexico 70 is about as posh as the people of Sunderland will tolerate, I fancy. My tacos were filled with Vietnamese beef shin, torched sweet peppers, agave syrup, watercress crema and Pico de Galla, who I thought played for Leeds. Eating my progressive concoctions perched on a stool in the front window, watching a Friday evening getting into its stride, I felt unquestionably happy. Some readers might not care for such brazen outbursts of feeling, but there it is. It was the being away, and the wet streets, and the fact that I'd survived the skiing, and the glistening Empire Theatre across the street, looking gorgeous and full of promise – that's what did it, that's what conjured the mood.

The Empire is an august establishment, its pale round tower beautified with pink bulbs and a green copper dome, the latter topped with a statue of Terpsichore, that Greek goddess of having a laugh, of cutting loose, of throwing some shapes. There's a showbiz adage that says that 'everybody dies in Sunderland', hinting at an unforgiving local audience. It would appear there's a speck of truth in the notion, for, back in 1976, when Sunderland was a town with a polytechnic and a river as busy as the Suez Canal, *Carry On* actor Sid James actually kicked the bucket at the Empire during a matinee of *The Mating Game*.

I know who wouldn't have struggled to win applause at the Empire. A local boy called Len Gibson, who passed away in 2021, having just reached his century. I read about Len in a brilliant book about Sunderland by Marie Gardiner, a few weeks after my trip to the city. In short, Len was a local lad who found himself, aged 21, in a Japanese Prisoner of War camp during the Second World War, tasked with building the Burma railway.

A keen banjoist, Len used his musical leanings to lift the morale of his campmates. He fashioned a guitar out of scrap wood, costumes out of mosquito netting, and then put on shows for the imprisoned. Even the Japanese officers would get in on the act, sitting cross-legged in the front row, dressed in their finest. For the length of the show, an illusion of peace prevailed, with sworn enemies laughing at the same daft capers. Len Gibson did three and a half years in that camp, catching malaria on twenty occasions and typhus whenever he had the time. One afternoon, after a shift on the railway, Len walked past the Japanese officers' hut and saw a couple of bigshots burning documents. Len feared the worst: he knew his captors were under orders to kill all prisoners in the event of a Japanese defeat. An hour later, one of the officers approached Len and told him the war was over and he should get back to Sunderland ASAP. I like to think the clemency those prisoners were afforded had something to do with Len's amateur dramatics, and the shared humanity they hinted at.

Across from the theatre is The Fire Station, a new venue for gigs and shows and whatnot, and next door to that is The Engine Room, a bar and restaurant in the habit of putting out beef cheeks and ceviche. The pair were opened in 2012. Wills and Kate popped up for the occasion. They weren't the first royals to visit Sunderland. When QEII came up in 1946 to visit a shipyard and launch a new tanker, she opted to have lunch in the shipyard's canteen. According to the *Sunderland Echo*, it 'was the first time a royal had sat down at a staff canteen anywhere', which goes to show how simple it is to distinguish yourself in that family. Prince Charles visited Sunderland with Diana in the eighties, and not to everyone's delight. A local lad chose to don a pair of massive plastic lugholes for the occasion, and duly got arrested. You'd have thought the copper would have just had a quiet word in his ear. Looking at The Fire Station, it occurred to me that I had already, in less than a day, seen a fair bit of this sort of thing – of Sunderland making sound use of old rope. There's the slag heap turned ski slope, the tram shelter on its way to becoming a café, and the old storage building in Seaburn that's now a seafood joint called North, where you have to book a month ahead. What's more, there's a big hole just along the street, where the ice rink used to be, and I'd bet good money that it's not being turned into a carpark.[5]

I went looking for a nightcap. There wasn't a shortage of options. Cleo's was a pink wonderland, Closet Bar wasn't keeping anything under wraps, Life of Riley looked a bit much for me, and I didn't think I'd last a minute in Infinity. Hundreds were pouring into The Point – though for what reason, I can't say. In the end I plumped for a pub – The Ship Isis, a nice old boozer with a fetching façade and bygone aesthetic. It was only after being told that the pub is haunted by the ghost of a serial killer who dumped her victims in the Wear that the barman asked what I fancied.

'I'll have a non-alcoholic beer, please.'

'Are you not from around here?'

'No, I'm on holiday.' (Yes, I know I say that a lot.)

'On holiday where?'

'Here.'

'Yeah, but where? Ultimately, I mean? Like Durham or something?'

---

[5] It's not. It will be Culture House. An events and gallery space scheduled to open at some point in 2025. And while I'm down here I should mention that an old industrial site up the river at Pallion is being transformed into a whopping film and telly studios facility, like nothing else in the country. Forget Shepperton and Pinewood, they'll be up in Sunderland in the decades to come. Brad Pitt will be bowling down Fawcett Street with a stottie under each arm.

'I'm on holiday here. In Sunderland. Nowhere else.'

'Fuck me, that's niche.'

There was a gig in train upstairs. I nipped up. The band was called Red Remedy. A fairly youthful outfit: the drummer kept being told to put his top back on by his mum. I nestled at the back, against a Victorian mantlepiece, where I chatted with the sound technician between songs. Yes, he was a Wearsider. Yes, he goes to the football. Yes, he's had the beef shin tacos at Mexico 70.

'Beyoncé played at the stadium a few months back,' he said.

'I didn't know she was a footballer.'

'It was £200 a ticket.'

'Bit steep.'

'That's ten games of football.'

'You're right.'

'It might be a load of rubbish, but the football gives you a reason, a target, a light at the end of the tunnel. It gives you something to moan about – again and again and again. I've got nothing against Beyoncé. I'm sure she's a canny lass. But she's got nothing on the football.'

On leaving the pub, I noticed an artwork on the side of a building around the corner. It said 'Eeeeeee!' in red neon. That was the extent of it. I'd heard the exclamation before, but didn't know what it meant or conveyed, so buttonholed a passerby who duly spilt the beans – or tried to. They said you say it when something's gone wrong. Or gone well. Or just *gone* – if someone has nicked your bike, for example. 'You might say it when you see a new bairn,' they said, 'Or when you burn your toast. Or when Boris Johnson comes on the telly. You can say it when you like, I suppose.' That cleared that up, then.

The artwork is called *The Mackem Shibboleth* (2023), which I dare say won't mean much to people outside of the region. And that's kind of the point. A shibboleth is basically something that's particular to a certain group of people. It can be a phrase, or an exclamation, or a principle or a belief – anything that serves to identify a person or a people. The use of shibboleths is mostly harmless these days, but in the past, they could be a matter of life or death. In medieval Sicily, for example, local partisans were in the habit of killing anyone that couldn't correctly pronounce the Sicilian word for chickpeas – *ciciri*. The Spanish did something similar with parsley, the Dutch with a seaside town called Scheveningen, and the Poles used lentils as a means of separating insider from outsider. The upshot of all this, as far as I can tell, is that you'd better know about *eeeeeee!* before you embark on a city break to Sunderland, in case you burn your toast or your bike gets nicked.

I made the mistake of getting a taxi. The cabbie was a Geordie, and was determined to share every thought he'd ever had. It wasn't the accent that gave him away – I can't tell them apart – but the nature of the op-ed that came at me with gusto. In short, Newcastle had been class all season. The Portuguese fella in midfield had been class, the manager had been class, the goalkeeper had been class, Ant and Dec had been class, and so had the supporters – the best in the country. He told me that while his mates worship the likes of Beardsley and Shearer and Ginola and Gascoigne, he's always preferred the players nobody else makes a fuss about, the ones who do a lot of good stuff but get very little credit, which is why his dog's called Barry Venison. (Me neither.)

As we approached my destination, and in an attempt to change the subject, I asked him what he thought about the city of Sunderland. At first he pretended he'd never heard of the place, before giving in to temptation and reciting what I reckon is probably his favourite monologue. 'Hadaway it's a city. It's a carpark, man. If you're in Sunderland, and you're looking at something, chances are it's a carpark. And the football team are a disgrace.

Mind yer divvent get recruited. Them Mackems will 'ave anything wi' two legs. Aw've a good mind te stay here and wait for ye – it won't take yer long te come te yer senses. That'll be eight quid, by the way.' The fare had gone up since he pulled over. I addressed the fact. 'Aye, it's goon up. You've been chewing me ear off, man.'

Heading to the hotel, something stopped me in my tracks – the din coming from the neighbouring establishment, a load of stacked-up shipping containers called Stack. I went in to investigate. It was absolute bedlam – but in a nice way. A group karaoke session was in full flow. The glad rags were out, and half off in places. About a thousand revellers were singing along to pop songs, following the words on a big screen. I can't say crowd karaoke is my thing, but with this lot it was irresistible. The choir was so unabashed, so happily unhinged, with each chorister wielding an inflatable oversize microphone. It was some spectacle, and it reached a crescendo during a recital of 'Hopelessly Devoted to You', with plenty of the singers giving every impression that they were anything but. It was a communal release, I guess, a collective end-of-week outpouring, a united kneading of that great knot of niggly emotion that builds up from Monday to Friday and needs somewhere to go. But I'm being presumptuous – they might all work Monday to Wednesday.

I made a peppermint tea and took it out onto the balcony, and there enjoyed the effect of a full moon on a dark sea as a mercifully subdued version of 'Angels' drifted across from the containers. I stared at the calm pane of dark glass, sturdy and ceaseless, bearing a path of moonlight which tapered on its way to Denmark and Holland. It had something of Sunderland about it, that moon over water. It was the scale of it, the wonder of it, the majesty of it, the play of dark and light – and the lack of people appreciating the damn thing.

Sunderland

Some of The Stack crowd had spilled out onto the promenade. I watched a squabble turn into an embrace, and then a pair of lads decide on a whim that they wanted to swap shoes. I'm not so naive as to think that such an early hours scene can't have an uglier side, a regrettable element, when it topples over from *joie de vivre* into fisticuffs and nonsense. But nor am I so cynical to think that such a scene can't be life-affirming and quietly glorious. A case in point: a canny lass just stripped down to her undies and made a beeline for the North Sea, while singing the chorus of 'Angels'.

Sunderland reminds me of home, in a way. Of Portsmouth. The sea, the history, the industry, the loss of it, the football, the war damage, the housing estates, the streets in the sky, the terraces, the flashes of architectural dash that are better for being uncommon. And the people. I can't claim to have met them all, but the ones I have met have been down to earth, willing to natter, self-deprecating, not indifferent to the occasional shandy, and as likely to save your dog as pinch your foldaway bike. Eeeeeee, I reckon I could live in the place.

The next morning, I took a bus into town. It dropped me on Bridge Street, outside the Fat Unicorn, an appealing peddler of cheese. I popped in for a sliver of something regional and was told by the cheesemonger that, looked at in a certain way, a rhinoceros is just a fat unicorn. Armed with that insight, I did a left onto High Street East. It was lower here. Closer to the riverside. Back in the day – the shipyards buzzing, women and girls wading waist-deep for small coals floating on the waves – conditions weren't exactly palatial in this neck of the woods. Things were tight. Things were dense. Things were thick and packed. Three, four, five to a room. As the job market mushroomed, so did the population. Hopeful immigrants from Scotland and Ireland and Sunderland's hinterland. With an effective sewage system still a long way off, the drinking water was nothing of the sort. As late as 1911, infant mortality was at 25% in Sunderland's East End.

Needing a boost, I entered Pop Recs, a venue, hub, forum, gallery and, happily for me, a café knocking out insane focaccia as though it were a given. I ate one of the best sandwiches of my life while reading some poems on the wall – it didn't take me long to decide that Pop Recs was my cup of tea. The community interest company was co-founded by Dave Harper, the drummer from local indie-rock outfit Frankie and the Heartstrings. Dave died in 2021 at the age of just 43. Pop Recs is a fine legacy. Finishing my sandwich, I clocked a sign saying that Pop Recs is no place for racism, sexism, homophobia, transphobia, misogyny and disablism. Gutted, I made a swift exit.

I popped into the museum, a Victorian whopper at the bottom of town. As well as a Nissan Bluebird and the fossil of a flying reptile, there were some paintings that Lowry did of Sunderland. Lowry had a major exhibition here in 1942 – the deliverymen dodging the bombs as they unloaded the frames – and another big one twenty years later, not long after he'd started ordering his roast beef and orange juice up the road in Seaburn. When I went upstairs to have a look at the Lowry stuff, I overheard a girl, no older than seven, sharing her thoughts. She didn't think much of them. Reckons the 'council are having a laugh'. Adjoining the museum is Mowbray Park, wherein I found a gorgeous walrus posing by the lake and the Winter Gardens. The walrus honours that poem of Lewis Carroll, 'The Walrus and the Carpenter', thought to have been conceived and composed around these parts. In fact, it is believed that Lewis Carroll got thinking about

Alice's rabbit hole while walking along Roker Beach, when he clocked a young girl emerging from a tunnel. I should mention at this juncture a wonderful graphic novel by Bryan Talbot called *Alice in Sunderland* (2007), which tells the history of the city (if not Britain) in a delightfully idiosyncratic and bravura fashion. It really is something else. Well worth a look.

Also worth a look is a local confection called the pink slice. I returned to the coast and picked one up at Fausto, a funky beachside café. Comprised of shortbread, jam and pink icing, the pink slice is a local delicacy that, if I'm candid, can stay local – I was getting palpitations after a mouthful. I welcomed the sugar, mind you, as I was just about to jump into the sea. To be more precise, I was going to have a go at coasteering – which is a bit like mountaineering but along the coast – with an organisation called Adventure Sunderland, who are based next door to Fausto. The instructor had my number straight away – not least when he clocked me fastening my helmet for the minibus ride up the coast to our first jumping-off point. For the next couple of hours, our group of twelve clambered over limestone crags and outcrops, which, while perfect to look at, are less than perfect to traverse and descend. As with the skiing, I found myself in a state of near-constant apprehension. The best part of the experience for me was just bobbing about in the sea. I liked the cold, salty water, and being wrapped in a buoyancy aid was like wearing a lilo – not unpleasant. Unfortunately, I wasn't permitted to bob about all day, and it was soon time to jump. The advice given was 'arms together, legs slightly bent'. In the event, I kept my legs together and slightly bent my arms. That'll be my contrary streak. The jumps got bigger. And so did my doubts. While the rest of the group managed the lot, I bottled the highest. 'Ha'way, man!' shouted the instructor, as I hesitated at the peak. The instructor put my reluctance down to my roots. Said he'd be adding an extra question to the health and safety form that people fill out in advance – *Are you Southern?*

After defrosting back at the hotel, and packing my bag, I took a slow walk back to the station. As I ambled through the backstreets, I asked a couple of lads playing football in the street – wingmirrors for goalposts – where the stadium was.

'Do you not know?'

'No, otherwise I wouldn't be asking.'

'You just follow the path.'

'You make it sound religious.'

'You what?'

'Never mind.'

The Stadium of Light was opened in 1997, on the site of the city's last standing colliery. Fans watched its erection in awe, in hope, in wonder. Tony Blair wanted the stadium named after Diana but the chairman said the name should honour those that worked underground, for whom the football was a shining light at the end of the week, a beacon at the end of the tunnel. It didn't surprise me to see that some of the stadium's bricks had the names of supporters etched into them. Margaret Leonard. John Tweddle. Robert Norman Junior. Tanya Fisher. The club is the fans – and that's not just a way of speaking. They constitute it. They make it. (Or mack it, rather.)

'A city without a cathedral. But not for long.' So said Gina McKee, narrator of *Premier Passions*, a fly-on-the-wall documentary series about Sunderland Football Club, made in the early 1990s, as the stadium was on its way up. The confusion of football and religion is also evident in the opening episode of a more recent docuseries, *Sunderland 'Til I Die*, when the local vicar is shown preaching to the converted about getting behind the team. In the final episode of the series, after some near misses

Sunderland

25

and low moments, Sunderland finally gain promotion, winning at Wembley in the play-off final. The episode is the most determinedly emotive thing I've ever watched. Every trick in the bag was used to pull on the old heartstrings. I was crying, for heaven's sake, and I'm a flipping Pompey fan.

As I said, Sunderland haven't won a major trophy for over fifty years. They came close in 1992, when they lost to Liverpool in the FA Cup Final. The Sunderland players, when they went up to be consoled by the Queen, were given winners' medals by mistake. Or maybe it wasn't a mistake. Maybe the Queen knew something good when she saw it, and made the executive decision to ignore the statistics and give Sunderland its due.

And as I also said – I could live in Sunderland. I'd get a flat at the top of one of the city's central towers. I'd be a regular at the Empire. Catch gigs at The Peacock, poetry at Pop Recs. I'd bowl around town with Roxy Music in my ears, or Brahms or Westlife, for there's no reason to think the world ends at Silksworth. I'd have a stottie once a week, and go to the football now and again – just the Tuesday night games, I fancy, for Saturdays would be for exploring – Northumberland Park, the coast, the North Yorkshire Moors, the Cheviots, the Pennines. I'd get my cheese from Fat Unicorn, have the odd saveloy dip, and head up Penshaw Hill whenever a wider frame was required. I'd take occasional forays across the Tyne into Newcastle (to deliver my condolences, of course). I'd take a brief leaf out of Bede's book, and knuckle down on one of my own – a nonsense novel about the day a Labrador was saved. I'd give pease pudding the cold shoulder, and pink slice a miss. I'd make time for Infinity. I'd become an expert skier and an amateur glassblower. I'd look out for those famous local faces, back home to see their mam, like Lauren Laverne or Jordan Pickford, like Gina McKee or even Jill Scott.

I wouldn't be Sunderland until I die. But I'd be Sunderland for a while. A good while. A good, happy while. Until some other complicated, bittersweet metropolis dug its claws into my heart, and I was compelled to skip town for a rival, a Stoke or a Norwich (or even a Chelmsford), better and brighter for having briefly been a Mackem.

Ha'way. It wouldn't be half bad.

2

Chelmsford

Three pies, three mash, and lots of chilli vinegar

The inclusion of Chelmsford in this book might come as a surprise to many, but the data doesn't lie (often), and I'm afraid it's simply the case that the historic capital of Essex, which sits thirty miles northeast of London, gets fewer overnight weekenders than any other city in the country. Which isn't to say Chelmsford isn't enjoyed or admired by its people, of course. It's only to say that it's not enjoyed or admired by anyone who isn't its people.

I can't say I knew much about Chelmsford before I rolled up there. I knew it had a river called the Chelm that might require fording. I knew it was roughly in the centre of its county and in a shallow river valley. I knew it was in old Essex, rather than the fresh stuff that came about after the Second World War, when the East End of London was rehoused in the neighbouring countryside. And I knew Chelmsford was awarded city status in 2012, mostly because Mo Farah had just won a gold medal and the Queen thought, *Ah, sod it. Why not? They make my jam near there, don't they?* (They do indeed, ma'am. At Tiptree, to be precise, which is fifteen miles northeast of the town – I mean city!)

Regarding Essex more broadly, most of what I knew came courtesy of a single episode of *The Only Way Is Essex*. In that episode, one of the first things said by Mark, the show's exaggerated protagonist, is that he'd like to stick his on/off girlfriend in the freezer for ten years, then get her out when he's ready to settle down. Charming. Elsewhere in the episode, Kirk vows to beef up, Lauren gets a spray tan, Amy asks Kirk if she can spend the night with him (presumably to sample his beef), and Sam undergoes a vajazzle, which is to say she has her pubic region decorated with crystals and glitter. When one of the characters says they're getting an extension done, one genuinely doesn't know what's being extended. The show doesn't present a cliché of Essex, but rather a cliché on steroids: a version of a version; a take of a take; a pumped-up, pimped-up shorthand – county as concept. I've got 383 episodes to go.

Fresh off the train, I studied a map outside the station. Many of the names on display – Mesopotamia Island, Central Park, Maltese Road, Swiss Avenue, Upper Roman Road – suggested that I could be in for quite an exotic afternoon. A larger map of the region, meanwhile, revealed such places as Bocking, Foulness, Messing, Fobbing, Mucking and Fingringhoe, which hinted at a county that knew what to do of an evening.

There was a good-looking pub across the street, so I nipped over for a look. The Brewhouse & Kitchen occupies a former Quaker meeting house. Anne Knight – I gleaned from a commemorative plaque – was born and raised in the property. Anne was a fair busybody, from what I understand. She was dedicated to the abolition of slavery, the promotion of universal suffrage, and the advance of feminism – and that was all before lunch. When Anne moved to France at the age of 72, it wasn't to put her feet up, but rather to take part in that country's revolution. She died in Strasbourg in 1862, nearly a hundred years old. Local author Sarah Perry gives a good account of Anne Knight in her 2020 book *Essex Girls*, a tome which provides ample evidence, were it required, that the ladies of this ancient terroir didn't limit themselves to dancing around handbags.

I put a question to an Essex girl waiting for a bus – 'I'm on holiday, what should I do?' – and before long a small crowd had formed around me. Its spokesperson was a lady in her seventies who said that she used to get up to all sorts in Chelmsford, not least at a nightclub called Dukes, but that these days she mostly fretted about her pension or dropped in on Sharon. These things not being available to me, I dropped into the Civic Centre instead, under the impression that it boasted a tourist information point, only to be informed that said tourist information point shut down ten years ago, it not having a point. Next door to the Civic Centre is the theatre. People were queueing up for a matinee of *Jack and the Beanstalk*, that cautionary tale about the ramifications of spaffing one's capital on a bag of nonsense – Essex indeed. (Stop it, Ben. You're peddling hearsay. See how seductive reputations can be?)

I followed Duke Street down to Tindal Square, which is situated at the top of the pedestrianised high street. Sitting at its centre, on an unmissable pedestal, is the square's eponymous judge, Nick Tindal. At the foot of said pedestal is a frankly gushing eulogy, presumably written by the bigwig himself. According to the inscription, Tindal was directed by serene wisdom, animated by purest love and justice, endeared by unwearied kindness, and graced by the most lucid style. Tindal would have done much of his serene judging in Shire Hall, the neoclassical whopper that sits across from his likeness. Despite its grand and illustrious appearance, Shire Hall was the site of many a

Chelmsford

31

miscarriage of justice (come to think of it, there's probably a positive correlation between the grandeur of a building and the number of indecent episodes associated with it), not least in the 1600s, when infamous witch hunter Matthew Hopkins got into the unfortunate habit of rounding up anyone he felt wasn't sufficiently graced with lucid style and effecting their execution – based on the fact that their neighbour had come down with smallpox, or they had a welt, or they walked funny, or for no better reason than they were a woman and available that afternoon. The court at Chelmsford hosted more witch trials than anywhere else in the country. Some claim to fame.

Shire Hall is one of the few buildings in Chelmsford that Niklaus Pevsner had any time for. The German émigré turned zealous observer of English buildings opened the Essex volume of his mammoth series detailing England's buildings thus: 'Essex has proved a difficult county to deal with.' For my part, I encountered plenty of good-looking buildings as I proceeded along the high street, which curves and slopes nicely as it heads down to the river. While it is true that Chelmsford suffered at the hands of town planners in the second half of the twentieth century, with their towers and carparks and ring roads and roundabouts, the core of the city remains anything but an eyesore.

At the corner of High Street and Springfield Road, I read that Charles Dickens once stayed the night in a building on this spot. Dickens didn't think much of his city break, I'm led to believe, claiming that Chelmsford was 'the dullest and most stupid' place he'd ever come across. (And that from a lad who grew up in Portsmouth.) Dickens should have nipped into Robins for a plate of pie and mash. He wouldn't have thought that experience dull. Established in 1929, and with shops in Chingford and Romford and Southend and Basildon, Robins is a bit of an institution. As well as pie and mash, the front window promised liquor. *Why not?* I thought. It's five o'clock somewhere in the world.

'Liquor comes on the side, does it?' I said.

'On top.'

'Fair enough. And what's that you're handling?'

'Jellied eels.'

'Pray elaborate.'

'It's jellied eels.'

The lady gave me a taste, sensing my circumspection. They weren't bad, not by a long chalk, but I can't say I thought much of the jelly. If I was going to have eels, I'd have them off the bone and in a curry, I fancy. Eel jalfrezi or similar. In any case, it was the pies I had my eye on.

'What are the options?'

'Pie.'

'But I mean on the inside.'

'We only do pie.'

'In which case I'll have pie.'

'Actually, there is a choice.'

'Oh yeah?'

'How many.'

I asked for one pie, one mash and liquor. The lady looked at me as if I hadn't finished ordering. And well she might. Mark Wright, the lad who wanted his lady in the freezer, has four pies, no mash and double liquor. Ian Dury had three pies, three mash and lots of chilli vinegar. I stuck to my guns and took a single pie to a marble-topped table. When I broke it open with a fork, a hot puddle of beef mince made its escape. The pie was delicious, and the mash wasn't bad either. I wasn't charmed by the liquor, however, which turned out to be a sad excuse for gravy, a thin stand in for sauce. When I heard a man in the queue – for it was bustling that lunchtime – say to his mate in a conciliatory tone, 'Nah, you've gotta get the liquor.

It's a sort of béchamel sauce infused with parsley', I almost flipped out. The man might as well have said the Pope was a sort of cheese infused with a parrot, for it would have been as true. On my way out, I was informed by a member of staff that the liquor is essentially the water the eel is stewed in, mixed with a bit of flour for thickness and a bit of parsley for colour. Béchamel, my arse.

At the bottom of the high street is a graceful stone bridge that spans the River Can. Here I spotted a lad doing an odd kind of fishing – magnet fishing. While most of his contemporaries busy themselves with stereotypical teenage pursuits, young Lewis Bright dangles his unusual rod in the rivers of Chelmsford in pursuit of … well, anything magnetic, I guess. Lewis has brought up trollies, bikes, unexploded bombs and a pair of tights full of money. Typically, Lewis either sells his catch to scrap metal dealers or attempts to get the items back to their rightful owner. Trying to do that with the tights must have proved an unusual errand. The lad has got 100k social media followers. The world is a funny place.

Overlooking the bridge and the river is a building called Cater House, which you might describe as a modern experiment – that went wrong. It was erected at the behest of those well-meaning planners back in the 1960s. I'm not desperate for architectural harmony in a place, and nor do I think that coherence is a prerequisite of excellence. I can take a fair bit of all-over-the-show – as there was in Sunderland – but this building took the biscuit. Perhaps it was meant as a deterrent, a rebuke to invading cockneys, because I can't imagine there are many who'll willingly go near the thing. The peculiar ornamentation on the south elevation was suggestive of a climbing wall. I wouldn't mind seeing the architect and the planner racing up its face, untethered.

I doubled back on myself to have a look at the new Bond Street development, which runs perpendicular to the high street, and includes a John Lewis department store and an Everyman Cinema, if you give a hoot about such things. The development is well done as far as these things go. Its task was to reconnect the high street to the riverside without being acutely depressing to look at. In this it is a success. I resisted the respective appeals of The White Company and L'Occitane en Provence, but couldn't turn down the Tiptree Tearoom. The people at Tiptree have been growing and preserving fruit in Essex since way back when, and have been supplying the royal family with all manner of spreads for almost as long. I ordered a pot of tea and a slice of bread pudding stuffed with Tiptree mincemeat, then took the opportunity to ask the young lad at the counter what his favourite thing about Chelmsford was. He gave it a lot of thought – to the upset of those behind – then asked if I'd ever heard of Wagamama.

Pressed for an alternative, the young man suggested either the bookshop next door or a place around the corner where you can throw axes and get pissed. (It's called Battle Bar.) I made the sensible decision, entered the establishment, then reemerged an hour later utterly trollied and with a nasty gash on my forehead, at which point I stopped telling fibs and entered the bookshop instead, where I took an almighty liberty by reading a great chunk of *The Invention of Essex* (2023) by Tim Burrows before deciding to buy the thing. There's a nice section in the book about the acute xenophobia that gripped Chelmsford in the 1960s, when an anticipated invasion of migrants was the talk of the town. The locals were right to be concerned, for the invasion occurred. And the poor indigenous people of Chelmsford – themselves descended from Normans and Saxons – have had to put up with a frankly hazardous number of Londoners ever since.[6]

---

[6] On the matter of books, Gillian Darley's *Excellent Essex* (2019) is also, er, excellent on Essex.

Before this report begins to reek of nothing but local history and the built environment, I'd better throw a spanner in the works and go ice-skating. Chelmsford's longstanding rink is contained in a large blue hangar next to the river and cannot be destroyed or repurposed under any circs because it is a back-up morgue in case of disaster. I hadn't been ice-skating for several decades, and not because I'm the sort of person that likes to deny themselves pleasure. I went roller-skating last summer for reasons that remain mysterious to me, and it occurred to me while doing so how generally content I am without wheels on my feet. I feel similar about steel blades, the addition of which just seems to be asking for trouble.

Gazing sheepishly at the rink as I queued for my boots, I saw some small skaters using fibreglass penguins to stabilise their progress. I guess the thinking is that the kids save face if their prop is a penguin. Huddled together behind the skate-hire counter, the surplus penguins looked kind of spooky. Their collective expression was expectant, hopeful, plaintive. It would prove to be one of the most moving things I saw in Chelmsford.

'Shoe size?'

'Eleven.'

'There you are.'

'That was quick.'

'I'm good at my job.'

'Any chance I can get one of those penguins?'

'How tall are you?'

'Six foot.'

'Then no.'

'Is it true the ice rink doubles up as a morgue?'

'Yes. You've got an hour.'

I don't mind saying that I hesitated rink-side for the best part of that hour, listening to the shapeless din of trepidation and pleasure, while visualising losing my fingers. I won't overegg it, but when I finally took to the ice, I was bloody awful. Because it was half-term, the rink was teeming with pint-sized obstacles. I had been told, by the girl who issued the skates, to keep my weight above my feet (as opposed to below them?), and to shuffle along like a penguin – clearly the go-to metaphor around here. So poor was my progress, that I soon attracted the attention of a steward.

'Mate. If you can't skate, why don't you stop trying to film yourself and just concentrate on what you're doing?'

'Nice to meet you. Can I get one of those penguins?'

'No.'

'Will you film me being rubbish?'

'Yeah.'

It transpired that Jacob was an Essex boy to the core, which is to say a figure skater with an interest in street photography. When I asked if he stacks it a lot, he said that because falling over is practically inevitable, the trick is to learn to fall in a way that doesn't hurt, or hurts less. The remark brought to mind that adage of Samuel Beckett, about failing, failing again, and then failing better, and reminded me – as if I needed reminding – that you never know when the wisdom of an Irish dramatist is likely to be invoked. Interestingly, doing those laps alongside Jacob, chatting away about this and that, my skating got immeasurably better, which goes to show that the less attention you give to something, the better the results tend to be. (Unless you're driving. Or operating on a brain. Or parenting.)

It was time to think about some accommodation. I asked at The Riverside Inn but they were full, and the same was true of The Ship Inn on Railway Street. I ended up at the County Hotel, which had the advantage of having a nice mural of Grayson Perry on its west flank, but the disadvantage of being inflexible regarding the room rate. I asked the inflexible receptionist if Chelmsford deserved to be unpopular.

'Thing is, it's a nice place to live but not to visit.'

'But isn't visiting a bit like living? And living a bit like visiting?'

'No, I don't think it is.'

'In that they involve similar things?'

'No,' they said, shaking their head sadly.

'But don't they overlap somewhat?'

'Not really, no.'

'Can't the visitor do some of the things a resident does?'

'No, I don't think they can.'

'But surely—'

'Look, would you like to attend one of the fine schools in the area?'

'Well, no.'

'Then how about we wrap this up?'

After dumping my bag in the room, I took a bus out into the beautiful, paintable, flat-as-a-pancake Essex countryside, where I hoped to be overtaken by the spirit of Constable and find a canny pub for a slap-up Lilley and Skinner.[7] The X10 went past two posh schools, a postwar housing estate knocked up to deal with London overspill, and a lot of solid suburban semis. Set down on Parsonage Lane, I walked the short distance to the Galvin Green Man, a charming redbrick building with a big garden running down to the River Chelmer. Back in 1975, two brothers from this part of the world, Jeff and Chris, started doing the dishes in a local restaurant for £3 a shift. Fast-forward fifty years and the pair have a brace of Michelin-starred joints

---

[7] Cockney rhyming slang for dinner, after the British shoe brand that was founded in 1835 and folded in 1962.

in London, plus this pub on the edge of Chelmsford. It's an old pub, dating to the fourteenth century, and was voted best public house in Essex according to a sandwich board outside.

I was here for the Michelin Bib Gourmand menu, a ridiculous name for something that, in short, is really rather simple: Michelin-level grub for a decent price – in this case, three courses for £30. While it was nice to read about the seasonal mushrooms and the whipped local cheese, it was nicer still to get them in the old north and south (gob, that is). I was interested to see that some of the wines on offer were being produced just up the road at New Hall vineyard. I was minded to see off my pudding and pay New Hall a visit, but unfortunately the local bus network couldn't accommodate such a recherché ambition.[8]

I walked back into town along the river. It was nice to be away from the built environment, amid ash and willow trees, and poplars and oaks, and beside the slowly flowing Chelmer. While by no means a mighty river, the Chelmer has a slight majesty, and a very real charm, as it follows its course, never the same as the second before. It was nice to pause and sit on a bench in the final sun of the day, to study the leaves of certain trees as they shimmered in the breeze, and, because you don't get to leave

---

[8] I visited New Hall some months later, for a self-guided walk through the vines and to dip my nose in a few samples. New Hall puts on several open days throughout the spring and summer, while the cellar door (for tastings and a chit chat) is open all year round. You can even rent a section of the vineyard, if you feel so inclined, and enjoy every liquid ounce that it issues. The girl tasked with renting bits of the New Hall estate happened to be called Anna Vine. If her sister Lisa opts to follow in her footsteps, it will be the best case of nominative determinism (names leading to jobs) since serial felon Robin Banks and insurance saleswoman Justine Case.

yourself at home when you go away for the weekend, to dwell on my nan's ill health.

We, too, are never the same as the second before. Case in point, an information board just made a dent in my ignorance by providing a small lesson on the slow worm, which is actually a legless lizard that can live for twenty years. Further along, another board spoke favourably of The Essex Skipper, which is a species of butterfly and no relation of Gooch or Cook or Ronnie Irani. Further along still, another board said that the easy-going nature of the river allowed for loosestrife to flourish. Call me pusillanimous but loosestrife doesn't sound like something you want to exist at all, let alone flourish. In any case, the aforementioned boards, and the stories and secrets they shared, are the handiwork of volunteers, who band together to keep the River Chelmer Local Nature Reserve spruce and attractive and educational to boot. I thank them for their efforts, and hope their ranks swell.

Having blown my budget on a finickity lunch, I was too poor for The Everyman (which might want to address the misnomer) and too poor for the theatre. Out of ideas and with drizzle in the air, I sat in the shadow of Judge Tindal, he of the lucid style and unwearied kindness, and gawped at the red neon of an empty steakhouse and the floodlit flint of an empty cathedral, the latter just apparent at the end of a narrow alley, looking all cold shoulders and good intentions. I walked around for an hour or so, through the subways and round the ring road, across the bridges and the retail parks, until I found what I didn't know I was looking for ...

I'll get this off my chest straight away: Hot Box must be one of the best places in Essex. If there is a better spot on an autumnal Monday for someone feeling a tiny bit lonesome and a tiny bit lost, then I cannot conceive of it. Housed beneath two arches of a venerable Victorian viaduct, Hot Box is a bar and a music venue and a hub for the community. Beneath one of the arches is the bar, at which I sat and had a cup of tea and chatted with the bartender (about gut health in the first instance and Chelmsford in the second). Beneath the other arch, where the gigs are held, a casual chess club was in session. The décor was maximalist. Shelves were lined with old books and nicknacks. Walls were decorated with flags and bank notes and record sleeves and posters. A Nick Drake album played softly, and a £2 fine was levied by the bartender each time someone talked about politics. (Undaunted, one lady spent a tenner making the case for electoral reform.)

Chess boards had been painted onto the length of the bar. I played the bartender a couple of times. As he walloped me on both occasions, he was good enough to feed me some lines about the place he calls home. He told me about a local musician called Rat Boy. He told me that the city used to make soft drinks and ball bearings and toothbrushes. He told me that you can kayak on the Chelmer if you're that way inclined. And he told me that I could sling my hook immediately for slagging off Cater House. I don't mind saying that Hot Box was my kind of tourist information point. Who needs Google when you've got the voice of the people?[9]

After reminding me that a bishop oughtn't behave in such a fashion, and after fining me two quid for bringing up the election, the bartender told me that Hot Box is a music venue at heart, and a bloody good one at that. Small venues like Hot Box are a key element of the British music industry. They cultivate the grassroots. They give new talent a platform, a sounding board, a springboard. And when there's a good act in and the place is full, then the atmosphere is electric. While I didn't doubt that

---

[9] Chelmsford never made toothbrushes.

Chelmsford

the atmosphere could be electric at the weekend, when a good act was in and the place was full, nor did I doubt that the atmosphere couldn't be perfectly lovely on a Monday, when the only sound is that of rooks claiming pawns, and Drake crooning of moons, and the bartender quietly commending the museum on Moulsham Street, and offering to make me a second cup of tea.

Like Pop Recs in Sunderland, Hot Box is a Community Interest Company, meaning it's not hellbent on a massive turnover. Instead, it's inclined to its people, inclined to its manor. Its idea of profit is the improvement and nourishment and protection of its community. It runs educational initiatives, puts an arm over certain shoulders, and looks out for marginalised groups. Despite being an indisputably valuable and brilliant place, it's been in debt since the pandemic, and is at risk of closing. That shouldn't be allowed to happen.[10]

Within ten minutes of leaving Hot Box, I was in bed listening to 'Dick Smith's A to Z of Pop' on Hospital Radio Chelmsford. The channel broadcasts throughout the night and has been on the airwaves nonstop since 1964. The DJs are all volunteers. Listening to Dick Smith transition silkily from Madonna to Meat Loaf, it occurred to me, and not for the first time, that it's people that make a place, that make it tick, that make it good. (It's also people that can muck a place up, but we won't dwell on that.) I fell asleep with Dick onto Prince and went on to dream – not of chess or Essex or eels – but of the former Conservative MP Rory Stewart.

---

[10] The Music Venue Trust, a charity which acts to protect, secure and improve grassroots music venues, is calling for a £1 levy on stadium gigs to support such venues, without which artists couldn't cut their teeth and emerge. Good luck to them.

The next morning, I set off for that museum the bartender had commended. I walked through the park, followed the river, turned right at the old stone bridge, then continued along Moulsham Street, the old Roman Road. A lot of the buildings on the street are medieval, albeit with modern concerns. I passed a bubble tea shop, another eel and pie house, and then entered an Italian deli called Ciao!, drawn by the exclamation mark as much as anything else. When the guardian of the deli caught me down on my haunches admiring his salami, he insisted I try a slice. Onto a good thing, I started admiring his cheese, and that too issued fruit – this time a sliver of Sicilian pecorino. When Julian slid an espresso under my nose while outlining the advantages of fusilli vs farfalle and celebrating the Roman temple discovered under the roundabout near Sainsbury's (the espresso had a long way to slide), I was putty in the man's hands. No surprise, then, that when Julian hinted that his mortadella and provolone sandwich was the best sandwich in Essex, I ordered one on the spot.

Although a bit of a trek from the centre, the museum was a delight. The building itself is a belter: a Victorian villa done in the style of Osborne House, Queen Victoria's favourite bolt-hole on the Isle of Wight. Over the course of an hour, and by dint of a number of well-written displays and timelines and exhibits, I came to know a bit about Chelmsford. I learned that Chelmsford was the only Roman settlement to be named after Caesar; that the toaster was developed here; that if you start digging a hole outside Julian's deli and carry on for a very long time you'll pass through gravel, crag, clay, chalk and slate, before hitting something called puddingstone, which sounds like my kind of material; and that a popular slap-up dinner among the local Roman population was stuffed dormouse served with a strong sauce made from rotten fish, which sounded infinitely more appealing than the liquor served up at Robins.

Chelmsford

The museum has much to say about a particular Italian immigrant. In the late nineteenth century, Guglielmo Marconi pitched up from Bologna in his mid-twenties to transform the world with wireless telegraphy. As a younger man, Marconi had taken inspiration from Heinrich Rudolf Hertz, the discoverer of sound waves. With the German in mind, and as all hot-blooded teenagers are wont, Marconi began conducting secretive experiments in the attic with his butler. Code-carrying radio waves were sent out from the attic across the garden to an improvised receiver strung up in a towering cypress tree, where the waves and the code were translated into a message – 'Your dinner's getting cold', for example.

After failing to win the ear of Italy, Marconi travelled to Britain to try his luck there. When he arrived at Dover, all his equipment drew the suspicion of customs officers, who notified their superiors. This intervention proved a stroke of luck. Marconi fell in with some influential people at the General Post Office, who, as chance would have it, were fed up with riding ponies around the country delivering invitations to supper, and in the mood for innovation. Before long, Marconi was transmitting Morse code signals across Salisbury Plain. Not long after, he sent the first ever wireless communication over open sea. With time, the masts grew, the antennas grew, the power stations grew, the receivers grew – and so did the distances covered. The radio operators on the *Titanic*, who sent the calls for help which were picked up by the *Carpathia* sixty miles away (and which resulted in hundreds of lives being saved), were employed by Marconi.

By this time, Marconi had a factory on New Street in Chelmsford, where all the components necessary for effective wireless communication were being produced. Chelmsford was at the heart of a social media revolution. Telegraphy eventually ceded to telephony – the sending of sound. Nellie Melba, the famous soprano remembered by a pudding, sang a song to the nation in 1920, and by 1922 entertainment broadcasts from Chelmsford were a regular occurrence – paving the way for the BBC, who took the baton and ran with it. The corporation's first broadcasts came from Marconi House in London a couple of years later. If you like *Gavin and Stacey*, or *Only Fools and Horses*, or *Desert Island Discs*, or *The Archers*, then you owe a debt to Marconi and Chelmsford. When Marconi died of a heart attack in 1937, he received a state funeral in Italy. Radios around the world fell silent for two minutes in his honour. The message was clear. Marconi had done stellar work – and at high frequency. *Grazie*, Guglielmo.

Another illustrious child of Chelmsford who was involved in progressive messaging, and is well stocked in the museum, is Grayson Perry. At the age of fifteen, Perry began going out dressed as a woman, and before long he'd been kicked out by his stepmother, who presumably didn't like Grayson borrowing her frocks. Over the following decades, Perry became a well-rounded artist, dipping into printmaking, drawing, embroidery and film. In 2023, Perry's documentary *The Full English* appeared on our screens. The question at the heart of it was 'What is Englishness?', and the answer at the heart of it was 'Just about anything, really'. In one episode, Perry goes to Munich to mingle with some England football fans ahead of their team's clash with Germany. One of the fans featured in the programme is shown wearing an enormous England flag embellished with vows of loyalty and devotion to Stoke City and Leek Town. Watching the man happily enwrapped in his flag, it was hard not to get the feeling that he would champion Earth in the event of an inter-planetary tournament. What I took from the episode, in case you're interested, is that we don't relate to one thing exclusively; that our identities are all over the place – but in a good way, a fruitful way, a way that results in our zones of interest and affection increasing and expanding as we travel, as we talk, as we listen, as we become more complicated people. Another guy featured in the programme says he gets the same buzz watching England play cricket as he does watching Pakistan. By crossing a border, and venturing afield, the man's affection had multiplied rather than switched. I like that.

Some of the ideas teased out in *The Full English* can be applied to the lavish breakfast that gives the show its name. Any attempt to pin down the Full English is destined to fail – the dish is unavoidably and unproblematically various. On one occasion, when I was a student in Manchester, my Full English turned up with a pair of merguez sausages. On another occasion, in Cornwall of all places, the chef asked if I wanted doner meat in lieu of bacon. And, just recently, a mate of mine was incredulous when his Full English turned up *without* avocado. When I make my own Full English, it's telling that I put curry powder in the beans, skip the toast altogether, insist on sriracha mayo, and, because some things are immutable, wash the whole thing down with tea (oat milk, of course). Why is that telling? What does my Full English say? It says that there's no one way of doing something, be that having breakfast, or being English.

Of the Perry pieces on show at the museum, I liked his cultural map of England, which instead of being marked with towns and motorways and boundaries and rivers, was dotted with people and things and programmes and bands, like Alan Bennett and Victoria Wood, like David Bowie and *Antiques Roadshow*, like Cheddar and Panto and Curry and Pret. Like *The Full English*, the artwork makes a good point about identity, about who we are, about what shapes and makes us. It makes the point that if you want to know an individual, or get closer to knowing them, ask not where they're from but what they value, not where they

46   SHITTY BREAKS

were born but what they treasure. Everybody has a map like Perry's, it just hasn't been eked out of them and put in a frame.

I also liked Perry's portrait of Chelmsford, or Chelmsford as he remembers it, Chelmsford as he *feels* it – because place is a personal thing in the end, built as much from emotion and feeling, from memory and impression, as any number of streets, or any order of architecture, or any volume of puddingstone. If I had to do a portrait of Chelmsford, along the lines of Perry's, I certainly wouldn't paint a city of 184,000 with eleven schools and seven retail parks. Instead, I would sketch the guy who runs the Italian deli who treated me like a guest in his home. I would transcribe the conversation I had with the bartender at Hot Box over several games of chess. I would illustrate the lad at the tearoom on Bond Street who loves Wagamama. I would show some of the city's street art, which is bright and bold and copious, and around every corner. I would portray myself in Robins having a jellied eel rammed down my throat. I would include an older lady launching an axe, and the fella on stilts who dishes out balloon animals on the high street, and a figure-skating Essex boy taking a spin on the ice. Few things can be said with certainty about places, but one of them is this: they are different every time we go, and every time we look. Which is partly why I love them – whatever they are.

3

Preston

Nothing is either good or bad but thinking makes it so

Let me put Preston in its place. Manchester, Liverpool and Blackpool are in the vicinity, the River Ribble is to the south, the Forest of Bowland is to the east, and the Lake District is about an hour north, assuming a speed of 40 mph. Now let me fill you in. The city has won national titles for least sun and most rain; is the birthplace of the industrial revolution (or one of them); and is famous for giving the world Andrew Flintoff and the butter pie, though not in that order.

Another thing about Preston – I'd never been there before. I'd changed trains at Preston a few times, before continuing onwards and upwards to the Lakes or Edinburgh – typical algorithmic travel behaviour, of which I'm now a trifle embarrassed. I could at least have left the station and wandered around for an hour to get a feel for the place, as the great Iain Nairn asked people to do in an episode of *Nairn's Journeys*, made for the BBC in 1975. Trouble was – and trouble remains – no one was telling me to do so. No one was inviting me to stop. No one was so much as hinting at the idea. I could have done with someone grabbing me by the lapels and saying, 'You haven't been to Preston? Are you butter pie between the ears, man? Take my e-scooter at once!'[11]

The results of a recent survey carried out by YouGov have done little to move the dial. In short, a sample of people were asked to give the thumbs up or thumbs down to a list of places. They were to base their decision on whatever they had to base it on – nothing, for example. Preston's approval rating was higher only than Bradford, Sunderland, Wolverhampton and Wakefield. Not ideal. In any case, the reason I've ventured up to Preston isn't because of that low thumbs-up figure, but rather because other people haven't – like all the destinations on my itinerary, Preston is statistically one of the least touristed cities in the UK and Ireland. Anyway, less preamble – let's go and see if they're all missing a trick, or wisely dodging a bullet.[12]

On arriving in a new place, nothing beats an initial clueless wander. (This is by no means a fact.) On leaving the big old Victorian station, and climbing its ramp up to the city's main horizontal artery, I was confronted with the slim spike of a distant spire set against a wholesome blue sky, and a red, sunlit lump that currently houses the county council, the Uluru of Lancashire. I turned right and proceeded along Fishergate. On any initial walk, you spot things straightaway, telltale signs, giveaway markers, like a red rose on a traffic bollard, a fetching old church that is now a French restaurant, a shopping centre called St George's,

---

[11] Yes, this is a nod to Bill Bryson. In *Notes from a Small Island* (1995), Bryson sketches an equivalent scene in which a character offers him his car to go to Durham at once.

[12] YouGov updated the survey in 2024. For some reason, Preston wasn't even asked about – so it's off the list!

a restaurant called Great Times that has seen better days, and a local busker singing of international affairs.

On a whim, I dropped into KFC. Not because I'm partial to the Colonel's secret recipe, but because I'd heard that this was the first branch of KFC in the country. As I bothered a table of customers by staring at a commemorative snap that proudly confirmed what I suspected, I couldn't help but wonder what I was getting out of the experience exactly. I nipped my sightseeing in the bud, and returned to Fishergate, off of which were a number of charming cobbled side streets. (Yes, cobbled streets are and always will be charming – like puppies.) The city's former wealth was written all over the face of the shopfronts – or some of them, at least. The building housing the Waterstones bookshop wasn't knocked up with a bottom line in mind, that's for sure. It was knocked up with neighbouring cities in mind – to let them know that Preston was going places, that Preston was onto something, that Preston was on the make. The results of status anxiety aren't always ugly.

The Sainsbury's Local is quite a dish as well. 'The best building of its type in Preston', according to that upright boffin Nikolaus Pevsner (though personally I'd say the Sainsbury's Local in Swindon is nicer). The building has more bays than your average bus station, while much of the sandstone façade has undergone a spot of the old vermiculated rustication, which is basically an attempt, misguided you might feel, to make the surface of the stone resemble a lot of wiggly worms (vermiculated coming from the Latin *vermiculus* or 'little worm'). The cotton that accounted for such buildings is long gone, and so is the money that it spun; but traces of that erstwhile largesse linger – with dignity – around and about town.

The Harris is such a trace. It is Preston's cultural centrepiece, and another peacock of a building. At once a museum, gallery and library, it is the legacy of one Edmund Robert Harris, a solicitor and railway enthusiast, and a rich one at that. Harris left £300,000 – some sum in those days – to the Preston Corporation to get something off the ground in his honour. The Harris opened in 1893, and was done, for a change, in the neoclassical style. On the front of the building, atop a row of tall columns, sits a rather impressive pediment, which is decorated with stony versions of Zarathustra, Aristotle and Plato, all of whom were local. The Harris is currently being transformed with lottery cash into something less damp and more permeable; less severe and more inviting. I'll watch this space.

Next to The Harris is a daunting modern job called Crystal House. The latter stands in place of the old town hall, which burned down in the 1940s. According to Pevsner, Crystal House is 'not a worthy successor'. The wording of that assessment, to my mind, gives every indication that the German émigré had, by this point in his survey of England's buildings, acquired the local talent for understatement. Incidentally, the architect responsible for the old town hall – Giles Gilbert Scott – also designed the red telephone box, of which there are a great many in this neck of the woods: indeed, Market Street boasts the longest line of them in the world. In a bid to add some pep and verve to this part of town – which they are calling the 'Harris Quarter' – I've since been told that the council has acquired the telephone boxes with a view to turning them into art installations, to be enjoyed at a rate of forty pence a minute.

A mite peckish, I tried to score a pot of parched peas from a longstanding food truck called the Hot Potato Tram, stationed nearby. Unfortunately, the boys dishing out the goods – known as The Spud Brothers – were unable to appease me – the local delicacy had sold out, and they only had jackets left. In lieu of peas, I was offered advice. 'Get yourself to the bus station,' said one of the boys. *Oh, not this again*, I thought, remembering that time in

Sunderland when I asked for a local attraction and was told to go to Durham. But the lad wasn't advising me to make use of the bus station. He was asking me to go and admire the damn thing.

Preston Bus Station is, mercifully some feel, one of a kind. The massive 1960s erection has the look of a battleship, with its curved concrete balconies that stretch on and on almost out of eyeshot. Why, it looks about to depart! I've never seen anything of the sort. It's 'giving science-fiction', to borrow a frankly objectionable new way of suggesting that something is suggesting something. It is the sort of bus station where you don't want your bus to come, because you're happy where you are. (Which is a sentiment unlikely to hold in the event of delays longer than fifteen minutes.)

But why so flipping big? Why so out of proportion? It has all the subtlety and appropriateness of a skyscraper in a village. The answer is that the bus station was built with a future conurbation in mind – a conurbation that never came to fruition. Back in the 1960s, a Central Lancashire mega city was on the cards – a merger of Preston and Leyland and Chorley, with all the gaps filled in. The plan faltered and was finally ditched by Thatcher in the eighties, which left Preston with an unnecessarily large bus station. For a long time, the local council wanted rid of it. They wanted it out of the way so a shopping centre could go up – the Tithebarn project. But when a recession hit and that project fell through, the city council sold the bus station to the county council for a quid (the latter council having the means to do something with it), whereafter it was brilliantly renovated and subsequently listed, with the result that it won't be a shopping centre any time soon. Now that it's a bit of a brutalist icon, people without any dependents or responsibilities flock to the station from all over to admire its bulk.

Looking up at the station, and thinking about its life story, it occurred to me that the structure is a bit of a totem, standing for more than just itself. It used to be an underdog, a sore spot,

Preston

53

looked down on, condescended to. The council wanted rid of it entirely. It was officially considered a stain, a problem, an issue. As such, people were invited to hold it in low regard, to think of it as a blot in the town's copybook. But now, having dodged several bullets, and because John Lewis pulled out, it is belatedly afforded the respect it deserves. The bus station's reputation has changed, and now it is seen differently, and thought of differently, and engaged with differently – as a prize, an asset, a landmark, a gem – despite the thing itself remaining fundamentally unaltered. Nothing is either good or bad, but thinking makes it so. That's what I'm getting at. Don't wait for an authority, or a rhythm or a chart, to tell you something's worth attending before you attend to it. I know life can be demanding and psychologically sapping and so full of decisions that it can feel quite nice, it can feel like a relief, now and again, to just be told what's key and hot and valuable and deserving and sexy and suave and whatnot – to have your thinking done for you. I get why we defer to others, to media, to the common sense, to the popular sentiment, to the algorithm when it comes to choosing (or not choosing) what things to engage with. But I reckon we should retain, if at all possible, a bit of headspace and mental bandwidth and cognitive agency to decide for ourselves what's decent and deserving and interesting and worthy and so on.

By banging on in this fashion, I'm not saying that it's just a state of mind (a way of thinking) that has pinned Preston down – or Sunderland or wherever – because of course it's far more complex than that. I'm not saying it's a state-sanctioned, media-driven, capitalist conspiracy to dupe the public into thinking negatively of a certain crop of spots. Not at all. I'm only saying that we'd do well to think for ourselves what is and isn't of value, because the received wisdom is often slightly off the mark, and is sometimes anything but wise. Which is to say, don't be shepherded uncritically to Manchester and Bristol, and Dublin and Brighton, and Prague and Budapest and Vienna and Rome, where you'll be one of a mob and duly overcharged. Go instead, now and again, once in a while, to those unthought of towns, those unconsidered cities. You may find them to be acutely upsetting, gravely disappointing, but you won't spend a fortune reaching that opinion, and you'll have fun forming it. If you don't, I'll compensate you. Not sure how, but I will. Promise.

Not far from the bus station, in front of Preston's indoor market, is a sculpture of Wallace and Gromit, the animated creations of local lad Nick Park. If you haven't seen any of the *Wallace & Gromit* stop-motion films, they centre on an adorable cheese-loving inventor (Wallace), and his savvy anthropomorphic beagle (Gromit). To give you an idea of Park's humour, Gromit is a graduate of Dogwarts, and a fan of The Beagles, McFlea, Poochini and Bach. Of the films, my favourite is *A Grand Day Out* (1989), wherein our plasticine protagonists, needing some cheese, take a trip to the moon, which is my sort of hair-brained undertaking. The sculpture went up in 2021. It has Gromit on a bench reading the paper, with Wallace nearby giving a big thumbs up while dressed in a recent invention. It's a cracking addition, if I'm honest. To those people who question its utility, let me say this – it is quite possible to sit next to Gromit on that bench and read over his shoulder. Charismatic sculptures like this one have the potential to become landmarks, to become local draws, to become keystones. Look at the *Manneken Pis* in Brussels, a sculpture depicting a little kid having a pee. If that pulls people in, there's no reason why this erection shouldn't.

I headed for my digs, which were just off Winckley Square, a gorgeous Georgian arrangement just south of the high street, and the equal of any such square in the country. There's an elegance and romance about the perimeter buildings, and the way the central park dips and climbs, and swings and rounds, lends further charm. One illustrious former resident was Edith Rigby. Rigby was an unmitigated rebel who pulled no punches in her effort to win equality and justice – for women, for the working class, for anyone unduly shunned or oppressed. For being such a rebel, Rigby won herself some time behind bars. She was arrested and imprisoned often, once for setting ablaze a bungalow belonging to Sir William Lever, who was in the soap business, I believe, and presumably in a right lather on learning of Rigby's prank. When asked about the incident, Rigby said it was meant as a question: 'I want to ask Sir William Lever whether he thinks his property on Rivington Pike is more valuable as one of his superfluous houses occasionally opened to people, or as a beacon lighted to King and Country to see there are some intolerable grievances for women.' I fancy Lever went for the former. In total, Edith was jailed seven times for her activism. On one occasion when the police came knocking, Edith hopped into some workman's clothes, hopped out the back window, hopped onto her bike, and then made a beeline for Ireland. Go on, girl! In 1928, women gained the vote on equal terms with men and became 53% of the electorate – in no small part because of people like Edith.

My accommodation was a room at the top of Winckley Stays Hotel, a terraced Georgian house just a stone's throw from Edith's old gaff. The room was nice. I'm not especially fluent when it comes to describing interiors, so forgive me as I point out the perky floral wallpaper, the curvy emerald-green lamp, and the, er, big bed, which if not a king was certainly in the family. If the room had to be compared to a celebrity, it would be Claudia Winkleman – unquestionably classy but with the common touch. Keir Starmer is a Travelodge room, in case you were wondering.

Below my digs was a restaurant called Aven – and by the grace of God may it stay there forever. I took one of the eight tables and, there being no alternative, agreed to receive the lunchtime tasting menu, £40 for eight courses. By no means cheap, but great value – especially compared to what you'd pay for such a spread in a more fashionable metropolis. The menu, in no particular order, starred a folly of cod in a pond of beurre blanc; the statutory mackerel that's had something unlikely done to it; a bit of pigeon dressed for a day at the races (it wore a fascinator of bright leaves and veg); and a pimped-up butter pie, a hot take on the local favourite. The latter was a highlight. Dauphinoise spuds, filo case, cheese custard, an onion and madeira sauce I would permit to flow through my veins: it was at once fine and hearty, just like the restaurant that conceived it. Aven is a string in Preston's bow – as sure as duck eggs is duck eggs.

Had a quick word with the chef, Oli Martin, a former finalist on *MasterChef: The Professionals*, who told me that Jay Rayner, food critic for the *Guardian*, recently waxed lyrical about a local backstreet caff called Roasta, run by a husband and wife from Hong Kong, just north of the Central Lancs university campus. Apparently the great Jay does a weekly radio show about food that's recorded at a different location each week, which gives him the chance to regularly sniff out something unassuming. Fair play to him. An eatery doesn't need to have been awarded or gushed over to be damn good.[13]

---

[13] I popped by but it was shut. When I read the review later, was pleased to see that Jay's impromptu lunch at Roasta really was a double win for the underdog. In an unsung, unheralded, somewhat overlooked Chinese diner, Rayner was served (and won over by) the unsung, unheralded, somewhat overlooked bits of a duck. The 'obscure corners and extremities of the duck, too often the parts left behind' were the parts that made his day. There's something in that. One person's trash is another's treasure and all that. Let's hear it for the weird bits!

That evening, I went to Club 3000 Bingo on New Hall Lane. My previous brushes with the sport occurred on coach holidays, when the whole thing had an intimate and slightly improvised vibe. Here the whole thing had anything but that vibe. The bingo hall looked ready for a colossal speed dating convention. The whole of East Lancs could chat itself up here. It was eerie at first, when I was the only one in the place, but it soon filled up. Nonetheless, the atmosphere remained austere and determined, rather than gay and frivolous as I'd anticipated. A table of ladies near me kept getting told off for talking and giggling when they should have been eyes down and dabbing. The lady across the aisle from me was lovely, mind you. She could tell I was miffed by the number of coupons I'd been issued – you could put out a Sunday broadsheet with the amount of paper I was given – so kindly leant across the aisle to whisper the significance of each. During a break in proceedings, she even led me across to see the prizes, which were stacked on the other side of the hall. When we got there, about an hour later, I was a bit underwhelmed, to be honest. It was a mountain of Bisto gravy boats – a right northern armada. Faced with the prize, I suddenly no longer wanted to win. I regret to say that I only lasted another ten minutes after the restart. When I whispered to Pauline that I was jumping ship because I had an inkling there was more to life than this, and donated her the rest of my coupons, she couldn't believe what was happening. She asked me if I was alright, thinking I'd come down with something nasty. She was properly concerned for about ten seconds – after which she was just cock-a-hoop to have the extra coupons.

In 1832, a certain Jo Livesley got the Temperance Movement going in Preston, at a pub called The Old Dog, where he drew up the first public pledge to stay on the wagon. Those in town the night I was there obviously didn't get the memo. In Hogarth's, the only thing they were abstaining from was polite conversation. They were on edge because of the football – Preston were away to neighbours Blackburn. I overheard the following:

'How are you?'

'Not bad, not good, getting older.'

'How's your missus?'

'Should have buried that.'

'Cuts hair, doesn't she?'

'You're having a laugh!'

'I could do with a cut.'

'Absolute twat.'

'Apparently, if you go to a Turkish one they do your ears.'

'Need to get your eyes tested, mate!'

'You off on holiday this year?'

'Bologna.'

'Nice.'

'Kids can't get enough of the stuff.'

'Italy?'

'Spag bol. Go on, my son!'

My next stop was a craft beer joint called Plug and Taps. A sandwich board outside invited me to come in for a girly drink – beer! The invitation was alluding to the fact that women have been brewing and boozing for thousands of years. There's a decent book by Mallory O'Meara on the matter. While I don't recall every word of *Girly Drinks*, not least because I read the bulk of it while under the influence of the titular refreshment, I do recall reading that the women of ancient Sumer were making pints millennia ago. The 'brewing priestesses' of Sumer would sing hymns to a beer goddess called Ninkasi (the hymns being beer recipes put to song), and do jugs in her honour. The priestesses chose to interpret the feeling of being a bit pissed as Ninkasi's divine essence surging through them. Cheers to that.

I had a pint of something by Northern Monk, which struck me as an oxymoron until I remembered old Bede in Sunderland and all the monkfish things he got up to.[14] I wandered around the space looking for somewhere to sit. It took me about four seconds. Then I wandered around again looking at the various artworks on display. Among them was a black and white photograph of a footballer making a tackle on a waterlogged pitch. I addressed a group at the bar, hoping one would know who the subject was. In the event, they all knew far more than was ideal. It was Tom Finney, legendary Preston winger, considered one of the greats of English football. Because footballers weren't laughably overpaid back then, Finney was also a plumber. The Preston Plumber they called him. Unlocked defences at the weekend, unblocked toilets during the week. Finney fought in the war for six years, never got booked, and retired at the age of 38 owing to a persistent groin problem, the latter detail being the only one I could relate to.

Any discussion of football in relation to Preston wouldn't be complete without mention of Dick Kerr Ladies FC. The team was founded in Preston during the First World War, filling a gap left by the factory's fellas, who were otherwise engaged. It all started one lunchbreak in the factory yard, when the female workers joined the male apprentices for a friendly match – and stuffed them. The team went on to play a succession of charity matches, gaining popularity with each one, drawing a crowd of 53,000 for a match against St Helens Ladies at Goodison Park in 1920. For this squad of talented trailblazers, the sky was the limit.

Only it wasn't. The Football Association saw to that. In 1921, the FA pooh-poohed the whole thing, arguing that the

---

[14] Some typos are worth retaining. Love the idea of Bede doing monk-fish things.

'game of football is quite unsuitable for females and should not be encouraged'. And they were true to their word. They didn't encourage it. The FA banned Dick Kerr Ladies from using any of the pitches or stadiums that were a part of the men's setup, a ban that remained in place for fifty years. Despite being forced to play on crappy pitches, DKL continued to draw massive crowds throughout the 1930s. The people liked what they saw, and voted with their feet, but the crusty bigwigs at the FA refused to backpedal or concede ground. As a result of their actions, the evolution of the women's game was halted for half a century. Stepping out of the Plug and Taps, it occurred to me that, with their fondness for playing football and burning down cottages, Preston girls sounded right up my street.

By my reckoning, I had a couple more in me, which is why I had another four. I looked in at The Black Horse around the corner because I was told it was fancy inside and had three addresses (it does, though how that improves the customer experience, I can't say), and then I caught the second half of a gig at a popular pub called The Continental, down by the River Ribble. When I pitched up, a fourpiece was in full swing in a barn around the back. The quartet were paying homage to a band called James – or a bloke called James, one of the two. I recognised a few of the songs, including one about sitting down. It was unexpectedly emotive stuff; the tunes and harmonies unapologetically uplifting. I fell for the music – or this version of it – just as I was falling for Preston.

I do fall for places quite easily. I'm quickly smitten – which can be handy when you've only got a weekend. I fall for the novelty, the stories, the people, the simple magic of being elsewhere. It all conspires to pull the wool over my eyes, to elevate the fairly normal into the somewhat amazing. At its best, and no matter its mode or vector or endpoint, travel has a weightless quality that is so at odds with the heaviness we ordinarily carry about with us that even a weekend in Preston can feel like an out-of-body experience. Trouble is, as with all moods, and all magic, the spell seldom lasts, and by the time I had taken a trio of nightcaps at a bar called Lonely People, and won an argument in the garden of Blitz (with someone who refused to believe that I had been curling that afternoon), I was treading the outskirts of disquiet, and feeling the beginnings of blue. Oh, to bottle that ten-minute feeling, when life is a kind of heaven!

You might be thinking, *Sorry, what? Curling? That afternoon? What's this clown on about?* Well, thing is, and at the risk of stating the blindingly obvious, you have to omit some of the stuff you do when recounting a trip like this, else the reader's hippocampus will likely rise from its armchair and quietly leave the room, and while I was massively impressed with Preston's Olympic-sized curling facility that is open to the public, and respected the fact that the Preston Curling Club have been at it almost as long as the Sumerians have been brewing, and appreciated the instruction afforded me at The Flower Bowl Entertainment Centre as to how I might slide the thing into the thing, the thing is, I didn't really enjoy it that much. Don't get me wrong, I'm glad I went. I'm glad I got down on one knee and gave it a shot. It's just that the actual experience – of curling solo on a Friday night in a faraway place – didn't have the heartwarming effect I had hoped for, and it hurt my knees a bit, which is why I omitted it from this record (and then didn't). I can't be sure, but I think it was the being on my own that did it. I'm usually pretty good on my own, but the whole time I was on that ice, pushing and sweeping, I couldn't shake the feeling that there are some things in life that aren't meant to be done independently, and that curling might be one of them. Hey-ho.

Winckley Square was looking idyllic the next morning. The sun was hitting the winter trees, as a twinkly dew embellished the grass. It was enough to inspire a good mood in the saddest of souls. I went up to Fishergate, swung a right, then sauntered towards a place called Rise, which was worth getting up for. About two years ago I promised to staple my thumb to a tree if I ever used the adjective I'm about to use, but what's a promise for if not to be broken, so here it goes – Rise is Instagrammable. Which basically means picturesque, noteworthy, remarkable – all good words already in circulation that are likely to outlive a social media platform. Rise is a small space with big windows and an open-plan kitchen. I enjoyed watching the chef as they lined dishes up on the pass, and the sight of poached eggs being briefly gilded by heat lamps before being whisked off to punters by a girl with pink hair. The place has a recognisable look, and a recognisable menu, but it's not playing at being a certain type of on-point café. It's legit, it's honest – just good and good-looking.

The café's in a good spot, as well. Part of Miller Arcade, which is another of Preston's high street sweet spots, architecturally speaking. The arcade, which dates to 1899, has got some class alright – a brass neck almost, handsome to the point of arrogance. There's something *gastronomic* about the building – it's got a sweet vibe, is giving pudding somehow. Then why so quiet? The ground floor was far from bustling and the upper floors, from what I could tell, were completely vacant. Ah, the high street. It'll get a break one of these days. First it was shopping centres – commercial adjuncts to the high street that nicked trade off the little man. When these started struggling, shinier alternatives were optimistically erected ... on the other side of the street, which succeeded only in shifting the local economy rather than bolstering it. Then the retail parks came, with their massive units and huge carparks, and then it was the turn of e-commerce to give the high street a kick in the teeth, the poor old sod.

In the face of all this, Preston council has come out fighting, and others are starting to take note. There is such a thing as the Preston Model, conceived by a Labour councillor called Matthew Brown. In short, it is an ultra-localist approach to tackling inequality and boosting the local economy. It involves getting the city's big spenders – the council, the university, the hospital, the police – to buy local. When the numbers were crunched back in 2013, they showed that just 5% of the £1.2 billion being spent annually by such institutions was staying in town. Whether to London-based builders, or global catering outfits, the money was leaving Preston. Not ideal.

With Brown steering the ship, Preston council, slowly but surely, persuaded the city's anchor institutions to use local suppliers. If a local supplier couldn't meet the demand of a contract on its own (for school dinners, say), then the contract was divvied up until the task was manageable. Between 2013 and 2017, the amount of public money staying in Preston all but tripled. According to Lynsey Hanley, writing in the *Guardian*, the Preston Model works: 'By 2020, Preston had achieved its highest employment rate and lowest levels of economic inactivity for more than 15 years, and in 2018 it was voted the UK's most improved city to live and work in. It also shows how local authorities, within the constraints of austerity and wider economic forces, can make choices that benefit citizens rather than companies.' Sounds alright to me.

It was time to get on my bike. I picked up an e-bike from a hire shop by the railway station, then proceeded with it to the beginning of The Guild Wheel, a 20-mile cycle- and walk-way that enwraps the city. It was some starting line: leftover spring greens, crispy autumn flotsam, a broad band of untroubled water, and, in the distance, a train crossing the Ribble, its image mirrored in the river. It wasn't HS2 by a long chalk, and nor will it ever be. In October 2023, after ten years of infrastructure development, the proposed northern branches of HS2 were summarily derailed and tossed in the bin. Forget the harrying of the north, now it's the tarrying of the north – the region's being held back, stymied. Or so it can feel.

Preston became a market town way back in 1179. Ever since, the locals have celebrated their right to flog turnips with a spell of festive carry on every twenty years called the Preston Guild. The Guild Wheel takes its name from this rare celebration. Said Wheel had, by now, led me to Avenham Park, which was verdant and undulating and opulent, with wide promenades and blooming gardens. A show-off rec if ever I saw one. I paused at the side of the river, and gave it a good thinking about. The Ribble is a biggie – 75 miles all up, starting in Yorkshire and finishing in the Irish Sea – and has always been integral to Preston's fortunes, not least when it comes to matters of the cloth. The city has shown a textile bent since the thirteenth century, its water supply being ideal for trousers. A big chapter in Preston's yarn involves a local lad called Richard Arkwright, who, back in 1768, contrived the spinning frame here (or a key component of it, at any rate), and so doing gave the industrial revolution a push in the right direction. It is not stretching the truth to say that Britain's industrial boom, and all that it issued, owed a lot to the endeavours of a certain Dick Arkwright. He wasn't thanked for his efforts, I understand, not uniformly at any rate. His invention made many people redundant, and poor Dick was chased out of town.

I left Dick behind and continued on my way, pedalling happily between an avenue of riverside trees, atop a carpet of crestfallen leaves, and through the shadows of elderly lampposts. I don't think you can rely on Lancashire for good weather, so

I won't make a big deal of it, but gosh what an effect it can have! And when it's winter and the trees are bare, there's less getting in the way of the light, less sunblock as it were, meaning the rays can get everywhere at once, and burnish it all. I slowed down as I passed a walker on the phone, hoping to eavesdrop on something that chimed with my mood. 'Get me one as well,' didn't really do it.

I came to Walton Bridge, four hundred years late for an almighty scrap. Oliver Cromwell's victory on this bridge, during the Battle of Preston in 1648, brought the English Civil War to a close and sealed the death warrant of Charles I. Cromwell and the Parliamentarians were up against the Scots in Preston, who were on the side of the King, who was in hiding on the Isle of Wight, or up a tree somewhere. The Scots had recently done a significant 180; had dropped a shoulder and turned on a sixpence. During the initial fighting to dislodge the monarch, the Scots had been allies of Cromwell. When the monarch was dislodged, the Scots, who just couldn't get enough scrapping, switched sides and set about getting the King back on his big chair, having only just got the poor sod off it. Led by the Duke of Hamilton, the Scots headed south, staying the night at an expensive gastropub in Windermere, until they were met by Cromwell and his groupies at Preston, who nipped their foray in the bud in indelicate fashion.

About seventy years later, another almighty barney unfolded in these parts. The battle of 1715 was, unoriginally, about who got to be top dog. On one side were those pesky Jacobite rebels, who wanted James on the throne, and on the other side were those who wanted George in the hotseat. The Jacobites lost, and the defeat put their rising to bed (for a while at least). The 1715 match-up was the last proper battle on English soil. On account of all the above argy-bargy, and its role in the old industrial rev, the historian Dan Snow – live on BBC Breakfast – called Preston 'one of the most important cities in the world'. Which is a much better tagline, from a marketing standpoint, than 'The Home of the Butter Pie'.

I entered countryside – unmarked lanes, low hedgerows, surrounding fields – and the silence was deafening. No, that can't be right … The silence was clear, was unmissable, was so obvious and arresting that I had to stop and stare at it, to respect it, to underline it. I got off my bike and admired the quiet fields and the stock-still ponies. By chance, I'd stopped at eleven – on the eleventh day, of the eleventh month. It didn't explain the silence, but it amplified it somehow, and forced on me some feelings that I would otherwise have dodged. Palestine. Ukraine. Sudan. And others, of course. A moment of reflection. A moment of reckoning. A fresh feeling that it's a ridiculous privilege to be on a bike on a Saturday, with nothing pressing ahead, and nothing troubling behind. Count blessings, I told myself, as I went on my way, and spare more than a thought for those losing theirs.

I'm not a cyclist. I don't own a cycle. And that's probably why the joy I now felt at finding myself upon one was quite so sharp. They take one by surprise after a period away – like shortbread biscuits. I would happily wager that when some anoraks four centuries hence get together to consider the vehicles of lore and nominate a winner, the bicycle will pip all others to the post. The combo of function and fun is unmatched. Look how children take to them with such elan, such glee, such unbridled, destabilised gusto. What's more, the bicycle is a vehicle in more ways than one – by hopping on the saddle, my mind had gained a brief licence to roam, to mosey around, to mooch as it were. It landed on war, and then it landed on joy. So it goes.

Some way further around the Wheel, I came to a nature reserve. Brockholes, managed by the Wildlife Trust, a leading

UK conservation charity. They've done a good job of it, I must say. Opened in 2011, the reserve offers two hundred acres of hides and trails, for spotting ospreys and otters and bitterns and lapwings. Walking around the floating visitor village, on the site of an old quarry, I could have been somewhere else entirely. The style and vibe (colluding with the weather) were transportive. I spent a happy ten minutes prospecting for goldfinches, the birds being due in town any second for a spot of overwintering. There have been some rare sightings here, I was told. A canny Mancunian was spotted once, for example. And so was a shaggy-crested belted kingfisher, which had been aiming for the Caribbean but wound up in Preston. A storm is believed to have diverted the bird, though I like to think it just fancied a change.

I bought a piece of cake that I didn't require because the reserve gets no direct funding, then mounted my e-steed and continued my loop – starting with a hair-raising climb through Boilton Wood, which I punctuated with pauses in order to catch my breath and catch a glimpse of the escalating view – of the Ribble, the Pennine Dales, the Forest of Bowland. The Tolkien Trail was out there somewhere. And so was the heart of Great Britian: the geographical centre of England, Scotland and Wales, just north of Blackburn, not far from Nelson and Chipping and Ribchester and Barley. Having got to the top of the wood, I asked some walkers which way to proceed, knowing that I hadn't time to do the whole lap. They said the quickest route back into town was through the Moor Nook estate, but they didn't fancy my chances. They reckoned I'd do well to get through in one piece. I asked when they last ran the gauntlet themselves. 'Well, I 'aven't ever done it in truth,' he said. 'It's just a known thing that you daren't.' Hm. The power of recycled ideas.

By no means can I commend every aspect of the Moor Nook estate, but I got through without fuss, and the chippy on Pope

Lane was a belter. I ordered a chip barmcake, not having a clue what the second word implied. It implied a roll, I discovered, or a bap, bun or cob. It was chips in buttered bread at any rate, and let's leave it at that. Most importantly, it was lush – and only £2.80. Pound for pound, it was up there with anything I'd eaten for months. That's the thing with places that don't get many tourists – the businesses need you to come back. They can't just dish out junk knowing a fresh busload will be pounding the pavements on the morrow. While a lack of tourism means, in all likelihood, more empty units in town, and a few quiet corners, it also means that those local businesses that are going strong tend to be – well, strong. The worst pizza I've ever had was in Venice, for heaven's sake.

On the train out of town, I thought back to Grayson Perry, and his portrait of Chelmsford, and wondered what I'd include if I had to conjure something similar in homage to Preston, which is to say something impressionistic and personal, rather than earnest and upright. I'd have Rigby on her bike, I reckon, giving a two-fingered salute to polite society and the status quo. I'd have Tom Finney holding his nose while unclogging a U-bend. I'd have Miller Arcade, and Crystal House, and Winckley Square on a sunny Saturday morn. I'd have the River Ribble, and Avenham Park, and a pair of Mormons in Plug and Taps. The bus station would be there (it would be everywhere if I'm honest), and so would that bloke who's off to Bologna with the kids. I'd have that long line of phone boxes, and Gromit on his bench, and Flintoff playing bingo, and the woman I argued with in the garden of Blitz. It would be quite the picture. A decent picture. Arkwright could supply the frame, I guess.

4

Wolverhampton

The best thing since avocado

When I mentioned my holiday plans to the lady on the train the prospect made her shudder. She tried to put me off the idea. Banged on about Birmingham for half an hour, as though it were the best thing since avocado. It turned out the lady was from Wolverhampton but had boycotted the place as soon as she could. Didn't flee far, only to a village four miles out. She told me that Wolves was voted the fifth worst city in the world by Lonely Planet. I thought she must have got the wrong end of the stick, but no, she hadn't. Some years ago, Lonely Planet ran a survey on its website. Asked readers to nominate the worst city they'd ever been to, crunched the numbers, then published them. Because Lonely Planet is a massive, highly regarded, international media company, the results went global – no matter that they were about as rigorous and meaningful as a tube of toothpaste. (The article I read about the rankings was published by the BBC.) I'm sure Seoul and LA – also in the bottom five – didn't lose much sleep over their ranking, but the reputational damage to a place like Wolverhampton, although tricky to measure, must have been considerable, and endurant. The council leader at the time, a guy called Neville, wasn't best pleased. He invited Lonely Planet to visit the city and make its own mind up. I'm inclined to think the invitation wasn't accepted, for when, sometime after my trip to Wolverhampton, I leafed through a Lonely Planet guide to England published in 2019, I found no mention of the city. Not a single line.

The station looked fresh off the rack. Black and gold, the colours of the city. It was covered in frost that cold, clear December morning, while the milky sunlight was having a dreamy Saturday effect. Bridging a ring road into the centre, I almost got flattened by a tram – didn't see that coming. Speaking of flattening, The Department for Levelling Up (and Housing and Communities) is here, on the right, in a new office building, doing its utmost to bring trade and attention and pride to places deemed lacking in such things. It's the first government ministry outside of London, unbelievably. Part of a plan to spread the civil service out, balance the books, even out the State. Why Wolves for this HQ? Well, partly because it turned blue at the 2019 election, after many years as a brick in the so-called Red Wall. The Department for Levelling Up was, in a way, a thank-you for ditching Labour.

I had an initial walkabout, as is my wont. The so-called Chubb Building is nice. Chubb are the lock and key people, if you didn't know. They've been keeping things safe around here for centuries. It's a graceful structure: well-built, redbrick, bit of a poser – the doorman of the city. It was converted into an independent cinema and offices, but the cinema hasn't survived, alas.[15] Just up the road is the Queen's Building. It's a good-looking

---

[15] Later discovered that a new four-screen independent cinema is set to open on the site in May 2025.

thing – plenty of decorative cornicing, two square turrets – but it looks a bit stranded, a bit out on a limb. It used to be part of the railway station, and then a part of the bus station. Now it's a listed foodbank, a protected one-stop, offering discounted grub and groceries. There wasn't a single foodbank in 1997. Now they're ten-a-penny, and not for no reason. To my mind, foodbanks are a manifestation of the public bailing the government out – of the Big Society that David Cameron dreamed of, operating nicely. Danny Dorling's *Shattered Nation* (2023) is a bruising examination of where we're at with respect to these issues, and plenty more besides. One of the most testing allegations in the book is that, in terms of quality of life, the UK peaked in 1973 and has been getting worse since. Ouch. Dorling could have done with coming to Wolves on a wintry Saturday. That would've cheered him up. It was cheering me up, at any rate. I just saw a topless man with a Santa hat on driving a convertible Escort. That was cheering. He went through a red light, mind.

And that's another reason to be cheerful – traffic lights. The first experiment with automatic traffic lights was conducted in Wolves in 1927. The experiment went well and so the trial was made permanent. The inaugural set of lights were positioned on Princes Square. The lights that stand at the junction today have stripey poles to mark the importance of the location. Drivers trying to clock the commemorative stripes have caused multiple accidents – a consequence that was unintended, one assumes. Just along from the famous lights is The Grand Theatre. Nothing shattered about this old dame. Muscular, fancy, but also restrained somehow – fabulous without even trying. Charles John Phipps was the architect, and it's considered one of his best designs – by people in a position to judge such things. The theatre was showing a panto. *Snow White.* Might pop in later, I thought. Might also pop into a pub called The Billy Wright. I think Billy used to bang them in for the football team.[16]

Queen Street offers quite an array – edificially speaking. Lots of venerable straitlaced Georgian stuff, the odd Dutch-looking bit, formerly glorious libraries and courts and dispensaries and mechanics' institutes, now otherwise employed. The old *Express & Star* building is here too. Has an American feel to it. Imposing Art Deco. One half expects Clark Kent to walk out the massive front doors. I guess the doors needed to be big so they could accommodate some of the personalities employed by the paper. Boris Johnson did work experience here, as a precocious four-year-old. Drafted opposing viewpoints on the matter of gobstoppers. I walked around the downtown streets for about an hour in total, and in that time Liverpool and Leeds and Ludlow and Luton were all hinted at by the buildings. Wolves is one of those places – it brings other places to my mind. A Georgian this. A Victorian that. A medieval the other. In short, the city is well-stocked.

I called in at a café called Sassy for a butty and a cuppa. At the neighbouring table was a paramedic off duty. At least I hope they were off duty. I suppose they might just have had a very relaxed attitude to work. Anyway, they were sharing stories with the owner of the café. So-and-so had a stroke. So-and-so tipped me a tenner while having a heart attack. So-and-so accidentally kicked me in the groin when I tried to clear their airway. It was nice to get a

---

[16] He didn't. He was a defender. And the former captain of England. First player in the world to win 100 caps for their country. Part of a showbiz couple, being married to one of the Beverley Sisters, a harmonious trio from the East End of London, who had a hit with 'I Saw Mommy Kissing Santa Claus', which I hope wasn't based on a true story. There's a clip online of the sisters doing a few numbers in Wolverhampton at The Grand. In between songs, Babs Beverley, Wright's wife, cracks a joke about Billy insisting on changing ends at half-time.

sense of the local lilt, and also the local mood. Based on what I'd seen and heard up to that point, I'd say the local mood was pretty good on the whole. Fairly buoyant. Fairly positive. I was sufficiently encouraged to lean across and ask the paramedic what he reckoned the best thing to do in Wolverhampton was.

'Leave,' he said.

'Oh, come on.'

'Have you been to Birmingham?'

'Like an avocado, is it?'

'What?'

'There must be *some* things you appreciate about Wolves. Imagine you had just one day left in the city. Before being exiled to West Bromwich or Dudley. And you had to do your favourite things. What would you do?'

He gave this some thought, then smiled, then laughed a bit, then said, seeing as I wanted to know, that West Park is lovely, and the city archives are fascinating, and there's a cracking Chinese on Queen Street. He finished his tea, mopped up the yolk, got to his feet, unlocked his ambulance from a distance of ten metres, and said, 'Now if you don't mind, there's someone out there about to have a terrible afternoon and they might tip me a tenner.'

The paramedic might have mentioned St Peter's as well. I went across to the church now. The building is thirteenth-century, but has been extended and refurbished over the years. Nonetheless, the church and its gardens are the oldest place in Wolverhampton. In one corner of the gardens, the bust of a sailor caught my attention. I walked over and, after scratching away at the ice, learned that I was looking up at a local lad called Douglas Morris Harris, whose features were drenched in fine, frozen thread. Douglas joined the Navy as soon as he could, towards the end of the First World War. He was given the job of dealing with the telegraphs on a boat stationed between the heel of Italy and Albania, one of several boats that had been strategically positioned to block access to the Adriatic. When a bunch of Austrian cruisers turned up, the Battle of the Otranto Barrage well and truly kicked-off. Douglas' boat – a drifter – came under heavy fire. Douglas stayed at his post throughout the onslaught, receiving messages, logging them, knowing they would be crucial to the outcome of the fighting. He was killed by a piece of shrapnel, then later found dead at his station, slumped over his logbook. He was nominated for a bravery award – but didn't get it. It was said, by the Sea Lords, that Douglas could have put up more of a fight. Douglas may have been overlooked by officialdom, but he wasn't overlooked by the people of Wolverhampton. When the bust before me was put up in 1918, most of the town came out to mark the occasion. People – as well as places – don't always get the credit they deserve.

While we're dealing with inanimate objects, let's have a look at a couple more, before we move on to do something less exciting. First up, in Queen Square, is a man on a horse, which is a bit of a local hotspot. The man is Prince Albert. When Queen Victoria came up for the unveiling, it is believed that she drew the curtains of her train carriage as it entered the city's outskirts. I'm told the sculptor committed suicide after spotting that he'd cocked up one of the legs or something, which is tragic if true.[17]

Next up is a statue of Miss Wolves, who has her back to St Peter's, her eye on the council, and appears to be carrying a

---

[17] It's not true. The sculptor lived for many years after the unveiling and there was nothing wrong with his sculpture. Thank you to those local historians behind historywebsite.co.uk for squashing that regional rumour. Fantastic resource.

copy of the local paper. Lady Wulfruna, to give Miss Wolves her proper title, gave the city its name. She inherited a farm on this spot in roughly 985, and what she did with it sowed the seeds for the town that would come. A certain Charles Wheeler sculpted the sculpture. Wheeler was a Freeman of Wolverhampton. It is my understanding that a Freeman can basically do whatever they want whenever they're in town, including bringing themselves on at half-time if Wolves are more than two goals down (a not uncommon occurrence).

As I said, Lady Wulfruna is facing the council offices, which have been done in the postmodern style, and are thought to resemble the poo emoji. I managed to resist a closer inspection, going instead under the ring road (which was starting to repeat on me) and towards the city archives, which are housed in the old Molineux Hotel, once home to the industrious family that gave the local football stadium its name. On the first floor of the elegant redbrick building, a woman called Lynn was poring over a compilation of newspapers – thousands of editions brought together in one tome. She does it for fun. Goes through said tome every weekend, picks out news items from yesteryear to share with the public: a woman arrested for pinching toothpaste, a man tipping a tenner while having a heart attack – that sort of thing. Elsewhere in the building, I found a collection of maps, dating back hundreds of years. It was fascinating to trace Wolverhampton's development. I studied one from 1935. There were so many factories: iron, brick, steel, varnish, coal. The workshop of the world, they called this part of the world. They also called it the Black Country, and not because it grew apples. The moniker either pertains to the pollution that was once rampant, or the massive seam of coal that cuts through the region, just below the surface, easily got at. Tolkien's Mordor is thought to have been inspired by the Black Country. The region was awarded

UNESCO Global Geopark status in 2020, for its geological heritage. That will get the cruise ships in.

An archives assistant took an interest in what I was doing, floated over and pointed out a few things. Low Hill Estate, West Park, the old railway down to Dudley, Wightwick Manor …

'You might want to visit Wightwick Manor,' he said. 'Nice old place. Arts and Crafts. Run by the National Trust.'

'And the Low Hill Estate?'

'As I said, you might want to visit Wightwick Manor.'

I studied maps from the 1950s, the 1970s, the 1990s, enjoying the slow spectacle of things evolving. East Park used to offer outdoor bathing. Rough Hills used to dominate the south. And when the ring road turned up – boy did it make a splash. Suddenly there was a wonky bull's eye in the middle of town, with roads coming off it like tentacles. It was as if a giant jellyfish had landed on Wolverhampton, determined to take over the map. Of course the road didn't just land, didn't just appear. It took 26 years to complete – suggesting they made a meal of it as well as a ring.

A map – any map – is a beautiful thing on closer inspection, on any inspection, in fact. The most unassuming artwork. The shapes made by roads and railways. The shapes made by all the bits in between. The haphazard form, the ad hoc arrangement, the elegant chaos. Add text and colour and it becomes a feast for the eyes. Light blue ponds, pale green parks, pink for pedestrianised. A vicarage, a reservoir, a trading estate – what an itinerary that is! A viaduct, a hospital, a temple, a golf course – even better still! All the bits and pieces of a place, gathered together, seemingly harmless and entirely good-natured, like nothing could go wrong there, not in a million years. It was a nice way to travel – next to a local, looking down on a series of old maps.

'Where would you definitely not go?' I asked.

'Erm. Maybe Bentley Bridge.'

'Bentley Bridge?'

'It's a retail park.'

'Ah, right. I'm with you. Yeah, fuck Bentley Bridge.'

I went next to the gallery, which is contained in a nice old building, done in Bath stone. There's an interesting frieze on the main face, showing sixteen characters representing the arts and crafts. The gallery is best known for its collection of Pop Art, that postwar movement that fired a shot at the canon, by asking questions about what art is and what it should feature and frame and so on. The movement was best embodied by Andy Warhol and his can of soup. Wolverhampton Art Gallery snapped up a load of Warhols when they weren't exactly fashionable. Canny acquisitions, you might say.

My favourite part of the gallery was the room featuring artworks selected by members of the local community. The chosen artworks are a reflection of local taste, of local leanings, and are a nice addition to the stuff picked and hung by pro curators. Further evidence that this is a gallery that's in touch with its people arrived when I was told that, once a month, something called Jolly Bolly happens in the Georgian Room, which is basically Bollywood dancing, for kids, amid oil paintings. What's not to like about that? Why shouldn't a gallery be put to such uses? Yoga with Titian, five-a-side among Turners, Keep-Fit with Rothko.

On my way out, I had a lovely chat with a volunteer called Sheila, next to a statue of Adonis in the foyer. There was a nice moment when, during an anecdote, Shelia absentmindedly leant on the old boy's marbles. By her own admission, Shelia's got a gob on her the size of West Bromwich. 'I'm a DJ on the local hospital radio station. Everybody knows me.' I could well believe it. Wolverhampton is that sort of place, and that sort of size. The city's scale allows familiarity – and fondness, therefore. Repeat encounters permit an escalation of concern, of kinship, of kindness. It can also go the other way, of course. I'm not so naive as to think that seeing the same person more than once a month is in all cases delightful.

Not far from the gallery is a restaurant called Bilash. It opened in 1982, and sits between St Peter's and The Halls, a recently renovated music venue that has already hosted the likes of Blur and Travis and the Red Hot Chilli Pipers. I spoke with the present owner of the restaurant, who told me that, back in the early eighties, his dad was up from London for a gig, saw a gap in the market, and resolved to fill it with curry. At first the locals were suspicious, but eventually they came round – and round, and round, and round. Now the son is at the helm, and The Bilash is winning plaudits from all over the shop. I had the Goan King Prawns, and believe you me, the dish deserves its capitals. Just two prawns, but they were the size of local authorities, butterflied and elevated with a dozen secret spices. The best was yet to come – a pudding called Gajar Ka Halwa, a blend of carrot and nuts that takes ages to make. It was a bit like sticky toffee pudding and carrot cake combined, which as far as I'm concerned is like combining Nigella Lawson and Romesh Ranganathan. I actually wanted to have my cake and eat it; wanted to scoff the lot and squirrel it away in my coat pocket, to be picked at during the pantomime.

And so I was back at the Grand, feeling a bit stuffed and sluggish if I'm candid. (Whoever decided that culture should be served after dinner was a twit.) Sean Connery performed at the Grand – I read going up the stairs – and so did Charlie Chaplin. Churchill gave a speech here, and was booed by the local ladies as he did so, who didn't like the cut of his jib or the thrust of his thinking. David Lloyd George dropped by after the First World War, got on stage and promised homes fit for heroes. You get the picture. The place has got history. Key figures have trodden its boards, have addressed its balconies, have confronted its stalls.

Nothing heavy on the cards tonight – just a version of *Snow White*, as I mentioned. The script had been written in house, by Buttons and his mate, so what I was being served was locally sourced produce. From the off, the humour and storytelling was operating on several levels, one for the kids and one for the adults. There was a smart silliness to it all, that took me out of myself, and held my attention. Which was just as well, because I was ready to conk out before I arrived, the prospect of 2.5 hours of *Snow White* hardly a wonderful one. I'd deliberately taken a seat at the end of a row in case a swift exit was needed. But in the event it was a riot, it really was. The tunes were uplifting and catchy and oddly philosophical, while the humour flirted with bawdy and toilet but always pulled up short. It was naughty but in disguise – it had to be, and was improved by being so. The bit that tickled me most – I'm embarrassed to say – was when Buttons looked at a member of the audience and said, 'Nice nose. Pick it yourself?' That's all I want after two giant prawns, four poppadoms, and a bowl of carrot cake.

While I was happy with proceedings, not everybody was happy with me. During the interval – and I admit that this was perhaps a mistake – I wandered around the theatre having a butcher's, up to the rafters, up to the Gods, looking at the ceiling, admiring the plaster work and the masonry. I was being curious, I suppose – and the fact wasn't lost on my fellow audience members. It didn't help that I was wearing a big winter coat and carrying a backpack. I resembled a dishevelled ghostbuster. In short, it wasn't standard behaviour for a panto-goer at half-time. I can see that now. But at the time I couldn't, which is why, when I returned to my seat before curtain-up, and the duty manager of the theatre approached to say that several members of the audience had expressed their concerns and reservations regarding wtf I was up to, it came as a bit of a surprise. Our chat went a bit like this.

'Pardon me, sir, but can I ask a question?'

'Sure.'

'Are you a creative?'

'Sort of. Why?'

'It's just that a few people are getting a bit suspicious.'

'I was on telly once. *Sunday Brunch*. You know the show on—'

'It's the backpack, you see. And you're alone. And you're wandering around. Looking at the ceiling.'

'And what do they suspect?'

'Well, it's not tourism.'

'Terrorism?'

'Yeah, and something else.'

'Crikey.'

'But it's alright because I said to them, "Look, I'm sure it's nothing to worry about. He's probably just a creative." Are you a creative?'

'I'm a writer.'

'There you are. Crisis over. Work in the theatre do you?'

'No, I'm a travel writer. I'm actually on holiday in Wolverhampton.'

'Sorry?'

'I'm on holiday here.'

'Oh god, now you're making me suspicious again …'

It was all good in the end. The young lad – who was only doing his job, bless him – was satisfied that, while far from normal, I was essentially harmless, and certainly not someone who was bent on blowing up the building, and I was permitted to remain where I was. And do you know what, I'm glad I didn't get handed over to the cops at half-time, because the second half was even better than the first.

I took a taxi to my digs – The Mount. I wanted to see the best hotel in Wolverhampton, and the consensus led me here. It used to be a family home: Mr and Mrs Mander, paint and varnish people, and a big deal locally. It's some gaff, although a bit twee, playing at being a castle. You can have a room here for about £100 a night, which is still steep if travelling solo, but not bad if you're splitting with another. Not sure what David Lloyd George was paying when he stayed in 1918. At any rate, David's stay proved invigorating – he called an election while he was here, before jogging back into town to make that speech at the theatre about heroic housing.

I had half a pint of bitter at the bar. There was a Christmas party in full swing. A window company, according to the receptionist. A few of them looked double-glazed, alright. I almost got yanked up onto the dance floor. When a song by Slade came on, 'Cum On Feel the Noize', there was an almighty roar of approval. Slade were from around here, you see. Got going in the 1960s, then began taking over the world – or the bit between Wolves and Walsall anyway. To increase the band's chances of success, their manager reckoned a different look was required, and turned the boys into skinheads. According to Dave Hill, the guitarist, they were the most terrified skinheads in the country. They soon switched back to glam rock and looking like wallies, and went on to hit the big time. Slade were the biggest-selling band of the seventies. Only ABBA had as many number-one hits. I wonder if Wolves could make more of Slade, as Liverpool wrings The Beatles for every posthumous penny. I wouldn't mind seeing where Noddy Holder played badminton, or where Dave Hill bought his flares, or where the band were chased up the high street by a set of legitimate fascists.

Wolverhampton

Just when I thought I'd got away with it, and they weren't going to do it, the DJ put on that effing Christmas song, the Slade one, 'Merry Xmas Everybody'. The song's creation story is an interesting one. For a bit of a laugh, the band were challenged to write a Christmas song by so-and-so's mother-in-law. Holder dug out a song he'd written years before that everyone said was rubbish, tinkered with the lyrics until they were seasonal, and then duly presented the band's biggest hit. Goes to show – just because something gets overlooked, doesn't mean it hasn't got legs.

My room was at the end of the modern extension, closer to Dudley than the main entrance. I made myself a tea, got into bed, then considered the people of Wolves from a statistical perspective. 0.1% pansexual. 12% Sikh. 0.2% working in agriculture, forestry or fishing. 46% semi-detached. 8.4% divorced. I did a quick calculation and deduced that the chances of running into a divorced pansexual Sikh working in agriculture, forestry or fishing were 0.0%, which struck me as a shame. I put the computer aside and read the opening chapters of Sathnam Sanghera's 2009 memoir *The Boy with the Topknot*, which I'd bought from the bookshop on Dudley Street. The author grew up in a Sikh family on a council estate in Wolverhampton – and not without incident. From a young age, he had different aspirations to those around him, different leanings, different dreams. He moved to London as soon as he could and, presumably to punish himself for fleeing the nest, got a job in the media. I couldn't wait to see how it panned out for the lad.[18]

---

[18] He acquired legendary status, basically. That's how it panned out.

It had snowed overnight. I woke up to a different city. Whitewashed. Freshly painted. But I knew it wouldn't last. Indeed, it had started to thaw before I'd finished my breakfast, which I ate looking out onto the snowy garden, where the children of a once eminent industrial family used to play hide-and-seek. They were in varnish, the Manders. The foursome next to me could certainly do with a coat or two of something. A faction of the Christmas party from last night, slouching through bacon, grumbling through porridge, sharing hungover stories of professional misbehaviour. I overheard the following. 'It was all I could do not to grab him by the balls.' I say.

I walked to Wightwick Manor, a significant Victorian pile that sits about a mile or so from the hotel. As I traced a curving snow-capped lane, I closed my eyes and listened to the snow under foot until I realised it was dangerous to do so. At the entrance to the manor and its gardens, I spoke to Sue, a volunteer. I asked my usual questions: what to do, where to go, that sort of thing. She said Shrewsbury was nice and so were the Shropshire Hills. 'But what of Wolverhampton?' I asked. She said it was empty now. Said it wasn't what it used to be. Pointed the finger at Amazon, Thatcher, Blair and Kardashian – 'And in that order,' she said, a touch confusingly.

Wightwick Manor was also owned by the Mander family. A bridge once joined the gardens of this place and my hotel. Generally speaking, I don't get excited by massive detached houses that used to be owned by rich folk. I don't care about the interior of my own dwelling, let alone someone else's. In the event, however, I quite enjoyed having a nose around. It was a very Arts and Crafts sort of place. There was William Morris wallpaper and wall hangings, and even the man's ideas had been used as decoration. One notion that got me thinking went as follows: 'If you want a golden rule that will fit everything, this is it: Have nothing in your houses that you do not know to be useful or believe to be beautiful.' I read the words with some trepidation, knowing that if my partner got wind of them, I'd likely be out on my ear. There was an indecent lack of beauty down in the servant quarters, I regret to say, one saucepan in particular striking me as immorally unattractive.

Call me a philistine, but the best element of Wightwick Manor was simply gassing with the volunteers, getting their take on the house and the people that have lived there. Sir Geoffrey was an MP. Miles was a sheep farmer and married an Indian Princess. Charles Marcus Septimus Gustav is a barrister in London and due to inherit the lot. Imbued in everything that the volunteers shared was a reverence for the house and the people attached to it.

'It's a *very* interesting family tree,' said one volunteer.

'Aren't they all?'

'Mine isn't,' she said.

'No?'

'Well, I don't know anything beyond my mum.'

'Then you should have a look.'

'Yeah, but you can't find out about normal people. Not unless you're Danny Dyer and you're on that show.'

'My nan managed it.'

'Did she?'

'She uncovered a relative deported to Australia for stealing rhubarb and flashing her knickers.'

'At the same time?'

'It was the same afternoon, I believe.'

'And where are they now?'

'The knickers?'

'The relative, you twit!'

'Long gone. This wasn't recently, Pamela ...'

'Probably eaten by a shark.'

'Yeah. Probably.'

After talking to Pam, I couldn't help reflecting on how funny it is how we come up with certain ideas, certain ways of thinking, about what's interesting and what's not, what's of value and what isn't, and then sort of stick with them, settle into them, like a nice pair of slippers. Some people don't conform to the standard patterns of thinking and regarding. Some people break the mould. One such person is Russell Shelton, who, after 35 years in San Francisco, working in Silicon Valley, loving life and getting a tan and making a mint, recently returned to live in his home city of Wolverhampton. Russell's relocation made national news. He told the BBC: 'I've travelled 6,000 miles to come back and tell you Wolverhampton is a great place to live.' I can imagine the reaction of some of the locals. 'Cool. Nice one. Now piss off back where you came from.' No, I'm kidding. I'm sure everyone enjoyed hearing of Shelton's change of heart, and respected his fresh perspective. After all, one of the bravest things you can do is admit that you were wrong. Apparently Russell is now working as a matchday steward at the football stadium, preventing fans from running onto the pitch in celebration. Must be the easiest gig in town.

On the bus back into town, I got chatting to a fella who reckons he was shot by a member of the Hells Angels on the Isle of Wight. He reckons the man that shot him had both a shotgun and a walking stick, which was novel even in those days. When we both alighted in the centre, he said I could do a lot worse than heading down to Major's in Bilston for the orange chips. When I asked what made them orange, he just shook his head, as if to warn me off that line of enquiry. He said he'd walk me to the tram stop.

I enjoyed the tram ride to Bilston. I enjoyed the light industry that went by (tyres, varnish), and a glorious old church that appears to have merged with a Sainsbury's. The way I was looking out the window, you'd think a stunning motion picture starring Clark Gable was going past. It wasn't, of course, it was only place and people, and the pair of them carrying on together, but there was something mesmerising about it nonetheless. Some, by instinct, marvel and wonder at the natural world. Some, by instinct, marvel and wonder at this. I've drawn the short straw, I reckon.

Major's is a family-run chip shop that has been going since 1975. I ordered a portion of chips (they come orange as standard) and a battered pig-in-blanket. The orange finish on the chips, which was somehow both a texture and a colour, had an almost ennobling effect. I don't know what ancient alchemy has to occur in order for the chips to turn orange, and nor do I want to know. Some things are better for being mysterious. There was another lad in Major's eating orange chips on his own. I got talking to him. His name was Tom Hicks and he was a photographer – of buildings mostly, the urban environment. Said he was a fair-weather photographer. Said he waits until the sun comes out, until the sky is completely and utterly blue, before grabbing his tool and hitting the streets. Said he may only work three days a month, but on those days, he makes Wolverhampton look gorgeous. He showed me some pics and, for sure, the lad is showing Wolves in a different light. Looking at his pictures, I couldn't help wondering whether beauty is always there no matter the conditions, or whether it needs certain weather in order to exist. I asked Tom about the orange but he didn't have a clue.[19]

---

[19] Check out *If Disappears, Still True*, a collaboration Tom did with a local poet, Liz Berry. Snaps of things on their last legs, set to poetry. It's lovely. Tom took the picture on the cover of this book, by the way.

I went to Bilston's indoor market and ogled the bangers, brooms, bags and blazers. Then I ogled Matt the baker as he bashed one out. Matt's apple pies are legendary. I watched him work, levelling up the pastry, wielding his pin like a wand, his fingers as thick as cucumbers and covered in what I took to be flour. He gave me a small custard tart on the house, bless him. 'That's what you get for being nosy,' he said.

I liked the idea – custard for curiosity. Who would have thought that having a butcher's in a bakery would pay such a dividend! Watching Matt make the apple pies was a bit of culture, as far as I was concerned. Not the sort you'll see on the telly, perhaps. Not the culture one thinks of when they hear the word, but culture nonetheless. I was reminded of an old episode of *World in Action*, made in the 1970s. The episode profiled a bloke called Jack, a factory worker, an ordinary chap, nothing special on the face of it. But the episode went beyond the face of it. It delved deep into Jack's life, into his thoughts and feelings, and by doing so it made poetry of the man, made his normal life appear noble and special and poetic. The simple provision of attention was sufficient to transform something dull into something that sparkled. They should make such a programme about Matt the baker turning out his apple pies at Bilston Market.

I got the tram back into the centre, then headed south on foot to a placed called The Yew Tree. It's a desi pub, which is basically a mashup of public house and Indian restaurant, and my kind of merger. Crisps and pakoras. Curry and football. Nuts and bhajis. Ketchup and chutney. The whole place was packed and it was a genuinely mixed crowd. There were people of all tones and types disputing decisions in a Midlands accent. I had the mixed grill, which was excellent value at just over a tenner. When the football finished, and they went back to music, I was hoping that something by Cornershop would come on, the band's music

Wolverhampton

89

being a chart-topping pickle of Indian and Britpop vibes. But it didn't. It was Ed Sheeran for an hour.

For a digestif, I went to the oldest building in town, The Lynch Gate, where I sat at the bar and weighed up my whereabouts: cosy, avuncular, the sort of place you need to have up your sleeve if you're living somewhere, in the event of a sudden downpour or a melancholic mood, when you could do with running into a few friendly faces and having a cheese cob and a half of Beowulf. I got out my notebook and started to scribble some thoughts. I got the feeling people didn't like what I was up to. I was being curious again. They're down to earth, Wulfrunians, and welcoming with it, but they're not above getting turned off by a plain clothes copper. A couple of lads nearby persuaded themselves I was keeping tabs on them. Got it into their heads that I was a bobby. Now I can't be sure, but if I was a bobby, I don't think my first move would be to whip out a notebook.

By now it was getting close to my home time. Tom the photographer had mentioned a racecourse, and I decided that that would be my final port of call. It took me about half an hour to walk there, but was worth the steps. It was a pretty big set up. There was a hotel, a grandstand, a floodlit all-weather track — and about fifty bookies stood on pedestals alongside dazzling charts of likelihood. I backed a horse called Probable. I had to with a name like that. It was the outsider: 50/1. I watched the race from the old-school grandstand: on my feet, leant against a railing, cradling a tea. Probable was evidently a misnomer because the horse came last. That will teach me to back the underdog.

After the race, I went and had a look at the parade ground, which is where the riders chat amongst themselves while their horses prance about. It's a ceremonial element of the whole thing that allows savants to spot dodgy ankles and hungover jockeys.

The jockeys were quite something. They looked dressed for a combination of dancing, war and golf. I got chatting to a couple of enthusiasts and they told me that the life of a jockey can be a tough one. Here one evening, there the next. Up at the crack of dawn, living off lettuce, risking their lives. The horses, meanwhile, get two weeks off between races, a final-salary pension, and spend a fair amount of time in the jacuzzi. 'They live the life of Riley,' said the couple, who must have firsthand experience of galloping four miles while jumping twenty fences.

I watched the next race from as close to the finish line as possible – just a few yards from the track. The sound of the pack coming down the home stretch was a delight. An earthy orchestra, pounding and mighty. After each race, the top three jockeys would head to a special area to be interviewed and congratulated. As the riders dealt with the press, the horses were circled, kept moving, led to water, their hides steaming. The whole scenario was novel to me, and therefore gently captivating. Over the course of two hours or so, I backed five horses, won £7.50, and drank three cups of tea. It wasn't a boozy affair. Not like Ascot or Aintree on a big occasion, like you see on the telly. Instead, the atmosphere was calm. Quietly dignified. Softly aesthetic. I returned to the same bookie each time. She was a nice lady, lived in the suburbs, hadn't been into the centre of Wolves for yonks. I told her about the theatre, Wightwick Manor, the gallery. 'Look at you,' she said, 'telling someone from Wolverhampton to do themselves a favour and nip into Wolverhampton. Now, are you sure you fancy Bruce Springsteen's a Legend because it hasn't finished a race for six years?'

Walking back to the station, I entertained myself by having a little think as to what I'd do with the ancient city of Wolverhampton if I had a blank cheque and diplomatic immunity. I'd ban Bentley Bridge, for a start. I'd get central government to tart up the old Georgian and Victorian buildings, and then I'd fill them with creatives (but only after a background check). I'd turn the ring road into a moat, for punting and paddle boarding, and to hell with the traffic consequences. I'd make it mandatory for those living on the leafy fringes of the city to enter the centre once a week for some light edification – a type of community service. I'd turn the man on the horse into a sort of buckaroo experience. I'd get Slade back together and make them do a gig at The Giffard every other Thursday. I'd get local lass Caitlin Moran to do a walking tour on Saturday mornings. I'd make sure any spare tickets for the theatre or The Halls were sent at random to locals. I'd close all the roads inside the ring road one Sunday a month so people could do what they wanted without the risk of being levelled. Oh, and I'd sign Erling Haaland on loan, and float orange chips on the stock market.

About twenty years ago, a poet called Ian McMillan wrote a poem about Wolverhampton. He compared the city to a favourite auntie who's always getting overlooked at discos. I'd say that was about right, if I'm honest. So do yourself a favour and drop in on your old auntie, would you? She might not remember who you are, and there's a chance she'll get pissed and start heckling your kids, but she'll definitely be happy to see you.

5

Wrexham

Too much love can kill a place

When I think of Cymru I think of Tom Jones, lava bread, leeks, lamb (and by extension sheep), the status anxiety of various Edwards, rugby, Snowdon, The Prince of Wales and his various embodiments, Abergavenny, Dylan Thomas (who wouldn't go quietly into the night and died at 39), that village in Anglesey with the very long name, Colin Jackson, my mate James, the late Gary Speed, the Gower Peninsula, the slag heaps of Blaenau Ffestiniog, the words *popty ping* and *smoothio*, Fireman Sam and English colonialism. And when I think of Wrexham? Well, it's just the Hollywood actor Ryan Reynolds, really, who, alongside fellow thespian Rob McElhenney, bought the local football club a few years ago. Before the club was taken over (and made the subject of a massively successful documentary series), Wrexham was rarely in the news. It wasn't prone to the back page, nor liable to the front. It went about its business (or lack thereof) largely ignored. As I headed to Wales on a Great Western service that was going oddly to plan, I typed Wrexham into the internet and spent an hour wading through the results. After about a hundred articles about the football club and its high-profile owners, I came to one about a local sweet chestnut that was voted tree of the year in 2023. After another hundred about football, there was a piece from 2014 about a 'riot' in the local Poundland store, which broke out when a half-price offer was abruptly halted with plenty of people still in the queue. A hundred more about football, and then an article about a nurse who was struck off when it was discovered she'd bonked a patient to death in a Wrexham carpark. A hundred more about football and then a piece about a seven-year-old kid with a cannabis habit. It's fair to say I was struggling to uncover anything that hinted that a pleasant city break might be had in the city.

Wrexham resides in the top right corner of the country, atop a coalfield and above a river, closer to Liverpool than Cardiff or Swansea. The English city of Chester is about ten miles to the north, and far too close for Wrexham's liking. As we pulled into the station – *Wrecsam Cyffredinol* – I plotted a path through town. Regent onto Hope onto High. It had a nice ring to it.

I enjoy walking in a curious fashion. I don't mean backwards and without bending one's knees, but rather with one's eyes peeled and ears to the ground. When you walk in such a fashion, things jump out at you, like bits of stimulating shrapnel. A dentist called Toothopia that promises transformative experiences; an optician called Jane Smellie; and St Mary's Church, which was once the headquarters of a certain Richard Gwyn, who was hung, drawn and quartered for being a Catholic. (This wasn't last week, I should add, but rather back in the days when Catholicism wasn't kosher around here, no matter the calibre of your soul.)

SHITTY BREAKS

From the off, the city had an air of maturity, as you might expect from a place that's been at it for ages. The branch of Halifax is upper-crust classical, The Royal Oak is half-timbered rustic, the Horse and Jockey is a thatched-roof boozer, and a string of elegant redbrick posers speak of a Victorian burst of commercial construction. I entered the bookshop on Regent Street and bought a copy of *Teach Your Cat Welsh* by Anne Cakebread. When I asked the bookseller where was good for food, they suggested, somewhat oddly, Lisbon or Levant. I thought they'd got the wrong end of the stick but no – Levant was around the corner and Lisbon was a few blocks down. The latter, I was told, had recently been favourably reviewed by Jay Rayner, who also bigged up that Chinese caff in Preston, you'll remember. It's funny which journeys your own accidentally echoes.

I found my hotel at the bottom of the high street, an Edwardian job called the Wynnstay Arms. A plaque on the hotel's façade informed me that the Football Association of Wales was formed on the site, back in 1876. Wrexham was one of the first clubs in the country, along with Swansea, Cardiff and Newport. Owing to a lack of Welsh opponents, the foursome were compelled to join the English League, where they remain. I went up to my room to eat the biscuits, wonder at the artwork, and unmake the bed – all the things one routinely does upon arriving at a hotel – and then went out for a walk.

Just along from the hotel is the Xplore! Science Discovery Centre (or *Canolfan Darganfod Gwyddoniaeth* to you and me), which is housed in a former department store. Money from the government and the National Lottery was used to repurpose the building, and in so doing inject a bit of life into this section of the city centre. I spent a happy hour hanging around the various scientific play stations: fiddling with this, experimenting with that, accidentally breaking the other. It was all very hands-on. Rather than reading about Isaac Newton, here you drop the apple. Rather than reading about air resistance, here you're blown over. Rather than reading about percussion, here you play 'Men of Harlech' – a stirring Welsh ditty that is essentially a middle finger to England – on a set of tubes with a pair of rubber paddles. 'Men of Harlech' wasn't the only tune available, I should add. That would be a bit outrageous. You can also play the Welsh national anthem. Elsewhere in the building, there was a theatre space for dumbed-down lectures (the perfect sort if you ask me), a gift shop with a range of inspirational rubbers, and the mandatory café. Energising, interactive, experiential – Xplore! is exactly the sort of thing that will help The Great British High Street weather an increasingly testing commercial climate.

The same is true of Tŷ Pawb, or Our House, which is just across the road from Xplore! The former covered market with a carpark on top now hosts a gallery, a performance space and a food court, as well as a range of independent vendors. I went first to the Court Café, one of several units dishing out nosh, and there had a bowl of lobscouse, a kind of lamb stew, which I ate alone at a communal table – so it goes. It was delicious. The peas, the mint, the carrot, the broth – the whole lot got better as the bowl went on. Sated, I popped across to the gallery to check out its latest exhibition. After completing a happy lap of the exhibited artworks, I can say with confidence that my favourite piece showed a pair of bananas spooning each other on top of the words: 'THEY WERE BENT FOR EACH OTHER'. All in all, it was a diverting half-hour and it didn't cost me a penny. Like Xplore!, Tŷ Pawb is a fine example of the upcycling of public space, and an obvious string in the city's bow. Props to all involved.

Having recklessly gorged on science and art up to this point, it was time for one of my five-a-day, and so I entered The

Drunk Monk on Overton Arcade, a craft beer place whose bartender was unable to teach me any Welsh because they happened to be from Stoke. Cosy, convivial, four stools at the bar – a similar vibe to Plug and Taps in Preston. While Tik Tok clips played silently on a telly (a girl had just eaten a pizza with her feet), I sat at the bar and studied a map provided by the hotel. Plas Coch, Mold, Offa, Acton. Faced with so many mellifluous options, I didn't know where to start. So I stayed where I was and had another beer.

Next, I went to a music venue called Rockin' Chair to see a band called The Declan Swans, who are enjoying an extended moment in the sun, after one of their songs got picked up by the producers of that documentary series about the football club that I mentioned. Upon climbing the stairs and entering the venue, I learnt very quickly that even Wrexham's hipsters are a relatively rowdy bunch. In their Converse shoes, and their Patagonia tops, and with their fairly trendy haircuts, it was easy to gain the impression that you could introduce the whole lot to your parents and nothing would go wrong. But on closer inspection it became apparent that, in spite of appearances, they were all batshit bananas. It was like they'd drunk nothing but bubble tea for the past six weeks. This impression was strengthened when I walked into the gents and confronted a lad dressed as a kangaroo. And the impression was strengthened even further when the band took to the stage and went straight into a song about gout, which was followed by another about diarrhoea, and another about the kangaroo I'd seen in the toilet, who duly hopped out from the wings during the chorus. It was perhaps one of the strangest gigs I'd ever attended. By the time the band got to their song about a bloke who nicked a Japanese car, I was on the brink of being utterly corrupted. I made my exit to the sound of the band's greatest hit, 'Always Sunny in Wrexham', the song featured in the doc. When I emerged from the building, and checked the weather with an upturned palm, I noticed it was absolutely pissing it down.

When I got back to the Wynnstay Arms, a karaoke session was in full flow in the bar. It was being hosted by a drag act called Shagger, who was no shrinking violet. Wrexham AFC would do well to sign them up. Pink wig, gold tights, a significant codpiece, sleeve tattoos – Shagger was quite the compère. Having spotted me lurking at the back like a soggy spare part, Shagger sauntered towards me, unzipped my jacket and said, 'You look like a right solid just stood there.' As I attempted to work out what a 'solid' was in this context, Shagger tried, and failed, to get me up on stage. In pursuit of a meaningful life, one has to draw the line somewhere. I went back to my room and watched a film wherein Hugh Grant measures the size of a Welsh hill, which was surprisingly moving.

※ ※ ※

The next day was New Year's Eve, and also a Sunday. I went up to St Giles, thinking I might sneak into the Mass. The church was founded hundreds of years ago, and is a fine structure – one of the Seven Wonders of Wales, according to an ancient rhyme. The Mass was delivered by the Reverend Jason Bray, who also did a turn on the organ. The first thing that struck me was how sharply the hymns contrasted with the tunes from last night. I felt a bit awkward at first, among the faithful, but a sign by the entrance had said that those without faith were entirely welcome, and so I settled into the solemn atmosphere. When I was asked by Jason to ponder my iniquities, I checked my watch to see if I had enough time. It wasn't hard to see and feel the appeal of the place. The meaning, the structure, the community. I'm not so naive as to think that faith can't lead to acts of extreme unpleasantness, but nor am I so cynical as to think it can't be altogether life-enhancing.

I stepped out into the churchyard and happened upon the gravestone of one Elihu Yale, who kindly gave his name to both the local Wetherspoons and a university in America. The inscription was quite something. It basically amounted to: 'Sometimes I was a wally, but hopefully I'll get into heaven.' I could relate to the sentiment. I sat on a nearby bench and watched, beneath a vast lancet window and a cloudscape that suggested a bunch of milky cherubs, the hands of a clock and the branches of a tree play against a canvas of green and black sandstone, the old rock gaining stain and moss with each and every hour. I remained on the bench for quite a while longer, just taking it all in. The everyday orchestra. The mellow drama. The snippets of overheard conversation. The spectacle of a small boy tripping over outside Lisbon and then furiously blaming his dad, who was nowhere near the kid when he fell. I'd live around here, I think, were I to move to the city. Somewhere on Temple Row, near the church, just a stone's throw from the high street. I'd come and sit here whenever I had a spare few hours and fancied going over my iniquities.

I went to Lisbon for an early lunch. It was a nice enough place, family-run, unassuming, certainly deserving of Jay Rayner's attention. I swerved the salted cod and went for the entremeada (wafer thin pork belly doused with lemon), and a small portion of feijoada, which is a traditional pork and bean stew. It was peculiar to be sitting among framed photographs of Portugal's capital – snapshots of a sunny elsewhere. Lisbon is a nice city, and chances are you don't need me to tell you that. It's one of the most visited cities in Europe – certainly not in need of a shout-out. It's overtouristed if anything. Whole parts of the city are strictly Airbnb. You risk introducing a certain perverse ghostliness to popular spots when you go down that road. Not so long ago, a few hundred people in Greece staged a funeral for the town they lived in, claiming it had been killed by overtourism. It's a serious issue: too much love can kill a place. Wrexham's safe for now, I reckon, but you never know. If Ryan Reynolds moved to Wrexham, next door to me on Temple Row perhaps, and started doing karaoke with Shagger on Sunday nights, it could be the beginning of the end for the place.

I wandered over to Waterworld. I couldn't not. The building invited me. It demanded my attention. In its own way, it's as striking and inexplicable as the bus station in Preston. I'm not sure what order of architecture it is. Out of order, perhaps. A bit like a train, a bit like a ship, a bit like a launch-pad, a bit like a bridge, a bit like a pyramid. If I didn't know it was a leisure centre I would have mistaken it for a NATO air base. I love it. Another wonder of Wales, if you're asking me, alongside the slag heaps of Blaenau Ffestiniog and Nessa from *Gavin and Stacey*.

Across from the leisure centre, on the other side of the carpark, a funfair was in train. You know the sort. Somewhat garish, somewhat improvised, somewhat chilling. The sort that will still be popping up in 4,000 years, during the next Ice Age. A ride called Toxic appealed to me. A vast pendulum, designed to swing until your insides revolt. I paid for my tokens, clambered aboard, and then wished with all of my heart to be back on that bench in the churchyard. I'll spare you the gory details but basically I thought at one point that my face was going to fall off. I worried for my nose and feared for my features. Great views of Mold and Acton, mind you. It was Type 4 fun, which is to say you didn't think it would be, and it absolutely wasn't.

I made a friend on the ride, though. Bloke called Owen, who said there used to be a police station not far from where we were standing, one of the most brutal, most peculiar in the world. He even showed me a picture. A vast concrete chunk sitting precariously upon a single stilt. Like a fucked-up lollipop made from cement. It was asking for trouble – which is about right for a copshop, I suppose. Eventually someone decided it was just too flipping weird and the whole thing was demolished. I'm told the ashes were scattered in Chester, and that the police are currently working out of Lisbon.

After nipping back to the hotel for a nap and a shower, I went looking for some merriment. First up, The Golden Lion. It was here that lager was first brewed in Britain, I read. Back in 1882, two brothers from Pilsner in Germany found themselves living and working in Manchester. Unsatisfied with the local ales, they decided to knock out a lager the way they'd seen it done at home, their thinking being, presumably, that when in Rome ignore the Romans. They went down to Wrexham to do their brewing because the lager producing conditions were superb there, the water from the Gwenny being top of the range, and the temperature underground ideal for storage. Fast-forward six months and the German bros had given birth to Britain's first lager, and they'd done so right here in Wrexham. For this alone, Wrexham should be immeasurably proud of what it has contributed to British culture – albeit via a pair of German fellas.[20]

I ordered a pint and took it to the only table available. It took some nerve to do so because the pub was crowded and loud with locals – getting their knees up, letting their hair down, having

---

[20] Wrexham Lager was recently acquired – or partly acquired – by the North American duo who bought the football club.

a singsong – and the table was right in the thick of the action. I stood out like a sore thumb, and then I stood out like an even sorer thumb when I pulled out my notebook and started scribbling words about Waterworld and the old police station that looked like a concrete lollipop.

A woman called Kathy couldn't suffer the sight of me scribbling away like a lemon on NYE, so staged an intervention. She leant across from the neighbouring table and shared a few thoughts, chief among them that I ought to buck my ideas up and do so sharpish. Kathy was a force of nature. It only took about fifteen seconds for me to get my head around that. She was as bright as a button, and didn't mince her words. She introduced me to her family, got me another pint in, then made me write down the following: *there is beauty in Wrexham and the people are good; please come again.* Then she took the notebook and amended the sentence so that it read: *there is good in Wrexham and the people are beautiful; by all means return.* (I wondered if it should be 'goodness' but, no, she was happy with how it was.)

When I told Kathy a bit more about what I was doing – going around, having a look, writing a book – she was far from impressed. She didn't mind the idea of the project, but didn't like how I was going about it. She said it wasn't research to sit in a corner on your own like a wallflower passing judgement. I pointed out that I wasn't sitting in a corner and I wasn't passing judgement but she was already up on her feet and saying that places are people in the end (and in the beginning as well), and that sitting on the sidelines wouldn't teach me a thing. She said while I was well within my rights to have a wander around and share my thoughts, I should bear in mind that those thoughts wouldn't count for much if I didn't get amongst it. Speak to them, she said. Be bold, she said. Not all of them will bite, she said. Don't wait for them to come to you, she said. Not everyone's like me, she said. And you should thank God that they aren't, she said. Wrexham is the people, she said, and the people are good and funny and honest, apart from when they're not. Yes, Wrexham has buildings, and history, and nature, but places are people in the end so stop sitting there in the corner scribbling about the fucking leisure centre and the pork belly at Lisbon and get on your feet and sing a song with my cousin Raquel. I can't sing, I said. Don't lie to me, she said. I'm not lying to you, I said. The burden of proof is on you, she said, grabbing me by the arm and giving me no choice in the matter. Racquel and I did a duet. I was in such a daze I don't even remember the song. I think it might have been something by Kylie Minogue.

When Kathy released me, I went to The Horse and Jockey, the pub with the thatched roof on Hope Street that I'd seen the day before. It was dead – the chalk to the cheese that was the pub before. I was on my own until a lad called Harry entered. I put my notebook away and asked what he was having. Local boy, early twenties, and a big fan of The Carpenters. He said that he didn't know a Kathy that fitted that description but it sounded like she knew what she was on about, then asked if I knew of the Gresford Colliery disaster of 1936, when 200 people died, the youngest of which was 14. Harry wondered what I reckoned of the fact that when the wives were given their dead husbands' wages for the week, they found that the men had only been paid for the hours they'd worked, rather than the hours they were meant to, which makes Harry want to reach for adjectives that he doesn't often want to reach for. He told me his favourite king was Edward VII, then told me why for the best part of an hour. He showed me pictures of his extensive collection of royal memorabilia, and said that the Princess Mary Adelaide of Cambridge mug was his favourite, followed by the Diana cushion. Said his granddad used to work at the Brymbo Steelworks, operating a crane, and when he got made redundant after forty-odd years he just wandered around Wrexham for hours and hours, not knowing what to do. When he eventually got home, Harry's nan said to Harry's granddad, 'What is it, love? You're the picture of bad luck.' At this point a Canadian entered. It was like the moment in a play or a film when something has to happen otherwise everyone's going to want their money back. The guy was called Jamie and he was in town for the football. Had flown in from Vancouver on a whim, having recently converted to Wrexham because of the documentary series. Harry took this information in his stride – had heard it all before, was accustomed to such nutters – but I couldn't believe what I was hearing. When Jamie asked Harry if he was local, and Harry got out his phone and showed Jamie some pictures of his extensive collection of royal memorabilia, I wished the pair of them well (though Harry especially) and went on my way.

I walked south in morning sunshine to the edge of the city, then continued along a muddy path through a patch of woodland, dodging the worst of the mud, ducking under loose branches, not knowing the way. I came to a field, bridged the River Clywedog, then followed a trail along a steep and bosky embankment, always in range of the river, which, at this point, was taking a corner with such gusto that it seemed in a hurry to get to Chester, as unlikely as that sounds. It was lovely and I was alone. The sight and sound of the meandering stream was an unspoilt tonic – and one that I was drinking just ten minutes from town. Happy New Year.

I was looking for Erddig Hall, a National Trust property, and the former pad of one Mr Yorke. Harry had shown me pictures. Had banged on about a period mansion with ample estate (every inch of it deserved, I'm sure), not unlike the house Darcy was renting in *Pride and Prejudice,* if that helps you to picture it. Mr Yorke doted on his servants, I understand. He gave them the time of day – so long as there wasn't bacon to be broiled or pots to be voided. Oh, I shouldn't be cynical. People can be good and kind and rich at once.

In the event I didn't get a glimpse of either Yorke or his Hall, for the whole set-up was closed on account of the bank holiday. Which was probably as well, because it was getting on for two, and the match began at three. I hastened up Erddig Road, cut through a leafy pocket of more affluent abodes, then passed the office of Sarah Atherton MP, a new blue brick in an old red wall. The sight of Atherton's office brought to mind an incident involving her illustrious colleague Jacob Rees-Mogg. In 2022, Rees-Mogg came to Wrexham to consider a council application for Levelling Up money, choosing to charter a chauffeur-driven limousine at a cost of £1,322 rather than just taking the train. The application was refused.

I don't want to go on too much about what's happened with Wrexham AFC over the last few years but seeing as we're on our way to a match perhaps a bit more context wouldn't go amiss. In March 2020, the club was at a low ebb. They were in the fifth division and may well have been relegated to the sixth had the season not been cancelled because of the pandemic. Meanwhile, across the pond, Rob McElhenney was told by one of his pals to kill some lockdown time by watching the football docuseries *Sunderland 'Til I Die.* McElhenney liked what he saw, felt an emotional connection with the subject matter, and started shopping for a football club. Wrexham emerged as a candidate because, in short, the club had buckets of pedigree and was practically at rock bottom. Ryan Reynolds was brought into the fold at this stage because McElhenney needed more dough. (My understanding is that Reynolds occasionally pretends to be a superhero called Deadpool and gets well remunerated for doing so.) Fast-forward some months (and miles of small print) and the pair were announcing their purchase of Wrexham AFC via a bogus social media ad for club sponsor Ifor Williams, who sell horse trailers. Wrexham's first game with Rob and Ryan in attendance was away to semi-pro Maidenhead, who had a window cleaner in midfield. When the celebrity duo did a walkabout in Wrexham the next day, a kind of meet and greet, I'm told it was a bit like Charles and Diana's visit in 1982. During that walkabout, Reynolds took some stick in a second-hand DVD shop, whose owner assured the actor that he wouldn't be able to shift *Green Lantern* (a romcom starring Reynolds as a milkman) if he had a million years and it was the only DVD left on the shelf. Throughout all of the above, Wrexham (both the club and the community) was being carefully documented. When the first series of *Welcome to Wrexham* landed (if that's what culture does these days), Wrexham's star well and truly rose, especially in the US. And when the BBC turned up for a cup match a few months later and Gary Lineker asked Ryan Reynolds what he made of Wrexham, and Reynolds said, 'You know, there's something special about it. You may not be able to say it's this or it's that, but it's a collection. A sum of all its parts,' its star rose further still. We pick up the action about ten months after that sentiment was shared, with Wrexham now in the fourth division, and ten minutes away from kicking off against the mighty Barrow. Phew. Get me a pie.

I was in with the away fans. It was the only way I could get a ticket. My plastic seat was made more uncomfortable by the cognitive dissonance I was hosting – being somewhat Wrexham and somewhat Barrow. The dissonance dissipated a notch when the away fans began sharing some thoughts with the home fans, in the form of a song called 'Where were you when you were shit?' In order to fit in, I had to bury my concern that the repetition of the personal pronoun 'you' was unhelpful when it referred to a different subject on each occasion. That said, even if I'd shouted out my concern I don't think anyone would have heard me. My, what a din! The Barrow fans were making a proper afternoon of it. (Mind you, I guess compared to Barrow, Wrexham is practically Las Vegas.) Though I do feel the Barrow fans crossed the line a touch when they began making unfounded allegations about what the home fans do with lamb – and they weren't thinking about mint sauce and rosemary.

Barrow took the lead in the first minute. I didn't find it hard to contain myself. For the next half an hour, Wrexham were awful. They were sluggish and complacent, and no one more so than big-money signing Steven Fletcher, a former Scotland international. Normally arrow-sharp, I can only think that Fletcher had one too many lagers the night before. At this juncture, my neighbour gave me a nudge with her elbow and shared an uncharitable assessment of Wrexham's televised rise from the ashes of non-league. 'Couldn't have happened to a nicer village.' It was as if the players had heard the woman's slur, because all of a sudden they started playing nicely. Fletcher, who I'd written off completely just moments before, even nabbed a second-half hat trick. Every time I took out my phone to photograph the Wrexham celebrations, my neighbour looked at me like I was the quintessence of filth. As enjoyable as it was to see Wrexham come from behind, it was the aesthetics of the whole thing that engaged me most.

The floodlit rain, the evergreen pitch, the blue and crimson tops, the stands of stoic supporters with their scarves and hats and belligerent wishes and unfailing dreams. At the final whistle, the Wrexham players, and not a few of the fans, could be heard knocking on the door of a second consecutive promotion. It finished 4–1.

Another entity elevated to something like stardom by the documentary series is the landlord of a pub called The Turf. For one reason or another, something about Wayne Jones' slightly dour vibe has gone down exceptionally well with vegans in San Francisco. Alas, when I entered the pub he was nowhere to be seen. He was probably up the road with Jane Smellie, getting his teeth varnished. I got a beer and found a seat – not easily done. The atmosphere was buoyant. There were raised glasses and raised voices and raised spirits. A few media types were in. Some random vlogger stuck a phone in my face and asked where I was from and what I thought. I said Portsmouth and not much if I'm honest. I chatted to the couple next to me, who were down from Liverpool for the day. They'd been following it all on the telly and thought they'd come down and have a look. Our conversation was nipped in the bud when a rumour started up, quiet at first, that Beyoncé was doing a shift behind the bar. Stranger things have happened: Prince William pulled a pint here once, and was forced to apologise for the size of his head. Paul Rudd's been in, and so has Will Ferrell. Must be some sort of celebrity apprenticeship scheme.

The couple from Liverpool weren't the only outsiders in The Turf. There was Jamie the Canadian, a few lads from Norwich, a group from the Isles of Scilly – all here because of what's gone on with the football. (See how the appeal of a place can alter when the messaging shifts?) It was good to see. I just wish there was something in Wrexham's success story that other cities could learn from, could borrow and apply. But there isn't, is there? Because the truth is that Wrexham got lucky. The truth is that what happened to Wrexham was akin to an act of God, a divine intervention; was like an almighty shot in the arm, courtesy of Hollywood. For a similar PR impact, the Pope would have to move to Nuneaton.

When things calmed down a bit, I asked a few locals what they made of Wrexham's unlikely renaissance, thinking I might catch a bit of cynicism or disquiet. None of it. Most thought it was all enjoyably crackers. A minority felt it was somewhat overdue, that the club should have been bought in the nineties by Demi Moore or something. A smaller minority were worried that they were going to wake up and discover it was all a dream. And one old boy, bless his heart, had the following to say: 'The Barrow fans were asking where we were when we were shit? Well, I told them. I was here. I was always here. And I'll be here for a while yet, because the club have agreed to bury me under the pitch.' It was a stirring outburst. I just wonder whether the club are going to wait until the old boy has kicked it.

Ambling around town the following morning, with two hours to while away before my train back to London, I was pleased to happen upon Bank Street Social. The coffee shop sits on an old narrow lane, alongside a nice run of independent traders, and is a credit to the city. It is socially as well as commercially minded, and is putting out some industry-leading cortados. But it doesn't do breakfast, not really, and so I was compelled to leave its snug environs for a place across the lane, Marubbi's, which has been in the same family for yonks, and is claiming to be the oldest café in Wales. A sort of twee greasy spoon, with lovely staff, homemade pies, and beans on toast for £3 – not a bad résumé. As I was finishing off my breakfast, and about to make tracks, a worker in high-vis overalls entered, carrying half the weather of Wales on his shoulders. He sat down, pulled out a newspaper (the dinosaur), then ordered the XL. It came pretty quickly but the toast was missing. The lad brought this up with the waitress a couple of times, but the toast still failed to materialise. He was lovely about it, though, this lad, as he asked for the third time. He said it happens all the time. And she said, does it happen all the time? And he said, no, I meant it's just one of those things. Call me sentimental, call me whatever, but it got to me a bit, this strapping lad with indelicate manners, wolfing down his three egg, three bacon, three sausage and so on, saying 'Don't worry, it's all good, no problem, okey dokey.' It was the 'okey dokey' that did it, that touched me. So gentle, so quietly kind. A bad person couldn't mutter the words. (Which is bollocks I know, but it's how I felt at the time.) Anyway, when the toast finally came, some five minutes after the lad had finished his breakfast, he folded up the triangles and squashed the whole lot into his mouth, waving an unseen goodbye as he went.

It might sound daft, but that's what travel is about for me, little scenes like that. I can hardly put the young man forward as a reason to visit Wrexham, of course. He might only eat at Marubbi's once a week, for a start, and what if the toast comes promptly the next time he's here? Why, you'd be denied the chance to see his unimportant sweetness in action, and might feel shortchanged. No, if you're going to come to Wrexham, don't come for the lad who didn't get his toast. Come for the things that can be depended upon. Come for the club.

And the river. And the feeling of a place going somewhere. Come for The Fat Boar, which is so popular I haven't been able to put my head around the door. Come for the character of the streets and the buildings, which add a hint of romance and drama to any amble around town. Come for the ancient sweet chestnut in Acton Park. Come for the amount of friendliness per capita, which is up there with anywhere I've been. Come for Britain's inaugural lager. Come, if nothing else, to acquire a few lines of Welsh, including *byddaf yn ôl*, which means, as chance would have it, I'll be back.

6

Limerick

A chicken fillet roll from the SPAR near his mammie's house

Before I visited Limerick, I had a phone call with a mate of a mate who grew up in the city. He was pleased to hear I was heading there. Said Limerick earned an unfair reputation some years ago that was doggedly reinforced and recycled by the media. Said it's an egalitarian city, unpretentious, wears its heart on its sleeve ('and it's a big fecking sleeve, so mind yourself'). Said, somewhat mysteriously, that I should avoid having any notions, else I'd be in for some 'slagging', which is the city's favourite sport, and basically amounts to taking the mickey out of anything capable of having the mickey taken out of it. Said there's the river, and the castle, and yeah you can go to Adare, the prettiest village in the county, but really I'd want to be just milling about, taking the temperature, talking to the people – or better still, have them talking to me. I promise you, he said, they won't take much persuading. In Ireland, displays of affection are a sign of softness in the head, but displays of unrelenting bullshit are par for the course.

On the plane to Shannon airport, in the Midwest of Ireland, a boy, aged three or four, was sitting behind me with his dad. 'Dad, listen,' the boy said. 'You've got to hear this. I've got a story for you ...' And then he went on to tell a story about the time he found a ten-euro note under his pillow from the tooth fairy. When he showed the note to his mum, and she said that tooth fairies don't pay that much and it should have been a two-euro coin, the kid was left wondering how the hell he'd been rumbled. The story went on for half of the flight, and included moments of high drama and self-reflection, and was a delight to eavesdrop on. A kid from anywhere else in the world wouldn't tell a yarn like that. Not with a County Mayo accent, at any rate.

I nipped to the loo at the airport – or the jacks as they like to say here, which comes, via a peculiar route, from John Harrington, who invented the flushing toilet in 1596. Anyway, there was a poster in the loo that was advertising city breaks. Budapest. London. Edinburgh. Lisbon. The likely lads. But to be fair to Shannon airport, and the scope of their offer, Birmingham and Frankfurt were also listed as options of equal weight and validity, at least typographically. The main image on the poster was Big Ben – or the Elizabeth Tower, rather, Big Ben being the bell. I'm not sure if that's a savvy selection. The totem pole of Westminster? The political heart of England? It was under Elizabeth, unless I'm mistaken, that most of Ireland was pinched and handed over to Protestants, both English and Scottish. And it was a member of that Westminster parliament, Charles Trevelyan, then working for the Treasury and in charge of famine relief, who said the Irish deserved the Great Famine for being idle and indolent and ungrateful and ungodly. I wasn't even out of the airport jacks and already the questions and provocations were raining down like old geezers and ponies.[21]

Outside the airport, I waited for the 51 bus in a storm. An Irish flag, proud at the top of its pole, was making the most of windy conditions. You'll know the colours: a white patch of peace between opposing religious views, green for Catholic, orange for Protestant. About twenty or so clambered onto the bus. I enjoyed the spectacle of a big industrial site drifting by to the south, dystopian seeming, Martian looking, apparently dormant. On the whole, Ireland isn't – and wasn't – an industrial country. Not the heavy, dirty type. In 1958, half of its GDP pertained to beef. It was agricultural, rural, agrarian, and especially so in County Limerick. When Ireland got a chunk of money from the US after the Second World War, a combo of loans and grants from the Marshall Plan, the stipulation was clear – with this money, we advise you to grow shit, and then export it. Got it?

The bus dropped us near the railway station, a solid stone specimen which had the look of a police station, nothing effete or dainty about it. The storm persisting, I sought refuge inside, where I ordered a tea from a café called Siege. The name intrigued me. Did it remember an historical episode? Yep, said the barista, a couple in fact, first it was your man Cromwell, and then it was William of Orange fifty years later. A pair of

---

[21] I read an article in the *Guardian* in May 2023 about Laura Trevelyan, the great-great-great-granddaughter of Charles Trevelyan, who is attempting to make amends for the doings of her ancestors. She quit her job as a BBC journo to campaign for reparative justice. Fair play to her.

non-Catholic do-gooders, sticking their beaks in. Do you want milk with that?

Standing in front of the station, hands on hips, I took an initial visual gulp: fairly flat, mostly Georgian, busy enough but certainly not vibrant (there was plenty of room on the pavement), and enough cloud to last a lifetime. The cloud made me think of *Angela's Ashes*, a 1996 Pulitzer-winning memoir by Frank McCourt that detailed the author's slummy childhood in Limerick. In the film adaptation of the book, it did not stop raining. Frank was up to his ears in it. Even when he was in bed. The book isn't universally admired around here, I understand. It was felt by some that there might have been at least one page of good weather among the three hundred. When McCourt published a sequel in 1999 called *'Tis*, the book was answered with another called *'Tisn't*, which tells you something.

I asked a wee lad twiddling his phones for directions to the Milk Market.

'Do you know Volcano Wings?'

'No, it's my first time.'

'Do you know Angel Lane?'

'Can't say I do.'

'Do you know the chipper on Leprechaun Street?'

'Afraid not.'

'Look, it's that way, so it is,' he said, pointing east. 'But if you get to a field, you'll want to be turning around.'

As soon as I started walking, Limerick started talking – started giving itself away. Men With Class Barber Shop. Molly's Bar. Palestine Butcher. Denmark Street with the Gaelic below. Green Acres. Son of a Bleach. Joe McKenna's Tool Shop. And then the Milk Market, which was buzzing with on-point artisanal producers – an hour ago. It had closed early on account of the storm. I asked one of the vendors what they'd do with their last day in the city. He said he'd go across the road for some dough bites, and then for a few drinks by the river, and then maybe to the castle if there was still time. Then he pointed to his son, and I thought the lad was being put forward as an attraction. 'The young one is after travelling. He wants to go but doesn't know where.' I looked at the young one in question and said: 'It doesn't matter where you go, it only matters that you go.' The kid didn't look impressed, just carried on packing things away. 'He was thinking of Thailand,' said the dad.

Given that it was chucking it down, and I was in the vicinity, I went and had a look at that castle, a gorgeous lump by the river, which was put up in the 1200s at the behest of King John of England. I spent an hour wandering around the castle and its indoor exhibition – reading the boards, watching the vids, pressing the screens. I must have downloaded 1,000 megabytes of info all things considered – about the castle, about the city, about Ireland – and yet by the time I was out in the open and up on the keep (the rain having waned), only seven bits remained: 1) In the 500s or so, then unsaintly Patrick was brought in on loan from Wales to get Christianity going. 2) When the Vikings turned up in Ireland they weren't in the mood to cohabit with the locals. They established exclusive strongholds at Limerick, Waterford, Drogheda and Dublin. 3) A few hundred years later, a lad called Brian quite liked the idea of becoming High King of All Ireland. Brian got quite far in pursuit of his dream job, then got stabbed in the back by a Viking in a tent. 4) By the end of the middle of the Middle Ages, Limerick was showing signs of hustle and bustle, and had a fledgling evening economy. 5) Oliver Cromwell laid siege to King John's castle in 1642 and in so doing provided

Limerick

117

the name for a railway station kiosk that would open 400 years later. 6) When William of Orange visited Ireland 50 years later, he basically cocked a massive Dutch leg and did a massive Protestant piddle all over the country. During the course of William's visit a decent amount of King John's castle was blown up, which is why one side of the building is now a gift shop. 7) For a good portion of the twentieth century, about thirty council houses were in situ within the castle walls, which is social security gone mad. The council estate was levelled in 1989 and in 2019 the castle was converted into an 'experience' – and a very good one at that.

I had something to eat at Canteen, on Catherine Street, a ten-minute walk in the direction of America, along those mostly flat, mostly Georgian streets. Spare, elegant, mindful – Canteen was just the right side of tragically hip. Because one of Limerick's nicknames is Pig Town, I ordered the pork schnitzel and took a seat in the window, where I watched all four seasons in the space of ten minutes. As I idly wondered to what extent the climate of a place determines the personality of its people, my schnitzel arrived, bearing a dribble of hollandaise and wearing a portion of matchstick chips. It was decent grub but I confess to being a touch troubled by the width of my chips. Why are they getting thinner and thinner? I mean, French Fries were already taking the potato. Matchstick fries bode ill, if you ask me, suggesting either a lack of raw material (which is hardly an ideal note for a chip to hit around here) or rampaging shrinkflation. They'll be subatomic before long. I asked the young one who served me what the best thing about Limerick was. He said it was the people. To be candid, I was getting sick of the sentiment. Couldn't it just be a theme park or something?

I went to Cahill's on Wickham Street, established in 1870. Originally a tobacco and snuff factory, Cahill's is now one of the best places to buy loose-leaf tea in the country, as well as cigars and teapots and lighters and hipflasks and pipes and so on. It's quite the emporium. Its chief operating officer is Eleanor, who I found dressed in orange and safely into her sixties.

'You're my man, are you?' she said as I entered.

'I hope so.'

'There's no point hoping – are you, or aren't you?'

Blimey, I thought, picking my wits up off the floor. 'I'm your man.'

'Grand. Now, would you like a cup of tea?'

My hour with Eleanor was a pleasant blur. I drank some tea and listened to her talk – that's the long and the short of it. She told me a lot of things, and I'm still, some weeks later, trying to process them. Some things pertained to tea, others to snuff, others to a painter called Brian McMahon, who rents a studio above the shop, and is better than Picasso according to Eleanor. I learned that Limerick earned the nickname Stab City when two houses alike in dignity got into a protracted spat that has long since been over. That tea got going in circa 4,000 BC when a leaf fell into the cup of a fella in China who was minding his own business. That the tea bag was invented by Americans in the 1910s, and that Eleanor wouldn't be seen dead within twenty metres of one. That the pub isn't a place to go in Ireland but a way of life, and that I could try a pint of that way of life next door at Flannery's if I was minded to. That the dog was in a mood because she was off to Mexico (Eleanor was, not the dog). That the actor Dominic West lived up the river at

Glin Castle. And that John Travolta got his haircut nearby. In short, I'd entered a tea shop expecting to have a quick nose and a bit of small talk, only to be treated like an errant nephew and gifted a stream of consciousness, every letter of which was delightful. On my way out, Eleanor slipped a packet of Limerick Breakfast Blend into my bag and a strainer into my pocket so I could make myself a decent cup of tea in my hotel room. Legend.

It was dark after Eleanor. And stormy still. I considered Flannery's next door, but hastened to my hotel instead, light-footed on the slick Limerick streets. At People's Park, I considered one person in particular, the fella up on the column, head in the clouds. I asked somebody emerging from the art gallery who they were and what they did. 'I'm Jim O'Doherty and I'm a milkman,' they said, with a wink. And then: 'The honest answer is I haven't a clue, but I bet he did feck all if they've gone and put him up there.'

It was a nice part of town – Newtown Pery. Named for Edmund Sexton Pery, an Anglo-Irish politician. Back in the eighteenth century, and wanting to do something with all the land he owned, Pery planted a grid of fashionable Georgian townhouses. Many are empty or part-occupied these days, which seems mad. I'm told that developers and the like are deterred from renovating such buildings by the costs and admin involved, preferring to build from scratch on the edge of town. By going after margin, they bulk up the donut and reinforce the hole. It's a sadly familiar story.[22]

---

[22] This is being addressed. The 'Living City' initiative, devised and implemented by the local council, provides tax incentives to anyone prepared to take on – and tart up – a portion of Limerick's vintage real estate.

I do like Georgian architecture. The sash windows, the iron railings, the straight face, the unimpeachable aura. It's a good look. What is it about the look that appeals? The relative lack of pomp and bombast helps, I think. Unfussy, unrendered, unadorned. Imagine a well-regarded person, confident but without being brash or boastful. They've done alright for themselves, but have kept the common touch. A bit of class, not shy of a day's work, got up in well-cut clobber, whistling a tune while doing the sudoku, awaiting the bus into town. That is Georgian architecture. Marriage material.

It was a nice hotel, too, No.1 Pery Square. Seamus showed me up to my room – up to Goldsmith. The rooms are named after writers, apart from Sash, which is named after the windows. I made a tea and put on the radio. It was a local station, Live 95. Apparently Munster threw away a lead last night, the hospital is full to bursting, and a nationalist politician called Mary Lou has a chance at the next election. Then it was the funeral forecast, which was new to me. Dylan Fitzpatrick of Patrickswell, formerly of Bottomstown, survived by two children and a dog, reposing at home until removal at midnight, burial on the morrow, Church of Immaculate Conception, donations to Munster Rugby. That sort of thing. It was quietly stirring stuff, and in paraphrasing I don't mean to poke fun, but rather to identify a cultural difference. The Irish are tighter to death. They lean into it. You won't get a forecast like that where I'm from.

I fired up the laptop and searched for articles pertaining to Limerick, hoping to have the bejaysus scared out of me. To be fair, it was quite a balanced selection: *A US tech company is to create 400 jobs. Munster win the league. Storm Brian lashes Limerick city centre. A pensioner is hit by a police chase car. Business magazine Forbes is forced to retract a baseless claim that Limerick is a den of iniquity.*

All things considered, not a bad write up. The article I most enjoyed reading concerned a local DJ who managed to scam a scammer. Back in 2019, chemistry student Ross Walsh received an email inviting him to invest £1,000 in a major businessman. Ross wrote back to the major businessman saying he wanted to invest 50 times that amount but his bank wouldn't let him until Solomon Gundi paid 50 euro into Mr Walsh's account, which Gundi duly did, and which Mr Walsh duly donated to the Irish Cancer Society. Lad.

I stepped outside and headed to Dolan's, a well-known pub and music venue on Dock Road. You can't miss it – green face, white windows, red neon trim. Just the place for inclement weather, hence its popularity. I took a seat at the bar. The till, I noticed, had buttons for each of the staff members. (It is this type of observation that distinguishes me as a travel writer.) Michael, Keith, Shane, Dylan. The till was giving Westlife vibes. I ordered the stew with soda bread – good food for a storm – and a Guinness 0. *The pint.* That's what they call it. Note the definite article. It elevates the drink somehow. Places it on a pedestal. A dais. Lends it status, substance, body. Not that Guinness needs more clout. The drink has an almost religious aura, an epic quality. At the brewery in Dublin, the master culture is kept under lock and key at -196°C; the drink's infamous darkness comes from charring the barley and imbues it with heavy significance; and then there's the ceremony of having to wait for it to settle, as though it had the devil inside of it. Even with its teeth out it was an impressive drink to sup.

I considered my surroundings. A corner reserved for musicians. A Munster rugby shirt. Old stone walls. Wooden floors. A fire blazing. Gentle lamplight. Dark red paint. Pictures of Beckett, Wild, Swift, Shaw and Synge. Below the Beckett, a quote of his. 'Perhaps my best years are gone, but I wouldn't want them back. Not with the fire in me now.' I don't imagine Beckett was on the old Guinness 0. There were paintings by Brian McMahon, the artist in residence above Eleanor's shop. It's nice how that happens. How an introduction allows a connection. How familiarity permits recognition. I won't labour the point. It's good to be shown things, and then see them again. Our fields of affection, inching forward.

Speaking of seeing, I asked Dylan what was worth having a look at locally. He said Kerry was deadly, and Tralee wasn't bad. I asked him to reduce his perspective, to wind his neck in and look closer to home. He did so – then suggested a chicken fillet roll from the Spar near his mammie's house. I paid no heed and had the pint again.[23]

---

[23] I have come to learn that the chicken fillet roll is arguably the most significant, pervasive, integral and culturally resonant thing in modern Ireland. It is a chicken sandwich that became a part of the Irish soul and is now refusing to budge. Blindboy Boatclub did a podcast on the chicken fillet roll. (If you don't know Blindboy Boatclub, get to know Blindboy Boatclub. He is a philosopher-shaman who goes around with a plastic bag on his head, and is the best thing to come out of Limerick since Terry Wogan.) In the podcast, Blindboy considers the components of the chicken fillet roll, traces its genealogy, sketches its roots, ponders its evolution and ubiquity. It is a startling disquisition, lasting over an hour, that touches on the potato famine, the Irish climate, human mastery of fire 60,000 years ago, his mum's habit of cooking frozen pizza in the frying pan, Irish shame and embarrassment and self-loathing, the Celtic Tiger, the advent of hot deli counters in Irish petrol stations, an Irish company called Cuisine de France, the country's accession to the European Union, the Global Financial Crisis, Barack Obama, and the insidious encroachment of multinational corporations on the Irish psyche. Blindboy reckons the chicken fillet roll is the 'great lie of post-Celtic Tiger Ireland', and suggests it embodies 'who the Irish would like to be'. Yikes. That's some roll. That's *the* roll. ('Nora, will you be having the roll this morning?' 'I'll be having the roll, Fiona, so I will.')

Sport was on silent behind the bar. American cousins across the pond, gaining yards. There was a beer called Treaty City on tap. Another of Limerick's nicknames. What was the treaty about? Dylan said he wasn't sure, so maybe I should just stick to the Guinness. If a treaty was being done in Limerick, I speculated, it could only mean one thing. Haggling with the English. Reducing the terms of subjugation. Tweaking the terms of their taking the piss. At this point the musicians arrived. Two old boys, neither the spitting image of woke. One had the stew, the other had the chowder. Both had the pint. And then they lifted their gear and made their music. A single stamping foot on old wooden boards. A strong spoken song. An accordion and a guitar. It did wonders for my meal. The drawn-out notes of the accordion felt fitting somehow, apt for a land so accustomed to struggle.

I waited for the rain to pass. When it didn't, I phoned for a taxi. At People's Park, I asked the driver about the fella on the column. He said he didn't know who it was but if there was any justice in the world it would be John Klein, boss of the Limerick hurling team, who had spearheaded great success of late.

'Do me a favour,' said the driver, as we idled outside the hotel. 'Get yourself on the YouTube and watch last year's final. Will you do it? Will you promise?'

When I got back to London after my visit to Limerick, I visited a chicken fillet roll pop-up joint called Emerald Eats. I asked the lad knocking them out what the chicken fillet roll meant to him. 'It's home,' he said. 'It's Ireland. It's all the crappiness of life, but all the good bits too. It's the weather and the grass and my first girlfriend Sinead. It's emotion. Will you be having the spicy mayo?' I took my CFR to a quiet spot, unwrapped it respectfully, then ate the boy's home and emotion. It was a chewy so-and-so. It certainly got the old mouth moving, the old jaw working. And maybe that's it, I thought. Maybe that's why the Irish love the chicken fillet roll so much. It reminds them of talking.

'I will.'

'And then will you come back for a game at the Gaelic Grounds? They get fifty-odd thousand in there. Old Trafford is like a church by comparison. The only thing you can hear at Old Trafford is all the Irish ones doing Hail Marys and slagging the referee.'

'I'll do it.'

'And make sure you watch last year's final. The grandchildren tell me it's on the YouTube. They're not paid, you know.'

'The grandchildren?'

'The players, you eejit! They're amateurs.'

I asked your man who he'd have in his taxi if he could have anyone in the world.

'Easy. John Klein up front and J.P. in the back.'

'J.P.?'

'That's right.'

'As in John Paul II?'

'As in J.P. McManus. And I'd have my late granda as well. If there was space.'

'There'd be space.'

'Grand. The Pope could go in the boot.'

❋ ❋ ❋

I resisted the basement spa, and its offer to scrub me with Sligo-based seaweed. I swerved the sauna too – wanting to keep the pint inside. Instead, I went straight to the dining room for a cooked breakfast. As I was tucking in, there was a slightly awkward moment when a fellow guest came over and asked if I was done with the yoke. He meant the pepper mill, that much became obvious, but for a second I thought he was after the best bit of my egg. Before stepping out for the day, I asked Damian on reception where he'd go for his last supper.

'Am I being banished or killed or what?'

'Does it matter?'

'Surely it matters.'

'Let's say killed.'

'In which case The Glen Tavern.'

'And what would you have?'

'I'd have the roast. With a lemon San Pellegrino.'

Why do I ask such questions? Why do I care where Damian would eat his last meal? Because I'm not after the best or the highest rated. I'm after places people have strong feelings for.[24]

The weather had turned and it was good to be outdoors and afoot. The Crescent, just around the corner from the hotel, is a gracious sweep that would be the envy of anywhere, 100 metres of curving loveliness. Nearby, the Irish Ancestry Research Centre gave me pause for thought. I had half a mind to nip inside and ask about my grandmother, Anne, who was invited by those that loved her most to leave the island of Ireland for having a child out of wedlock. The baby was given up, and my nan banished to Portsmouth, where she breathed no word of her expulsion. It was only after her death, when the child that had been taken from her got in touch with my dad, that the truth was revealed. Both children were called Thomas, which chances to mean 'twin' in certain ancient tongues. So it goes.

Speaking of things coming apart, I entered Rift on Upper Mallow Street, wanting the 'posh coffee' mentioned by Dylan at Dolan's. They take their extraction seriously at Rift, that much was plain. My cup had no handle, which is always a warning sign, and was served on a small rectangle of marble, beside a vial of brown sugar and a teaspoon. Notions, I'd say.

---

[24] I went to The Glen Tavern and the roast was bang average.

It was bloody good, mind you. Pungent, but in a nice way. Went straight to my head. I sat in the window and spoke with a student of medicine. She said the city's got bucket loads of *je ne sais quoi*, which must present challenges to the marketing department. 'And it's not robbing you like Dublin. It's cheaper here. Less tourists inflating the price. Less mercenaries flipping apartments. It's been up and coming for 35 years. Never quite getting there. To the relief of the locals.' It was an interesting take. It showed an awareness of the pitfalls of tourism, the drawback of renown, the imperfect consequences of popularity. Before I left, I asked the barista about the name of the café, thinking it might allude to The Troubles, or the protracted spat mentioned by Eleanor. It doesn't. It refers to a Kenyan mountain range. The barista, who chanced to be the owner, told me he lives just around the corner. Said he bought a small place for about 150,000 euro – which is expensive for Limerick. He said he wanted to see more footfall in town, and so decided to walk the walk. Fair play to him.

I found an inconvenience store on Lucky Lane. A kind of ad hoc curiosity shop, full of things you didn't know you wanted or needed. A Trump first edition. A dramatised version of the Bible (as if it wasn't dramatic enough already). Old adverts for Guinness suggesting that the pint is perfect for fatigue. Monochrome snaps of the River Shannon, of the docks, of People's Park. A poster for a musical called *Oliver Cromwell Is Really Very Sorry*. Vintage gear, vinyl records, an arcade machine. I chatted with the lad in charge. Asked him what he fancied locally. He said you stop seeing things when you live somewhere. I moved on.

I went to a book shop on O'Connell Street, O'Mahony's, which has been on its feet since 1902. Its elegant black and silver frontage shone in the unexpected sun. I chatted with

Limerick

127

Stephan O'Mahony, captain of the ship. Like Eleanor at Cahill's, Stephan is an ambassador of Limerick, which is not to say he's blind to the issues the city faces. The waterfront could be improved. Parking and access are an issue. Out of town distractions mean too few people in the middle. 'And the reputation is another thing. The message needs to change – and it deserves to change too. The West Coast of Ireland gets a lot of tourists. Limerick should be a part of the itinerary. It should be a gateway at least.' I asked for a tip and was given a couple – a book about Ireland called *We Don't Know Ourselves*, and the International Rugby Experience just across the street. I set off with the former, and in the direction of the latter. It was an easy building to spot. Once seen, not easily unseen. A tall, broad-shouldered, redbrick newbie. ('Meaty', said the *Guardian* building buff Rowan Moore.) Lighthouse vibes, with a touch of church about it. It was a good building to see in more senses than one – being an attractive attempt to bolster Limerick's high street offering. The chief midwife of the International Rugby Experience was J.P. McManus, the local businessman and racehorse owner (who's currently in the back of that bloke's taxi). Four derelict buildings were fused together and dramatically revitalised. Props indeed.

Inside is a celebration of rugby and its underlying principles. Different rooms are devoted to the values that are believed to underpin the sport: solidarity, respect, integrity, passion, discipline. I savoured the first four but, true to form, skipped the latter. The whole thing is truly, carefully, cleverly, and relentlessly interactive. Not a museum, not a gallery – experience is the right word. You watch, listen and play here. You can do the haka (or try to, anyway). You can pick your all-time fantasy team. A digital Johnny Wilkinson offers kicking lessons. A virtual Keith Earls tells you how to sidestep. By being interactive, the IRE is also accessible – even to rugby innocents like me. My only dalliance with rugby came when I was twelve, when my maths teacher punished me for answering back by putting me in the scrum. I came out of that equation with a bruised nose and less lip on me.

Up at the top of building, in an enclosed loggia, panoramic views of the city are available. It was quite an eyeful. The castle. The cathedral. The rivers Shannon and Abbey. The low, stone bridges. Acres of rooftop and pavement. A fruitful hinterland. Weather that was brilliant and awful at once. When the rainbow I was hoping for failed to materialise, I descended to the gift shop on the ground floor, where I couldn't resist a jumper. It bore a list of cities: New York, Paris, Milan, London – the usual suspects. Amid the aspirational pack, however, in the heart of the scrum, was Limerick. A tongue-in-cheek inclusion, but not off the mark. Call me easily pleased, but I rank the likes of Limerick up there with London and Paris and that prized coterie. In terms of return on investment, in terms of pleasure per pound, in terms of history per square metre, I swear a feather would tip the scales. If you took all the stuff in Limerick (historical episodes, decent spots to eat, edificial appeal, volume of craic) and divided it by the number of people going after that stuff, and factored in the long-term benefit of spreading the love and the attention and the travellers' cheques, you're left with a pretty decent idea. I asked the girl who flogged me the jumper what she would change about Limerick given a wand and carte blanche. 'The perception of the place,' she said. 'It's all here. And it's only going to get better. We just need people to know.'

It was dark now, and I went to the river. Wide and lovely, nicely lit. Swans milling about, not a care in the world. Old mooring bollards, to be leapfrogged these days, that once caught the slung hooks of to-and-fro merchants. The river was calm

Limerick

now, but it wasn't always so. An informative panel spoke of emigration to Canada, of locals catching a ride to the much-promised land, and lodging with cattle in the hull. People don't tend to take such measures, to make such moves, if things are cushy at home. The Great Famine took a million lives. It forced another million abroad. The population of Ireland decreased by roughly a third. And yet, at the same time, merchants were exporting 400,000 barrels of oats. Yes, there was blight. Yes, the potato crop failed. But the people might have been fed, kept alive, rescued. If any Irish person has a chip on their shoulder, chances are an Englishman put it there.

I continued along the river to the Easter Rising memorial, which shows three men and an unshackled lady – Mother Eire. The sculpture remembers the time the Irish revolted, when a certain Patrick Pearse declared a Republic from the General Post Office in Dublin. The Easter Rising wasn't pretty. It wasn't a calm attempt at persuasion. It couldn't afford to be. It had to be fierce. As fierce as the oppression which had prevailed for centuries. In 1921, five years after the uprising, Michael Collins went to London to do a deal. When he returned, and showed what he'd done, and his compatriots saw that it involved six counties in the north remaining a part of Great Britain, not all were best pleased. A split emerged between those for and against the deal. A civil war ensued. Irishman against Irishman. Family against family. Brother against brother. Each faction fighting for their conception of the right way to proceed. The pro-treaty forces came out on top, and the Irish Free State was born, at the cost of Northern Ireland.

Newly and imperfectly independent, the Free State struggled at first. It wasn't easy for the country to earn enough, to turn over enough, to develop enough, to compete with what was on offer elsewhere. As a result, the people continued to leave.

Not one or two, but hundreds of thousands. The country was vanishing. In the 1950s, the only two countries in Europe that were shedding citizens at a significant rate were East Germany and Ireland. East Germany built a wall to keep the people in. The Irish Free State didn't and they continued to leave. By the middle of the twentieth century, the population was a quarter of what it had been a hundred years before. An unbearable reduction.

Things changed. They always do. Ireland stopped aiming for strict self-sufficiency and opened its doors to international business and trade. Cue the Celtic Tiger, a period of rampant economic growth in the nineties and noughties, which saw the Republic of Ireland become one of the richest countries in the world. Multinational companies were seduced by tax breaks. The country reconnected with Europe. People stopped leaving and they started arriving. Mother Eire was purring. But no Tiger lasts forever, Celtic or not. The Global Financial Crisis of 2008 delivered a crash and a slump, a drop and a crunch. But it was a drop from a position of strength, and the country remains, from an economic standpoint, a vastly different beast to the one that almost vanished.

A riverside pub called The Curragower was buzzing with clocked-off workers and distracted students. A trad pub on one side, a well-heeled dining room on the other, and with just the right amount of wattage and plants, it was an easy place to like. I had the fish box – scampi, squid, hake and chips – but only required a third of it. Another Guinness 0, to moisten the load. As the fatigue fell off me, I recalled the famous Guinness ads, white horses in the surf, a fish on a bicycle, tick followed tock followed tick followed tock. Let's have some of that maverick messaging in the service of Limerick, I thought. Blindboy is trying. He made a telly programme about Limerick for RTE, the national broadcaster. He signed off thusly: 'This is Limerick City, and if you don't like it, you can feck off to Cork.'

I was wearing four layers and I was still somehow frozen. I stood by the river and watched the water rushing, sliding darkly west, Atlantic bound. Channels of black emerged from shadow beneath the arches of the bridge, giving an impression of sudden appearance, as if the flow was being printed, rolled out, issued; the bridge a machine, churning out Guinness. On that bridge, I had my first encounter with Limerick's motto. Translated roughly from Latin: *an old city good at fighting.* As well it might be.

On the other side of the bridge, Treaty City Brewery is doing its thing in 400-year-old premises. I had a gander at their Renegade, a taste of their Outcast, and was invited back for a tour. A pedestrian crossing, made up like a rainbow, led me to my final destination: The Locke Bar, a way of life by the river, and a fine spot for a nightcap. The pub was busy. Abrim. Abustle. More craic than the Grand Canyon, and this was a quiet night. The pub does trad music and dancing every night – that's what gets them in. Three young ones were at it now. The fiddle was magic, lifting the whole thing up a level. Another young one arrived to do the Irish dancing. It was like she was trying to keep as little of her feet on the floor for as long as she could while staying in sync with the music. Less inhibited when I'm off the sauce, I had half a mind to get up there and join in. 'Dance first. Think later. It's the natural order.' There's another bit of Beckett for you. The only other line I know is the one about us all being born mad but only some of us remaining so. You might reckon me mad when I say that Tayto crisps are not a patch on Walkers. I just had a bag, and they didn't do it for me.

I roamed the building looking at things. I enjoyed the framed pictures especially. There were a fair few of the Munster rugby team, group shots from down the years, candid stuff from tours overseas. One picture from 1985, of a few of the players in a hotel room, drinking from cans, a post-match celebration, or postmortem perhaps, though it might have been both, I suppose. Anyway, the picture was oddly and unexpectedly poignant. It seemed to silently scream that we're only here for a while, that we're just passing through. I've got a mate from Waterford, Davy, and he's got one hell of a voice. About ten years ago, alongside a Pole and a guy from Argentina, the two of us went around Europe in my clapped-out campervan, busking as we went, living off the proceeds. Davy did a cover of Leonard Cohen's 'Passing Through' and the sentiment never wavered, never waned, no matter how often he sang it. It always got under my skin, and now this unextraordinary photograph was doing the same. The dancing stopped, and so did the fiddle. It was time to move on. I was glad I came.

7

Newry

The kind of landscape that makes you think twice

When I think of Northern Ireland, I think of Rory McIlroy. And the big hole in the middle of it all, full to the brim. I think of the Peace Road, of *Derry Girls*, of a border in the sea. I don't think of the cold details. I don't think of 1.4 million people, fourteen counties, five cities and 167 towns. And I don't think about Newry.

And nor do the folk at Lonely Planet think much about Newry either. On the inside cover of my *Lonely Planet Ireland* is a map of the island of Ireland, with key towns and cities and attractions marked. Poor old Newry is entirely obscured by an info box banging on about Belfast. If that's not a case of being overlooked, I don't know what is.

Newry railway station is out on a limb. Not knowing of the free bus into town, I phoned a taxi. The driver knew how to talk. 'Sure I've been over to London. Went across at sixteen, looking for work. Got three years of the stuff in Coventry, which was more than enough. No, I didn't mind England. Which might surprise you. Foreigners get in my car and say, "The Irish hate the English, is it so?" And I say, "Feck off where you came from spouting bollocks like that." The English are grand. Especially when they're in England. 99% of people – and this is no word of a lie – are decent people no matter where they're from. Apart from Tipperary, where it's 92%. That's you. Mind how you go. £5.30, but let's call it 6. I'm only joking. Let's call it 7. You're English, after all. And I don't care if your ma's ma was from Cavan. I should charge 15 with heritage like that.'

Newry is a small city located between Belfast and Dublin. It grew up around the River Clanrye, which passes through the city on its way south. The river empties into Carlingford Lough, close to Warrenpoint, which is where old Jo Biden's forefathers set sail. Obama also has Irish heritage, incidentally. To honour the fact, he came over and visited the petrol station in Offaly that had been named after him. Let's hope he did his duty and had a chicken fillet roll.

Following partition in 1921, Newry became part of the North – just. It retains a Catholic majority and a Catholic leaning. In 2021, according to the census, three times as many residents of Newry identified as Irish than Northern Irish. No wonder it was a hotspot during The Troubles. There would have been a fair few around here who would've happily bidden the British farewell. During The Troubles, it's fair to say that Newry wasn't set up for tourists. Providing a warm welcome wasn't high on the agenda. Now things are changing. House prices went up 371% in the ten years after 1996 – which tells you how in demand houses were in the years up to that point. Unemployment has fallen significantly, and visitor numbers have picked up, albeit from a pretty deep baseline.

The taxi dropped me at the bus station. I buttonholed a fella and asked for some tips. He didn't say Belfast. He didn't suggest Dublin. He didn't say Dundalk is nice. He didn't ask if I'd brought my trunks because the Isle of Man is but a good swim away. He was kind about Newry. He wasn't surprised I was there. He said the towpath to Omeath, Courtney's on a Thursday, Ned Kelly's for your tea, and Brass Monkey if there's time. The man's advice sounded like a poem. A rush of appealing gibberish.

The man might have added the local library to his list. It's an unassuming building on Hill Street, but worth dropping into. I considered the shelves. *Parliament of Northern Ireland: Common Debates, 1969–70* had me champing at the bit. I would have spent the afternoon with the tome if only I could reach the thing – it was top shelf stuff. They've not debated since from what I could tell: the instalment before me was the last in the series. I know Stormont's been dormant, but has it been that long?[25] The library was hosting an exhibition in its gallery space, in conjunction with the Prison Arts Foundation. The artwork of inmates was on show. There were some fine sentences, some moving sentiments. One poem, 'Concerning Mental Health (in the style of Brecht)', deserves to be quoted in full.

> There will only ever be one you
> you are unique
> you will never
> pass this way again
> develop your personality
> attitude, determination, pragmatism
> moral fibre

---

[25] The Northen Ireland Assembly, which sits at Stormant, was out-of-office for a couple of years up until February 2024. The Democratic Unionist Party had been holding things up on account of concerns about post-Brexit trade arrangements.

think

it's the sensible thing

never give up.

I didn't mind that. Goes to show that you can never say with confidence whence good art will emerge. I was invited to leave some feedback and I did so. 'Keep it up. Make it permanent. It's the sensible thing.'

They've made Pat Jennings permanent. They've set him in stone around the corner from the library, launching a counter-attack. Jennings was a legendary goalkeeper, for those not in the swim. As well as Newry, he played for Spurs and Arsenal, and was the first player to make a thousand senior appearances in English football – which was some feat (and some hands as well). He carried on playing for Northern Ireland into his retirement, making his final appearance at the World Cup in 1986, against Brazil, aged 92. Incidentally, Pat's appearance record was later surpassed by Peter Shilton, who played for Stoke, Derby, Plymouth, Leicester, Southampton and Bolton. Perhaps this is wishful thinking, but with a CV like that, I'd say Peter was well positioned to write the sequel to this book.

The Pat statue is outside the town hall, which was built in 1893, from red bricks and granite. It's a town hall you can imagine living in, suave but also homely. Interestingly, it stands on a bridge over the river – thus being a bit in County Down and a bit in County Armagh. Its capacity to straddle reminds me of Pat's repping both Spurs and Arsenal, while its inbuilt compromise brings Canberra to my mind, which was constructed a ridiculous distance from Sydney and Melbourne, in the middle of nowhere, so that both could save face. Diplomacy, it would seem, can involve some heavy lifting. In front of the town hall, a massive Palestinian flag was flying at full mast.

It wasn't the first such flag that I'd seen. They back the underdog around here, I fancy.

On any urban wander, a dozen things will jump out, will catch your eye, will catch your ear, will demand a line or two. Danske Bank is a fairytale structure, the stuff of legends. One half expects Rapunzel to appear at its uppermost balcony. The cathedral is a neogothic rocket that should be in Dundalk. (The architect got his briefs in a muddle, and sent instructions for Dundalk to Newry, and instructions for Newry to Dundalk. Or so they say. The legend has an unmistakable whiff of bullshit about it.) An outlet called Around a Pound has an expensive exterior and will surely be Around a Pound Fifty before long. A bakery called The Cake Granny didn't inspire long-term investment. A mural of a child making a peace sign was obscured by ongoing construction. And a billboard promoting a BBC show called *The Tourist* had had the heart ripped out of it, as if the word tourist were a dirty word around here.

Near the outdoor market, I found a run of shops that was after my heart. Glambition, Fireworks Galore, and an IRA gift shop – all in a row. I tried – and failed – to imagine the circumstances in which a person might require all three on the same afternoon. In the window of the latter were images of prisoners, presumably republican, while inside there was a range of merchandise: things to wave, things to wear, things to stick on the fridge. The lovely lady manning the hub said she didn't mind me sticking my head in and being nosy, but suggested that if I'd been carrying on in a similar fashion thirty years ago the same might not have been true. She also recommended Ned Kelly's. They love an insurgent around here, don't they?

At 9^2 Coffee on Monaghan Street, I put my head round the door and asked for Ned Kelly. The lad laughed, then persuaded me to wait until later, said it was the sort of place you went after eight pints at the pub, not for an afternoon small plate.

'I'm on holiday in Newry,' I said.

'Good luck with that.'

'What would you do with a spare afternoon here?'

'I'm smart but not that smart. Emigrate?'

'No, come on. There must be something.'

'Dolce Vita.'

'Now you're talking.'

'They do this pizza.'

'I'm listening.'

'With chips and chicken kebab on it.'

'I've stopped listening.'

I was speaking to Ryan McCoy, a DJ and self-described foodie. He was adamant about the pizza. Not since the Brexit referendum have I heard such a spirited apology. And for a pizza. With chips and kebab on it. Remembering what my old friend Winnie said about rosé wine, the pizza struck me as nothing more than the outcome of indecision. I promised your man I'd think about it. Ordering a coffee, I noticed a plea for donations on the counter. To support a ward at the hospital, in honour of the care given to a local guy's late wife. I mention this because the amount of donations was considerable. The list of names and pledges, just from today, went on and on. I made a note: 'Good café. Friendly. Worth a nod.'

Speaking of nods, when the young ones do it around here, they produce a gust of fecking wind. They're all fringe these days. Ryan McCoy's packing one, that's for sure. While the style is by no means unique to Newry, here the problem is especially serious. Epidemic levels. Acute cases. Indeed I'm told the amount of fringe per head is starting to interfere with the microclimate. If the trend continues at the current rate, they'll soon be tripping over their forelocks, like some order of latter-day monks. I know what I'm talking about. I'm mostly fringe myself these days. Have been since I went in and asked for a simple haircut at Men With Class Barber Shop in Limerick. I somehow came out with more fringe than I went in with. We move on.

Modern Newry was built on reclaimed marshland. The original centre was further east, on higher ground, and grew around an abbey that had been founded in 1157. The abbey was dissolved in 1548, as part of Henry VIII's great indelicate protest, when he offered a middle-aged middle-finger to Rome and the Pope. Four years after the abbey's dissolution, the Marshal of the English Army in Ireland moved into the property. Walter Bagenal had the place heavily fortified, clearly not up for locals popping over to borrow some sugar. Bagenal's castle, as it became known, is now the local museum.

When Ken saw me struggling with the audio guide, he decided to steal ten minutes away from his desk and show me around. It was excellent to have him briefly at my side, pointing out this, nominating that, illuminating the other. There was some great stuff on show, to put it plainly. A torch used in the evacuation of Dunkirk. An original poster promoting passage to Canada aboard the *Lady Caroline*, in the wake of the great famine. A wee autograph book, owned by a man who went on to lead Sinn Fein, open at the page where Michael Collins put pen to paper. A map of Newry from the 1700s, by the esteemed French cartographer Jean Rocque. A few pieces of work by Seán Hillen, one of Northern Ireland's leading contemporary artists, known for his provocative collages, for beautifully combining Darth Vader and Jesus.

It wasn't all eye candy: there was much to compute and to reckon with. I learned that after the Ice Age, around 10,000 years ago, nomadic hunter gatherers crossed over to Ireland from continental Europe. I learned that Dublin was repeatedly mistaken for Belfast during the Second World War and copped a lot of German bombs as a result. I learned that when the museum put in a lift they discovered the bodies of 35 people. And I learned that Bagenal's daughter was snapped up by his arch enemy, one Hugh O'Neill. It was a different experience to the one I'd had at the rugby place in Limerick. I didn't get to kick anything for a start, and I wasn't ranked against other visitors. Nor did I leave the attraction with a sweatshirt under my arm equating Newry with San Francisco and Venice. No better. No worse. Just different.

Also different was the sky. When I stepped out of the museum, and looked to the heavens, there was nothing to be seen. The new sunlight applied a layer of gloss to everything around. Taking advantage of the weather, I roamed the city's East Bank for an hour. Monk's Hill, Maryville, Mount Pleasant, Windmill Winds – I wouldn't mind that paper round. I paused outside a cottage. A cottage that was also a shrine. Red front door, red railing, *You'll Never Walk Alone* plastered above the doorway. You get the picture. The owner doesn't support Everton. As I stared, the front door opened. The occupant had clocked me. He didn't appreciate my nosiness, and now I was in trouble. 'The manager's gone,' he said. 'My phone hasn't stopped ringing.' He compared himself to a sports car, said he was out of petrol. I thought to myself: all cars need petrol, but there you go. 'Have you seen the tennis? Get in here and take a look. It's gone to a fifth set.'

His name was Jimmy. And that's how he greeted me. The Liverpool manager's departure and a tennis update. He was 74 and recovering from a heart attack. Had lived in Newry for fifty years but they still called him Belfast. Inside the house, Jesus and Steven Gerrard were given equal footing on the mantlepiece. He made me a coffee, told me a few things. Said his daughter was a journalist on *The Irish Times*, that his son was in Newcastle, and that Liverpool needed to get Henderson back. It was only at this juncture that Jimmy paused to wonder, 'So what brings you here, Ben?' First he welcomes, then he asks. It's an admirable order.

We watched the tennis, and drank our hot drinks, as Jimmy told me a bit more about his life. Said he went over to London when it kicked off in Belfast. Worked at Dulwich Hospital, at White Hart Lane, at the Supreme Court. Wherever there was electricity, there was Jimmy. He got a few funny looks when he opened his mouth, so he did. He was held for seven hours for no reason once. Not long after the Guilford Four. People were on edge and not without reason. He said he was married for thirty years, and that it still hurts that he isn't anymore.

'Much going on with you today?' he said.

'Fair bit, yeah.'

'Well, you may as well stop a bit longer then. Watch the fifth set. Have another coffee.'

'OK.'

His mum was a Catholic and his dad was a Protestant, and the fact that they loved each other taught Jimmy a lesson. A lesson without thinking. It taught Jimmy that one could be this and one could be that and the result could be love. 'What more do you need to know?'

'Don't get me wrong,' he continued, 'I'm not against nailing your colours to the mast. When you're into something, by all means do it with passion. Just don't get cross if others have their own ideas. There's room for the lot of us, so there is.'

He took my mug, went to the kitchen, put the kettle back on.

'Was it one sugar or two?' he called from the kitchen.

'One, please.'

Newry

'And you're happy with the Fernando Torres mug or are you wanting another?'

'I'm happy with Torres.'

'I stopped using it when he went across to Chelsea. Was that a cheer for Djokovic or the other fella?'

'The other fella.'

'Brilliant. Could be a tie break.'

'Looking like it.'

'It's grand you stopped by, Ben, so it is.'

Pat's Carry Out looked nice in the early dark. Steamy windows concealed the action within. A neon sign said OPEN. I made a peephole with my sleeve. It was a chip shop. Or a chippy. Or a chipper. I put my head around the door. It might as well have been a brass neck, the reaction I got. When I asked for directions, the young one working had more cheek than a puffer fish. She said, 'Yeah. What you do is, you go into your pocket, and you get out your phone, and then you type in where you want to go, and then – strike me down if I'm talking out me arse – *it tells you how to fecking get there.*' But she was only slagging, only teasing, for when push came to shove, and she realised I was about as tooled-up as a Cistercian nun, she spent more time than she could spare performing how I might proceed to the industrial estate. By way of thanks, I ordered a portion of onion rings. They were huge. Like the battered rings of Saturn. I hadn't seen onion rings in a chipper before, but then I don't count myself worldly. I said, 'If I end up in Derry, I'll be coming back to complain.' She said, 'I'll be getting my hair done, so I will.'

I went down Warrenpoint Road, past the bowling club, a cemetery on the hillside, and a pair of floodlit outdoor tennis courts. Didn't think I'd see the latter in Northern Ireland in January. Two women were disputing whether it was in or out. 'If that was out, Leanne, then I'm Saint Patrick.' 'Denise, it landed in Ballymena, so it did.' Just when I feared that it might come to blows, or result in a backhand across the forehead, they broke out in laughter, and agreed to take a point each.

I came to my destination. Formula Karting. It was a proper setup: three indoor tracks, a bar, a viewing gallery, £25 a spin. By coming here, I was behaving out of character. I'm not exactly a petrolhead. In fact I drive like a granny. (Assuming, that is, that grannies drive like me.) My first car was an F-reg Renault 5, for which I paid £300 in 2004. I was promised it could do 54 mph but I never took it past 38. Cyclists used to overtake me. I'm just not a thrill seeker, I guess. My idea of a good time is playing charades with a friend I haven't seen for six years. Given the above, you won't be surprised to learn that I quite enjoyed the safety briefing I was given before my time on the track, during which I was given ample reassurance and stuck in a onesie.

For the next twenty minutes, instead of burning rubber, I went around and around as though constantly approaching a pedestrian crossing. It was fun nonetheless. Adrenaline, endorphins: basically my brain had its belly rubbed for a while. The activity offered a lesson in perspective, too, about how the same thing can be perceived so differently. You see, I was under the impression that I was going reasonably fast, and yet, when I was shown some footage, it turns out I was hardly moving. The lads that kitted me out delighted in showing me how slow I was. One of them wondered if I was actually shitting myself, because that had happened before. They were called Tommy and Fridge.

'Fringe?'

'Fridge.'

'Fridge?'

'Fridge.'

'Why?'

'Ah, let's not get into it.'

Lovely boys. Both seventeen, doing A-levels. Sharp. Quick-witted. A softness to them. A warmth also. Qualities I encountered a fair bit in the young ones in Northern Ireland. I don't imagine they're all like that, but I met enough to know that they're not a rare breed. Tommy is after a job in a factory, but quite fancies the idea of travel writing now I've mentioned it. Fridge, on the other hand, is after going to the university up in Belfast. He seemed a touch embarrassed when admitting to this plan. But his pal Tommy is supportive. '100% you're going,' said Tommy. 'You'll be deadly up there. Introduce that mob to a bit of class and sophistication.' They were both surprised to learn that Newry was a city.

'The Queen bestowed the title before she died,' I said.

'Died?'

'Yeah.'

'Feck me,' said Tommy. 'I miss all the carry on. Who shot her?'

I went to a hotel for dinner. Canal Court. The big yellow one that you can see from outer space. Built in 1998, I read. Two brothers wanting the town to turn a corner, away from the carry on, away from before. They bought an old mill, turned it into a big glamorous hotel, no expense spared. Gym, spa, suites. It's a nice conception story. Anything but immaculate. I went through to the Granary Bar, where I ordered a wimpy Guinness and considered the menu. My luck was in: the hotel did that mad pizza recommended by the DJ. They were doing a collaboration with Dolce Vita. I reckoned myself a right lucky so-and-so until the pizza turned up. It was quite something. Blindboy Boatclub has probably done a two-hour monologue on it. I can't give it my blessing, though. It was structurally unsound. The chips, which were carrying two types of squeezable sauce, kept tumbling off. One got into the pint, for feck's sake. The young one who served me said that people come all the way from Belfast for one of these. *Christ*, I thought. *Can't be much of a food scene in Belfast.* They also come for the chicken burger at Friar Tuck's, he said. But he won't go near the place. He was dumped in Friar Tuck's, you see, by his first and only love, and his body won't let him go back. 'I've tried a few times,' he said. 'Because I bloody love that burger. But my legs know best. Too much trauma. Will you be having another pint?'

I wasn't having another pint. I was moving on instead. The lad suggested Cobbles for karaoke or the Bridge Bar for a quiet one. I opted for the latter. It was a cosy place, not unlike Dolan's in Limerick. A refuge on a blustery afternoon, or an evening full of sleet. I treated myself to a whiskey, then treated the whiskey to a lap of the premises. A framed newspaper article provided some intel. The Bridge Bar was owned for a long time by a Mr Toner and his wife. It was known as the most peaceful pub in the country, bringing together people from all walks, all sides, all classes and creeds. Mr Toner ran a zero-entertainment establishment. No pool, no darts, no music, no fruit machines. People had to talk. Duly inspired, I had a chat with an old boy at the bar. I was hoping he'd say something flattering about Newry. Or share with me a secret of its past. Or introduce me to another feather in its cap. Or tell me some tall tales about life here as a boy. But he didn't. And he couldn't. Because he was from Oslo. I turned to the *Newry Reporter*. A pensioner has been given a two-year suspended sentence for peddling counterfeit handbags, and Newry has the most potholes in Northern Ireland. That was enough for me. I pushed the *Reporter* aside.

There was a game of Gaelic football on the television behind the bar. A mash of soccer, rugby, Aussie rules and basketball. Like that pizza but on a sports field. The goalkeeper had lost the run of himself. He was wandering all over the pitch, as though out walking the dog. Within ten minutes it was clear you get none of the carry-on that you get with non-Gaelic football. None of the theatrics. They don't stop play for injuries, even if the lad's head's fallen off. The players aren't getting paid, and you have to be from the county you play for. As a result, there's an honesty to it, an intensity. Not everyone was as impressed as I was, however. Listening to the woman at the other end of the bar, you'd think she'd narrowly missed out on selection herself. 'You might have done that an hour ago, ye fecking eejit.'

Around the corner from the pub, there's another statue: the Newry Navvy, pickaxe in hand, looking ready for a pint. The statue remembers the navigators that dug the canal here, that guided it south, from the inland coalfields all the way to the Irish Sea. Opened in 1742, it was the first of its kind in Britain and Ireland. It was hard, thankless work – but work that is remembered at least. A goalkeeper and a navvy. Newry's chosen two. It's interesting which folk a place will put forward, will put on a pedestal. It can be a bit predictable, to be honest, and regrettable too, which is why certain statues end up in canals. It is a matter of representation. The question being: who best, and most justly, stands for this place? And the answer in Brussels is a kid taking a leak.

Newry is situated between a rock and a hard place – but in a good way, a beautiful way, with the Mourne Mountains to the east and the Ring of Gullion to the west. It was towards the latter that I set off now – having booked a treehouse for the night. When I boarded the 43 bus, I tried to pay the driver in euro. You're not where you think you are, she said.

The bus dropped me in Forkhill, a few miles southwest. I would have walked to the treehouse had there been enough light, but I couldn't see the end of my nose, so the owner of the treehouse, Carter, kindly picked me up. I'm not mad about Airbnb but when I saw Carter's creation I had to enquire. Besides, this thing was built for visitors; it was never anyone's home.

The treehouse made a good first impression: propped between a tree and a mountain, between sycamore and granite, and surrounded by the Ring of Gullion, seven hills covered in heather and bracken. It was built over three years and would make a decent hotel blush. You have to cross a wooden suspension bridge to get to it. It has a jacuzzi, a flushing jacks, a stargazing hammock complete with electric blanket, an alfresco shower, and there was champagne in the fridge along with eight types of chocolate. On the sideboard, meanwhile, were bread, butter and blackcurrant jam. Having arrived unprepared, they made a fine dinner. You can cook if you wish, or order in if you prefer, but I was content with my slap-up picnic.

I didn't take to Alexa at first. It felt rude to demand, to pester, to put out. But I soon got the hang of it. Soon picked up the knack. Soon got demanding. And so there I was, up a tree, in a hot tub, miles from anywhere, asking Alexa to play Harry Styles. ('Are you sure?' she said.) Carter had shown me what Alexa was capable of. If I wanted to turn on a light, I had only to say. If I was in the grip of a hangover, I had only to mention the fact and Alexa would close all the blinds and play two hours of whale music. (The bedroom was something else, by the way. A glass and wooden cube designed for weighing up the heavens.) Over the course of the evening, my questions of Alexa significantly escalated. What is a cloud? What is a strawberry? What is Ireland? What am I? Alexa answered the latter question thus: 'You are somebody who asks very interesting questions.' I was genuinely flattered.

Newry

Snuggled up in bed, I asked Alexa for a famous Northern Irish sitcom. I know you're not meant to watch telly when you're up a tree and connecting with nature, but you're also meant to be true to yourself and so I watched an old episode of Alexa's suggestion, a long-running sitcom called *Give My Head Peace*. It was an episode from 1999 called 'Two Ceasefires and a Wedding', in which a Catholic activist weds a Protestant copper. The show is basically a piss-take of the sectarian divide in Northern Ireland – which isn't the sort of brief I'd readily accept. When explaining why he has to conduct his secret IRA meetings in the kitchen, Da says: 'Cal loses interest in the struggle once *Noel's House Party* starts.' Elsewhere in the episode, a young Royal Ulster Constabulary copper, Billy, is worried that the rumoured ceasefire will cause him to miss out on overtime, and Ma is shown doing some ironing in the front room, getting the creases out of a pile of balaclavas. Later on, Emer and Billy are out in the countryside, having a roll in the hay. Emer nips Billy in the bud. 'Billy, do you not think you should wear some protection? Just in case?' 'Right enough,' says Billy, rolling over and reaching for his bulletproof vest. It was grand. When the episode climaxed, I asked Alexa to play something that would send me to sleep. She stuck on Graham Norton reading his own novel. Harsh.

I woke before dawn. I could see from my bed the outline of a mountain, Slieve Gullion, the biggest in the ring. There was an early buzzard, the beginning of bluebells, a hint of purple in the heather. The quiet coming of colour. I thought of that Larkin poem, 'Aubade'. I asked Alexa to read it, but she didn't have the right. Suddenly a dog appeared. An Alsatian. On the other side of the bridge. A drawback to kipping in a treehouse – wildlife. Then, as abruptly, the Alsatian was joined by a French bulldog and I began to relax. Carter had mentioned a French bulldog called George. And here was Carter now, come to show me how to get the tap to issue boiling water (which I'd been struggling with). It turned out to be a simple operation. But then I'm a simple sort, meaning the two things had cancelled each other out nicely.

I was left alone until checkout. In the clear light of day, I studied my whereabouts. The furniture came from the landscape, was fashioned from sycamore and ash. The glass was stained, the pipes were copper, the shower was wild. It was all beautiful and purposeful at once – which isn't a combo I'm ever likely to master. It is a truly special place: but how to spend my final few hours? I wrote in the guestbook ('Keep it up. Make it permanent. It's the sensible thing'); attempted and failed to meditate four times; then gathered up the remaining Ferrero Rocher, got in the tub, and asked Alexa to play the greatest hits of Luther Vandross.

I walked up the mountain I could see from the treehouse. Carter said it would be criminal not to. The view evolved as I climbed. Took shape. Gained content. Grew in stature and scale, just as the morning had. The estuary at Dundalk. The other mountains in the ring. A distant historical folly. The slightest hint of Belfast. In a long window of sunshine, the going was grand. The path, although crude and rocky, was sound. As I went, and as I climbed, I was reminded of the Camino de Santiago, that pilgrimage in Spain. The rewarding simplicity. The kindness of nature. The unexpected mood swing. The kind of landscape that makes you think twice, that brings you up short. Without doubt, it was fine countryside. (It inspired *Game of Thrones*, for heaven's sake.) And it was on Newry's doorstep. It *was* Newry's doorstep. Hard to think of a city with such a fetching backyard.

I reached the top. The scant clouds were still in spite of the wind, and the far-reaching view was an answer to any town or city. I wasn't alone. Also here, at the top, was an ancient passage tomb, a prehistorical burial site. I got down on all fours and followed a low, narrow tunnel into a sacred place of rest. I paid heed, closed my eyes, reflected on my personal insignificance, then pulled out a large slab of Milkybar, rescued from the treehouse. I tried to think of the chamber's creators, but my imagination – and with it my heart – wasn't up to the task. Instead I whistled a tune – Boyzone's 'No Matter What'. A pebble caught my attention. It had been written on. It said, simply and neatly, and in Tippex I think, 'Well Done'. Not meant for me, I know, but you take what you can. I left the note upturned, for someone else to happen on.

8

Milton Keynes

Radical Optimism

If you can't have a good time in Milton Keynes, there's something wrong with you. The city is weird and that's why I loved it. Its strength lies in its oddity. Its charm depends on its anomaly. Let me explain.

Everyone's parents are odd. MK's parents are an Act of Parliament and an urban theorist called Melvin. On paper, MK was conceived in 1967. In practice, it grew up over the next ten years or so, coming of age on 8,000 hectares of surplus farmland in Buckinghamshire. The planned city was carefully positioned equidistant from London, Birmingham, Leicester, Oxford and Cambridge – so it didn't get in the way, I suppose. The railway station, at which I now arrived, was opened by Prince Charles in 1982, just months after he married Diana. When I stepped out of the station I immediately turned on a sixpence to see where I'd come from. The station was glassy, boxy, shiny. Not a brick in sight. Not a hint of a column. Not a whisper of granite or puddingstone. It looked ... *formerly modern,* somehow – like eighties synthpop, or an episode of *Tomorrow's World* from 1976. I was standing on Station Square, a stony plaza bordered on three sides by sparkly midrise office blocks. A chunk of *Superman 4* was filmed on Station Square, and not because it exudes olde-worlde charm. An information board said that the local park took its cue from the Big Apple; that Campbell was an answer to Central. Evidence that Milton Keynes looked abroad for example. That MK looked to NY for its USP.

For better or worse, most towns and cities evolve organically, higgledy-piggledy, ad hoc. MK, contrastingly, was entirely preconceived. It was a 1960s new town, the most ambitious of a postwar bunch, brought into this world to deal with overcrowding and substandard housing in London. You only have to spend ten minutes in MK to see that the city's designers didn't mind a bit of glass and steel, that modernism was the watchword, that concrete ruled, that it was a case of function first and ornament second. Befitting this leaning, the city's masterplan included a grid of roads for easy-going driving – automobility was reckoned the ultimate way forward. The roads would bend with the land, would curve with the contours. It would be a grid, but an irregular one. The grid roads created grid squares, home to a hundred hoods, each one of the squares somewhat autonomous, with its own local centre. More egg box than donut, therefore. There was to be a three-storey height limit outside the centre – no building taller than the tallest tree – and a six-storey limit downtown, though that has since been scuppered, or razed rather, judging by the lofty hotel at the top of the strip, named La Tour.

All the design principles, all the thinking and whatnot, were laid out in a document called *The Plan for Milton Keynes* – which became an unexpected bestseller and knocked a three-year-old Richard Osman off the no.1 spot. All the top bods were recruited to chuck in their tuppence worth, to contribute their vision: MK was going to be a showpiece of British design. It was going to turn heads. And it did. And it does. It was considered a marvel then and, in certain circles, is considered a marvel now. No expense was spared, no detail overlooked. Cornish granite. Ample green space. Bespoke benches. They even turned the grid a few degrees to the left at the very last minute, so that the mid-day sun would stream down Midsummer Boulevard on the longest day of the year.

Who did all this? Who was in charge? Who were these cutting-edge top bods? Power rested in the hands of an appointed Development Corporation. MKDC wanted to break ground in more ways than one. The Corporation wanted a city that was 'non-hierarchical' – which is to say, all over the place. The idea was to spread out the assets and appeal, not have all the good bits clustered and contained in the middle. Decentralisation was a guiding principle. A central concern.

When Milton Keynes comes in for stick, it tends to be the city's downtown core that cops it. This is perhaps unsurprising. For one, this is the part of the city that non-residents are most likely to confront – and therefore critique. And for two, this is the part of the city where people typically expect to find all the 'good' bits – like atmosphere, for example, and history. Back in 1980, the president of the Royal Town Planning Institute described central Milton Keynes as 'bland, rigid, sterile, and totally boring'. But the thing is, the middle of MK was never going to appeal to conventional mindsets, because the middle of MK was never meant to be conventional. The chief architect of MK, the inap-propriately named Derek Walker, claimed that the true 'father of the city' was a certain Melvin Webber. Melvin, an American urban designer and theorist, believed in 'community without propinquity' – community without rubbing shoulders – and for-mulated the idea of the Non-Place Urban Realm, which sounds

Milton Keynes

155

dreamy. Melvin doubtless envisaged the residents of MK existing in a massive WhatsApp group, from which they would derive both meaning and updates while proceeding smoothly in Ford Cortinas. Let us be clear: MK's blue-sky thinking was not – and is not – everyone's idea of cake. But this shouldn't be a deterrent, for isn't the proof in the pudding? Just come for the day. Come for a nibble. You never know, you might just acquire a taste for the place.

I left Station Square and came to an underpass, part of an extensive network of cycle and walkways (known as redways) meant for those residents who refuse to enter the modern world and get themselves a motor. MK's grid roads are rarely crossed – they are bridged or passed under. A cyclist never has to encounter or be alongside a vehicle. And there are no steps in MK, I'm told, so my friend Anthony, who uses an electric wheelchair, could safely bowl around for hours without getting pissed off. Nice.

I came to a temporary road sign. One of the yellow, triangular types. It was in the middle of the pavement and pointed to COFFEE. I paid heed and was led to Bogota – a decent indie with a banging long black and old-fashioned punters reading poetry on sofas. The café's owner had come back from Colombia determined to inject a bit of character and indie spirit into MK. As well as Bogota, he has opened Canal St Coffee, which is up by Campbell/Central Park, where the cakes are done by a *Bake Off* star called Tracy (and are very, very good). A city – any city – needs big characters nudging the agenda. Well-meaning movers and shakers. Entrepreneurs who aren't only after the coin, but who sense the bigger picture, the greater good. I took my coffee away. Walked north along Midsummer Blvd, the main central drag. As I did so, I felt a sharp sense of being *someplace else*. I'll say it again: MK is an urban anomaly. The layout, the look, the intent behind it all – it amounts to an oddness that is almost exotic, and is certainly arresting and provocative. Milton Keynes gets you thinking. I'd already suffered at least seven trains of thought since turning up – which is more than I suffered during the whole of my twenties. Here's something that got me thinking: the local JD Wetherspoon. It stopped me in my tracks – and not because the price of the bitter was sweet. Situated on the corner of Upper Fourth Street and Midsummer Boulevard, the pub had no name, was simply called Wetherspoons. Perhaps the publican couldn't decide. Like an indecisive parent, torn between Jack and Jill, plumping for neither, opting for nothing.

Unless you've been living under a rock, you'll know about the Wetherspoons chain. It started with one boozer in Muswell Hill, London, back in 1979. Now there are nearly a thousand Spoons in the UK and Ireland, and they've all got flipping names. I went inside the one before me, damaged my amygdala by having four and a half americanos for 69p, then looked into the matter of its missing identity. I went through a list of all the Wetherspoons pubs – it took me about a week – and discovered that the one in central MK is the only one without a name. There's The Whispering Moon in Croydon. The Man in the Wall in Wimborne. The Red Lion and Pineapple in Ealing. The Three John Scotts in Hull. The Up Steps Inn in Oldham. The Mechanical Elephant in Margate. The Electrical Wizard in Morpeth. The Wouldhave in South Shields. The Asparagus in Battersea. The Bottle of Sack in Sutton Coldfield. The Bobbing John in Alloa. The Kirky Puffer in Glasgow. The Malcolm Uphill in Caerphilly. The Bank Statement in Swansea. Cool names. Weird names. Creepy names. Poetic names. Clearly anything goes. Clearly a Wetherspoons pub can be called just about anything. And yet the one in central MK is … nameless. What are we to make of that? It's as if the company were conspiring with the stereotype, colluding with the received wisdom,

Milton Keynes 157

that MK is a bit blank and characterless, a bit of a non-entity. It's a tragicomic oversight. An almost offensive act of neglect. If the only thing that comes of this book is that the Spoons in MK gets a name, I'll be happy. Call it Melvin's the Daddy. Call it The Vacuum. Call it Whatever. Just call it something.

I proceeded to the Church of Christ the Cornerstone, not far from the pub. Stylistically, it's quite the mishmash, nodding to both modern and classic at once – which is how you pull a muscle. The diverse style is fitting, however, as it's an Ecumenical church, meaning it hosts many branches under one canopy. It is a coming together of ideas, not unlike the city that hosts it. Church of England, the Baptist Union, the Methodist Church, the Roman Catholic Church and the United Reformed Church – they all get stuck in under the same roof. It's a practical approach with a good-looking result. I wonder if that German building boffin Nikolaus Pevsner said anything about it.[26]

I kept on walking until I was brought up short by a striking interaction: two girls sharing some gossip, sat on a railing. Called *The Whisper*, the sculpture hints at intimacy and friendship (as well as subterfuge and conspiracy), and is nicely done. I reasoned that the pair were keeping it down because they were outside a library – but it turned out that couldn't be the reason, because it was pumping in there. No whispering going on at all. Melvin would have been appalled by the amount of propinquity. Lots of collisions, engagements, encounters – more than is conducive to satisfactory exam results, I happen to think. But it was good to see the place busy. Full to bursting almost. I overheard

---

[26] He didn't. Though he did say that the shopping centre in MK was the best of its kind in the British Isles. Which was probably as close as Pevsner got to a gag.

one teenager, a proud Milton Keynesian, dissing Northampton in colourful terms.

As in Newry, I chanced on an exhibition in the library's gallery space, put on by an organisation called Living Archive, who have been telling the stories of MK and its residents for the last forty years. The walls were decked with a sweep of portraits with accompanying bios, the snaps taken by Sagar Kharecha, a local photographer. There was Naseem Khan, who owned a restaurant called Namji, where she employed women from minority ethnic backgrounds who had never worked, getting them into the kitchen and helping them learn English. There was Zainab Manji, who was forced to flee Uganda when Idi Amin gave the country's Indian minority ninety days to leave, and was now a key player in the local volunteering scene. Great people. Not household names. Not celebrities. But beauty is as beauty does, and they deserved to be on display, the focus of a show, the heart of an exhibition.

Elsewhere in the library, there were some great paintings by Boyd & Evans, a pair of artists from Hertfordshire who, back in the 1980s, were invited by the Development Corporation to reside in MK for a period and get the place down on canvas. The artists ended up staying put, and live in the city to this day. I reckon MK is that sort of place. Not many are seduced, but those who are tend to stick around, probably because the reality of MK surpasses the received wisdom. There was one painting by Boyd & Evans that held my attention for ten minutes, which is a long time as far as me and paintings are concerned. Created using documents and pictures from the local archives, it was a montage of scenes and snapshots, capturing everyday life in the city. Called 'Fiction, Nonfiction and Reference' – which is probably a suitable title for most artworks – it showed the city's ubiquitous black pergolas, the famous steel benches, Willen Lake,

Campbell Park, children on shoulders, a sense of warmth and hope and calm – and a number of pedestrians dead on the tarmac, having been mowed down by cars.

On the ground floor of the library, I studied a selection of aerial shots from over the years, showing the city at different stages of its development, black and white patchworks riddled with stream and lane, later conceding to grid and growth, boulevard and carpark: MK as a nipper, as a teen, as it entered its fifties. I was intrigued to see a grid square called Coffee Hall, and another that shared a name with an ex-partner of mine who dumped me for being too short – good old Stacey Bushes. I would later listen to a podcast about nomenclature in MK. (*Under the Grid* is a series put out by the MK Museum, and is worth a listen if you're interested in MK's unusual bio.) While it was enjoyable to learn how certain roads and roundabouts got their names, I couldn't help wondering whether just having a guess wouldn't be more fun. Looking at MK, all sorts of things occurred to me. The neighbourhood of Tongwell was surely barbecue country. Bury Field had the makings of a cemetery. Downhead Park was built during a depression. And Fenny Stratford surely remembered a high-status character in an erotic drama set in Detroit. And what about Milton Keynes? Where did that name come from? Well, in short, the appellation came from one of the preexisting settlements that was embraced by the development. A Labour politician involved with the creation of MK considered Milton Keynes to be an appropriate name as it combined the idealism of the poet and the good sense of the economist; the blue-sky thinking of the former, and the bottom-line thinking of the latter. (Though it could be argued that economists have it in them to be more fanciful than poets, but there you are.)

160   SHITTY BREAKS

I couldn't get out of the library. No sooner had I stopped day-dreaming about Stacey Bushes than I was diverted by something else on display. This time it was a fossil – the complete skeleton of an ichthyosaur, to be precise. It looked like a mixed-use household utensil – for combing hair and prising things open. A librarian called Michelle was on hand to tell me that ichthyosaur means fish-lizard in Greek and that the example in front of me had been dead for 3 million years.

'David Attenborough adores ichthyosaurs. He's potty about them. And to think – there's one here, in Milton Keynes library. It's enough to keep you awake at night.'

'Why, does it snore?'

'Pardon?'

'Where did you find it?'

'MK used to be a seabed. They found it when they were digging Caldecott Lake.'

Call me a dinosaur, but I think most technology is just asking for trouble. The first time I had a worry along these lines was back in primary school, when a kid called Alan threw a biro at me. The resultant injury made me desire the wholesale return to a strictly verbal way of life. I mention this because I had just bumped into a delivery robot. I had been warned: MK is a bit of a hotspot for experimental urban technologies. The little fella that almost felled me was produced by Starship Technologies, an Estonian company based in San Franciso, set up by the pair who brought Skype to the world. When ST launched their delivery robot, MK was well up for it. At the time of writing, the city's fleet, which is the world's largest, has covered 10 million kilometres. The robots run on electric, ride on sidewalks, and have a maximum speed of 3.7 mph, which is about as fast as I was going in that go-kart in Newry. They are a sensitive bunch, employing a range of sensors and cameras to dodge potholes and kerbs and bins and prone scooters and whatnot. As well as sensitive, the robots are also chatty. 'Asher' speaks like a university student. 'Sunshine' is always upbeat. While 'Harry' has the voice and manner of a British butler. Someone from Starship Tech is on record as saying that while the residents of MK tend, on the whole, to respect the well-being of the robots, they do sometimes get kicked, especially Harry. That MK was well up for the robots shouldn't come as a surprise. It fits with the city's founding ideals – modern, resourceful, forward-thinking, somewhat inhuman. MK is also trialling driverless buses, which I'm not on board with. You see, I manage a veterans' football team, and bus drivers make up a quarter of my squad. If all bus drivers were given the boot, more would be available for selection, and we'd never win again.

It was time to check out The Shopping Building: low-rise, lots of light, modelled on something in Milan.[27] Initially the building had no doors – God knows why, perhaps budget constraints – but the loophole was closed when joy riders started racing around the building's interior. I quite like The Shopping Building. If nothing else there's lots of room in which to privately despair. (I'm not a natural shopper.) There's also trivia dotted around, to break up the experience: 250,000 floor tiles, first McDonald's outside of London, opened by Thatcher in 1979, takes two months to clean the windows, only shopping centre to have hosted *Question Time*. Poems have also been scattered around to lighten the load. The work of local children. One started on the front foot. 'This is my city, this is my home / If you've never lived here, what do you know?' Fair enough. Not going to argue with that. There was

---

[27] In October 2024, centre:mk (formerly The Shopping Building) put out a glossy televised advert, the purpose of which, presumably, was to get lots of people interested in visiting Milton Keynes. They filmed it in Glasgow.

another one that was less a poem and more just a series of thoughts. From the look of the poem, I got the impression that Ruby had just been practising how to use the return key, and the result was mistaken for poetry. It happens more than you think.

At the north end of The Shopping Building is that lofty hotel I mentioned, La Tour, which is taller than any tree I've ever seen. I popped my head in, got quoted a price, then popped it back out again. I whipped out my laptop and actioned my back-up plan – the Travelodge. At £25 a night, it made a lot of sense. Sure, there would be no aspirational hand cream or views of Leighton Buzzard, but there would be money left over to pump into MK's evening economy.

You can do a lot of things in Milton Keynes – waterskiing, snowboarding, rock-climbing. Taken together, the list of optional diversions almost reads like an apology. As time went on, perhaps there was a growing awareness at some level of local government, that the nature and character of Milton Keynes, while admirable and interesting for reasons explained, was putting the population at serious risk of ennui, with the result that an array of pursuits and diversions was introduced to keep the glum-rate down. You can ice skate. You can mountain bike. You can help clean the windows of the shopping building. And you can skydive, *indoors*, which is what I did now. I entered XSCAPE, found the skydiving corner, and was inducted to the sport by Nora, an iFLY instructor. In quick succession, I was issued advice, a helmet, a boiler suit, and earplugs. I felt delightfully snug, all wrapped up in my outfit. I could have nodded off during the briefing. When Nora advised me to keep my legs straight, my chin up, and my arms above my head, I was reminded of a motivational tea towel my nan once had that conveyed much the same message.

I was joined up with two families. I was pleased with this development; pleased to learn that the hour-long session was going to be split between the lot of us. I had worried that I'd be skydiving for an hour, which would have been like commuting from a distant star to Bradford-upon-Avon. In the event, each participant got two dives, each one a minute or so in length. As I weighed up the vast upturned hair dryer that was keeping contestants airborne inside a massive plastic tube, I became, at that late hour, nervous. Nora had taught us a bit of sign language so we could have short conversations while diving – OK, chin up, legs straight, fuck you, that sort of thing. Unhelpfully, my mind had filed these new signs alongside the ones I'd picked up during a British Sign Language session I did a few years ago, when I learned that the sign for lesbian was the same as the sign for Liverpool. On the brink of my dive, I worried that I'd make a mistake and accuse Nora of being an OK lesbian or similar.

I was the last one up, having kindly allowed the others to go before me. (Women and children first and all that.) When my moment came, I wanted to back out. At the very last minute, stood on the threshold, I wanted to say no. In actual fact I did say no, but Nora couldn't hear me on account of the conditions and the earplugs, and so in I went, horizontal I got, airborne I became. And do you know what? I took to it. I felt calm. I felt relaxed. I felt at peace. When my minute was done, Nora had to wake me up. The second dive was nice but there's nothing quite like doing something for the first time. Novel experiences carry an inherent bonus – unless, that is, the thing you're doing for the first time is eating canned tuna. (Can't stand the stuff.)

At the end of my skydiving experience I was given a little certificate, which went straight in the recycling bin. On my way out, I wasn't surprised to see that digital evidence of my dives could be purchased and uploaded. I studied myself in flight. I looked … better than ever to be honest. Perhaps everybody has an optimum set of conditions in which they are most likely to achieve a kind of fleeting bliss. For me, that optimum context involves being airborne and in a onesie. I took a picture of the picture – it pays to be meta sometimes – and escaped XSCAPE with a spring in my step.

I went to a different grid square for dinner. This involved going back to the station and taking the train to Wolverton, four minutes westward. Itself a new town, Wolverton was purpose-built in the 1800s to house those employed at the local railway works, and was one of the preexisting settlements embraced by MK when the city had its growth spurt. There is an obviously different look and vibe to Wolverton – evidence that MK, contrary to rumour, is no one-trick pony.

I was here for a pub, The Craufurd Arms. When I turned up, some people were playing board games, others were enjoying a gig in the back room, and others still were tucking into Korean fried chicken, dished out from a food truck in the carpark. Stained glass windows, communal tables, Bowie on the speakers – it gave me Dragon vibes, which was my go-to tavern when I lived in Poznan, Poland. I asked if I could do the quiz, but was told that they were full, always are. Happily, the quiz master, Jessie, managed to source me a pair of regulars to cling onto at the bar.

Steve and Phil both work at the big Tesco, Steve on veg and Phil on trolleys. Both nice lads. On account of his trench coat and trilby and Star Wars t-shirt, I wasn't surprised when Phil told me that he was into *Dr Who* cosplay. Steve turned out to be an absolute brain box. He supplied at least eighteen correct answers, including giraffe, X-ray, beaver, Justin Fashanu and Princess Anne. I don't mind saying that my biggest blind spot was in the celebrity department. Steve was appalled that I couldn't identify Dua Lipa. I was good at the raffle, however – got it bang

Milton Keynes

on first time, meaning I was invited to play a game of Higher or Lower, a little bonus side-show carried out in the interval, with a £100 jackpot. Stuffed it up royally when I guessed the next card would be lower than a 5 and it wasn't, going to show that it doesn't always pay to be counterintuitive.

Throughout the quiz, it was my teammates that provided the best entertainment. Learning their stories, hearing their opinions – on Milton Keynes; on Charles III; on Dua Lipa's latest album, *Radical Optimism*, which Steve suggested was exactly what I had demonstrated by coming to MK on holiday. I learned that the late Queen's train was built at Wolverton. That there's a statue of a long jumper on one of MK's roundabouts. And that Frank Bruno is a regular at the cinema where Phil used to work. I also learned that Phil lives in Stacey Bushes, which is where the concrete cows are.

'The what?' I said.

'You don't know about the cows?' said Phil.

'Nope.'

'They're a 1978 sculpture, created by an American artist, who was probably concerned that the residents of such a futuristic new town would forget what a cow looked like.'

'What do they do?'

'Nothing.'

'Right.'

'I tell a lie – one was beheaded.'

'Yikes.'

'And another was kidnapped and held to ransom.'

'Blimey.'

'The original herd were moved to the museum. Probably for their own safety. The ones out there at the moment are replicas.'

'I'll add them to my to-do list.'

'Really?'

Another interesting thing Phil told me was that the inaugural 'cock and bull story' – meaning a story that might not be entirely accurate – was told up the road in Stony Stratford. The term refers to a pair of pubs at either end of the high street – The Cock at one end, and The Bull at the other. A story would start in the former – Dennis bought a tractor – and by the time it got to the latter it would have acquired a different quality altogether – Dennis stole a tractor and drove it into the vicar's conservatory.

After the quiz, I had a quick chat with Jessie, the quiz master, who told me she was originally from Northampton but now lived round the corner.

'What's Northampton like?' I said. 'I heard some kid dissing it in the library.'

'Oh, it's dire.'

'Really?'

'That's why I left.'

'So why Wolverton?'

She gave this some thought. 'I guess it reminds me of Northampton.'

There really is nowt as queer as folk: we can't stand what we're used to, and yet we won't have anything else! The laws of attraction and repulsion will never cease to amaze me.

It was the price that attracted me to the Travelodge, and it was the noise that repulsed me. On the train back from Wolverton, I'd been looking forward to a decent night's sleep – and I continued to look forward to it for the next eight hours. I got very little kip, is the gist of it. £25 worth of very little kip. A group on my corridor spent the night visiting each other's bedrooms. The pitter-patter of feet, the rat-a-tat-tat, again and again, all through the night. What errands were they running? What news or gossip needed to be shared at three in the morning? What sort of commercial travellers carry on in such a fashion? I was tempted to intervene, but I am essentially averse to confrontation and so put up with it. If anyone from Travelodge is reading this – yes, I am interested in compensation. I shared my thoughts with the receptionist the next morning.

'Sorry, love,' she said. 'It was a school trip.'

'A school trip?'

'Yeah, a grammar-school lot with an interest in cryptography.'

'And an interest in each other as well, by the sound of it.'

'That's what happens when you drop the prices too low. You attract riffraff.'

The noisy grammar-school lot had been to Bletchley Park, or Station X to those in the swim, home of Second World War codebreaking. It was towards Bletchley Park that I was presently headed. I took the train one stop east, again just a few minutes. Bletchley railway station looked more like a 1950s infant school than the gateway to extreme military know-how. (Cunning.) At the main entrance to Bletchley Park, I had a chat with a porter called Jonathan. Like an addict in rehab, Jonathan told me how he ended up in MK. Basically, he was travelling home one day when his train broke down outside Milton Keynes. When everyone in the carriage started badmouthing MK, Jonathan instinctively stood up and made a passionate defence of the city, despite never having been to the place. A bit fed up with Birmingham anyway, Jonathan decided to put his money where his mouth was and move to the city he'd vouched for. He'd regretted it every day since. No, he hadn't. He was very happy with his decision. 'Milton Keynes is misunderstood,' he said. 'That's the point I'm making. And I make it about a hundred times a day.'

Also misunderstood were most of the text messages sent by the Germans during the war, for the simple reason that they were encrypted and encoded by various machines, the most famous being Enigma. Enigma wasn't one machine but thousands, all of them operating (and obfuscating) along similar lines and via similar means, i.e. a series of discs or rotors which would rotate each time a letter was punched, ensuring a significantly scrambled outcome, turning straightforward communications – 'get some milk, then target Exeter' – into unspeakable gibberish. To their detriment, the Germans didn't bank on the determination, or capacity, of the Allies to decipher. They didn't bank on Bletchley Park.

My free guided tour started in the old Victorian manor house, which is set in lovely grounds and opposite a lake. The house was erected in the 1890s, for a wealthy stockbroker and MP called Herbert Leon. When the government's codebreaking arm acquired Bletchley Park just before the war, Herbert's old pad was its one and only office. At first it was all rather ad hoc. The billiards room for traffic analysis, the ballroom for Enigmatic activity, and so on. By the middle of the war, however, Bletchley Park had become a veritable intelligence factory, employing thousands. At no point in its life was Bletchley Park ever just Alan Turing in a garage being independently brilliant while surviving on Pringles. It was a huge team effort. Credit doesn't always get where credit ought to go.

As I was shown around the site, the scale of the place – and the range of its activities – became clear. In this hut they were eavesdropping on Hitler. In that block they were unscrambling Japanese gossip about the state of German tanks. Of the things I saw, and heard, and read, a good many have stayed with me. The story of Betty Webb, a recent centurion, who joined the codebreaking effort at Bletchley because she wanted 'to do

Milton Keynes

169

something more for the war effort than bake sausage rolls'. (At one point, almost 75% of employees at Bletchley were women.) The tale of Alan Turing, who did admirable work throughout the war before being hung out to dry for not being straight. A film shown on loop (in Hut 8 or 9) that did a great job at explaining the crucial role Bletchley Park played in preparations for D-Day. The details of Operation Fortitude, which was basically a concerted attempt to lead the Germans up the garden path, to get them thinking that an invasion would land at Calais, rather than Dunkirk. And the needle in the haystack analogy – in which the cryptographers were less looking for the needle and more removing the haystack – will also stay with me. (In fact, it's an approach I've started using whenever I can't find a sock.)

A moment of light relief arrived when someone in the group asked a question about the type of person that would make a cracking cryptanalyst. The guide said that if you're able to watch five episodes of the quiz show *Only Connect* and get every single question right, then you might well have got a job at Bletchley. I know for sure I wouldn't have got a job at Bletchley – not even in the gift shop. If I'd been employed in the area during the Second World War, it would have been as a scarecrow in one of the surrounding fields that, some twenty years later, would be earmarked by government as a way out of a housing crisis.

I was interested to learn that one means by which Bletchley recruited its brainpower was via the *Telegraph* crossword. In 1942, the *Telegraph* made their crosswords extra flipping hard and cryptic, and held live events, exams almost, where they would test unsuspecting cruciverbalists against the clock, with the War Office looking on. Anyone that completed the puzzle in under twelve minutes was invited to work at Bletchley. It would have taken me twelve minutes to find the right end of the pencil.

In the museum's café, where I paused to decompress at the end of the tour, I was amused to see that the menu had been cleverly encrypted – unless, of course, it is actually £4.10 for a milky coffee these days. My final thought on leaving BP – may the record show – was that MK was lucky to have it.

Having stepped away from Bletchley Park, I found myself in the mood to behave in an incomprehensible way. I did so by heading to the Wetherspoons around the corner. This one had a name, of course – Captain Ridley's Shooting Party – and there was a story attached to it. When the undercover MI6 lot arrived at Bletchley Park to check out Herbert Leon's gaff and suss out whether it would do the job as a war station and intelligence factory etc., they went under the codename 'Captain Ridley's Shooting Party', and gave every appearance of being a group of old chums in town for a shitty break. Nice.

I got the train back into the centre, walked up Midsummer Boulevard, took a left, a sharp left, and then another left, before having the best jacket potato of my life at the YMCA. To be more exact, I had the spud at the YMCA's attached café, a classy joint called Home Ground. (I'd read about the café on a blog called Sophie etc., which covers MK's burgeoning food scene.) The YMCA bit of the enterprise – the accommodation above and next to the café – is home to about 240 people, aged 18 to 35, each of them needing a helping hand in some way. The residents are housed and supported and counselled under the same roof – an integrated, joined up, one-stop approach which I'm told is working really well. Residents can also work or volunteer at the café, to gain skills and confidence. A lad called Remy did my jacket potato. I asked him what his secret was. He said he works butter and cheese into the spud-fluff before whacking the chilli on top. If you're not into spuds then there's always the daily soup option, the contents of which are grown in the roof garden, which is fertilised with the coffee grounds from downstairs. (It's that sort of place.)

Post potato, I went to the art gallery, which is at the top of town, and in the shadow of La Tour. I'd come to see an exhibition of photographs by Saul Leiter, a New York Jew who snapped and painted prolifically, searching for everyday beauty and unremarkable delight. Leiter's photos are improved by the imperfections they carry. Nothing is ever cleanly or completely portrayed. The images are incomplete, obscured, unfinished. There is always mist or shadow, rain or condensation, a blind or a curtain – something getting in the way of the subject, but elevating it at the same time. As much as I liked how the photos *looked*, I liked what they implied even more, about beauty and value – how they are partial, how they are imperfect, how they can be anywhere at all. I also enjoyed the sentiments and feelings of the artist, which were displayed around the gallery. 'It is not where it is or what it is that matters but how you see it.' I'm onboard with that notion.

You might call this part of MK the culture quarter, for the gallery is just across from the theatre. It's a 1,500-seater. Punters come from all over the region – Woburn, Newport Pagnell, Aylesbury, those well-known dens of thespianism. I popped my head in on the off-chance, and managed to score a cheap ticket to see a comedian called Tom Allen, who you may have seen being sassy and acerbic on the telly. He didn't have much of a set, if I'm candid. It was all rather ad hoc and off the cuff, which I didn't mind at all. Tom basically went along the front row taking the piss out of his fans, treating them to his brand of insincere snobbery. Tom signed off by saying: 'I love you MK, no matter what they say.' My thoughts entirely.

Because they do say things, don't they? As much as I'd love to wish it away, MK does have a bit of an image problem.

SHITTY BREAKS

What can be done about it? Well, little chapters like this aren't going to help much, that's for sure, and nor is *EastEnders*. I refer to a recent episode wherein Bianca Jackson, after many years off-screen, returns to the show as a resident of MK. So far, so good, I thought – maybe the episode is going to portray Milton Keynes as a place where you can live a healthy and balanced lifestyle while saving a bit of money on rent. None of it. Within fifteen minutes, Bianca has thrown a brick through someone's window and a twelve-year-old kid has been caught eating out of a bin. I was actually rather annoyed. Because it's one thing presenting Coronation Street – which doesn't exist – as a place so diversely dangerous that the average life expectancy is 32, but it's another thing entirely when the place you're throwing under the bus to serve your dramatic purposes is actually legit. They should do another episode. I'm going to write a letter to the BBC about it. And in that letter I'm going to suggest that instead of throwing a brick through a window, Bianca should be shown doing something a bit more representative of the average resident of Milton Keynes, like mugging a delivery robot.

9

Bradford

A pair of alpacas called Blur and Oasis

I received a mixed message upon arriving at Bradford Interchange. On the one hand, a bright mural said, 'Welcome home sexy!' On the other, a portal labelled 'Welcome to Bradford' was indisputably shuttered. The latter was the entrance to the bus station, closed because the concrete ceiling of the underground carpark keeps falling off. You're prepared to accept a certain amount of risks as a motorist, but that's not one of them. I walked down Bridge Street and into the thick of it. Sun was lighting the city's old sandstone, a lucky rock to have on tap. At every turn there was a puffed-up edifice, august and Victorian, built on the backs of countless sheep. Straight off the bat, visitors are forced to confront Bradford's former glory. That the city was once a global bigshot is everywhere plain.

Bradford didn't get going in the 1800s, mind you. It was on its feet and firmly established way before its industrial flourish. Evidence of an Anglo-Saxon settlement can be found by the cathedral, and it's well known that Bradford was well and truly harried by the conquering Normans, for having the gall to be northern. Thereafter, for a hundred years or so, Bradford was basically owned by the de Lacy family, a mob of French-Viking heavyweights, who I'm sure were all lovely. Similarly, the medieval village of Milton Keynes used to be owned by the de Cahaignes. Top Normans ruling the roost. It's a part of British history we don't tend to dwell on or romanticise. Just how continental we are.

Bradford has seen a few arrivals over the centuries. During the city's industrial boom years, the population grew by a factor of thirty. Job opportunities – however grisly and backbreaking – attracted people that were struggling elsewhere, like the Irish caught up in the potato famine. German Jews also came in large numbers, to flog yarn from massive sandstone warehouses in a part of town that became known as Little Germany, which is largely intact and as it was, with a heavy concentration of listed Victorian whoppers, now being put to different uses. Economic growth isn't always good for the health, mind you. All the chimneys pumping out all that smoke took its toll on the people. Around that time – Bradford's so-called heyday – about a third of children born to textile workers didn't make it past fifteen.

Bradford's boom eventually settled, and then waned, and then wallowed. In the years after the Second World War, skilled workers from Bangladesh, India and Pakistan came to fill a labour gap that was a spoil of war. Before long, however, the new arrivals were all surplus to requirements. It was a case of bad timing – the new arrivals were the last ones to board a sinking ship. A hundred years after its boom, Bradford was pretty much bust. Like many post-industrial cities, it had to deal with the pursuant social issues: the poverty and unemployment, the tension and angst. Needless to say, it's less than ideal when an industry that had supported hundreds of thousands of people disappears within a decade or two.

I came to Bradford City Hall. A sandy gothic palace, its midriff adorned with long-gone rulers: William, Richard, Henry, Stephen. (Stephen?) When these monarchs were initially hewn, they cost £63 each, which is cheap considering the cheek on some of them. Speaking of cheek, Oliver Cromwell is up there amongst them. Bradford backed Cromwell during the English Civil War, mostly because his adversary Charles I had peeved the locals by selling Bradford to pay off some gambling debts. City Hall stands on Centenary Square, which was named and pedestrianised in 1997 to mark a hundred years since Bradford was made a city. The square is dominated by a network of contentious waterworks; hundreds of sprinklers and fountains, plus a mirror pool the size of Barnsley. All up, it's the largest public water feature in the world, I believe, and just what the doctor ordered for a flagging post-industrial heavyweight. But I shouldn't be cynical. These things can have a measurable impact. Case in point: 12% of the local population are now employed as lifeguards.

Looming over one side of the square is the Museum of Science and Media. Born in 1983, it is a mecca for movie and telly and internet buffs. The museum boasts three cinemas, including Europe's first IMAX, and has 3.5 million items in its archives, including the first negative and the first telly footage. Bradford is also a UNESCO City of Film, and was the first such city in the world. It earned the status in recognition of its contribution to shooting and cutting and screening and whatnot. I've seen a few films made or set in Bradford. *Rita, Sue and Bob Too* (1987), written by Andrea Dunbar, is one such film. I saw it when I was about ten, and I can't say it made me want to hasten northwards, or meet anyone called Bob. At any rate, the museum was closed. It was getting spruced up in readiness for the city's stint as City of Culture in 2025, more of which anon.

A statue of local lad J.B. Priestley stands in front of the museum, his coattails flapping in the wind, asking to be clung to, to be reached for. One of my favourite scribblers is Priestley. He died aged 89 in 1984, after a career as a playwright, novelist, screenwriter and general left-wing bigmouth. At one point in his life, he found himself on George Orwell's famous list of suspected communist sympathisers, basically for saying that we ought to spare a thought for the poor, and think twice before acquiring an A-bomb. Priestley was an important broadcaster during the Second World War. Addressed millions on Sunday nights. Rallied the troops, bucked up morale, did a famous piece about all the little boats going across to Dunkirk. After the war, his leftie sentiments influenced the formation of the welfare state – and were, therefore, not to everyone's taste. Alas, J.B. was nipped in the bud, was taken off the airways, with Winston Churchill leading the calls for his canning. *Pipe down, Priestley.* That was the gist of it. As it stands, the statue is fenced off, which some might consider an advisable quarantine. His works aren't off limits, however. Have a look at his *English Journey* (1934) if you're new to the man. The author went travelling in England during the Great Depression and then reported back – thoughtfully, beautifully, humanely. He makes England look both dreadful and delightful at once, which sounds about right to me.

I'm sure J.B. would have frequented the Alhambra back in his day. The theatre is just across from the museum, and is another marquee building, fit for any urban stage. It was modelled on a palace in Grenada, Spain, for reasons that remain a mystery to me. All the travelling stuff from the West End of London ships up here, plus some decent local productions. Next door to the theatre is the old Odeon cinema. When the cinema was put up in 1930, it was the largest outside of London, taking 3,000 at a time. It's been dormant for decades, to the chagrin of the locals. Though better dormant than dead – more than once was it brought back from the brink of extinction. On one occasion, 1,000 people gave the building a massive hug to get their point across. It is set to reopen as a mixed-use venue later this year, relaunching as Bradford Live. Watch this space, however, because in my experience long-awaited erections don't tend to be punctual. But I wish the revived Odeon well. God knows that some of these old cinemas deserve a new lease of life. If it can't happen here – in the first UNESCO City of Film – then where can it happen?

Having seen a few sights, I went looking for some less obvious fodder – and found some. A copper being admitted to the Police Museum – a busman's holiday if ever there was one. Two nippers having a tiff outside the Peace Museum. A post box that had been cheered up with a crudely painted smiley face, the paint running and hinting at tears. The ground floor of the Royal Hotel, now an American candy store. A tent in the doorway of an old bank or similar, beneath the city's overbearing motto, *Labor omnia vincit*, work conquers all. You get the picture – Bradford is full of them. I don't know a more arresting city. It's chock-a-block with visual spats, with odd alignments and ironic combos; glancing arrangements that bear accidental grace, beauty by ricochet, compelling by chance. One reason the city is so photogenic is because the fabric of Bradford is a dependable backdrop against which another element – passing, fleeting, ongoing – can briefly coincide. You can't call this knack or habit of Bradford's a tourist attraction, but it floats my boat.

The old Wool Exchange, a once frantic hub of barter and trade, was looking gorgeous on that sunny Saturday morn. It's some building. Sandstone again. Venetian Gothic, I'm told. It is a romantic edifice – the stuff of fairytales. A show-off construction, conceited even. It's got notions alright. Around the time of its launch, that famous snob John Ruskin was invited up to comment on its appearance. He didn't think much of the building at all – owing to the nature of its purpose. Ruskin felt trade and exchange were crude and ungodly. Reckoned the best of buildings were pious and pure. I wonder what he would have thought of that leisure centre in Wrexham.

Saint Blaise was pious and pure. Had he been a building, Ruskin may well have approved of the fellow. Bradford's patron saint can be found posing on the exterior of the Wool Exchange. Blaise was tortured with a wool comb before being beheaded, and thereby martyred. It was the wool comb detail that secured his selection as Bradford's saintly patron. Had he been tortured with a lobster he wouldn't have stood a chance. These days the Wool Exchange is home to one of the finest bookshops in the country. Because the shop has a toilet, I made use of it. (I'm approaching that age.) I found a nice piece of graffiti within. 'Big Up Bradford' had been penned onto a block of sandstone beside the cistern. Trying to take a nice picture of the sentiment, the banging on the door started up again, and I was forced to nip my artistry in the bud and get out of there.

The bookseller suggested paying Tony a visit at Pizza Pieces around the corner, an underground institution marshalled by a heavyweight Italian, Antonio Barbiero. It's a lowkey basement restaurant, busy with students tucking into Hawaiians. Queuing to order, I read a framed newspaper snippet, in which Tony offered the following: 'To make a business last in Bradford, you have to be a larger-than-life character.' From what I could tell, the guy was a case in point. There was something colossal about him. Like he could govern an entire city by recourse to facial expressions alone. I had the minestrone soup for £2.50, then a vast slice of margherita for about three quid. The pizza was decent: skinny and crisp, indulgent and piping, easily folded and dipped into mustard (I know, I know …). I expect Jay Rayner was in here last week, had the lasagne for a fiver, and is penning his thoughts as we speak.[28]

Walking off the above, I stopped to snap a rooftop pig, perched on the edge, either threatening to jump or hoping to fly. There was something of Bradford in that striking ambiguity. A man entered the frame. Came out of the pub on which the pig was stationed. He spotted me.

'Why don't you take a picture of me?'

'Huh?'

'Why don't you take a picture of me?'

'Because you're not as interesting.'

'What's that?'

'I said you're too good-looking.'

'Fair enough.'

'You'd break the camera.'

'Now you're talking.'

'What's that pig up to? Do you know?'

'What fucking pig?'

His name was Sandy. He'd been barred from his village, was alcohol dependent, and should've been at work. He also had a tattoo on his neck. A quaver or a crotchet.

'I play the guitar,' he said. 'Write songs. It calms me down. You play?'

'I can only play two chords.'

'You can get good music out of that.'

'You reckon?'

---

[28] He wasn't. He was at a Nepalese place in Hartlepool.

'You can get good music out of nothing almost. What you up to, anyway?'

'I'm on holiday.'

'No you're not.'

'Yes I am.'

'Where?'

'Here.'

'In Bradford?'

'Yeah.'

'No you're not.'

'I'm pretty sure I am.'

'What wally goes on holiday to Bradford?'

'Me, I guess.'

'Fancy that. Bradford on holiday. Fair play to you, though. Got to have a look, haven't you? I'm Sandy.'

He offered me his hand. I took it.

'You're cold,' he said. 'Should get yourself inside for a brew.'

'Yeah, I might do that.'

Sandy turned and looked up at the pig. 'It's a boar by the way. And given its track record, I'd say it ain't going nowhere.'

As I walked away I had the following thought: I would never have spoken to Sandy, and come briefly to like him, if he hadn't entered my frame. There's something in that.

I took Sandy's advice, sought a cuppa indoors. Entered a café called Lefteris, which means 'free' in Greek. Taking my vase of mint tea to a table by the window, I couldn't help wondering whether the boss might have been better off going for one of those randomised pairings that you see a lot of these days, like Slipper and Horseradish, or Kumquat & Spleen. Terrence was at the helm, up to his elbows in sourdough. Said he opened during Covid; that this was less than ideal; that the city centre wasn't getting enough footfall. Terrence wasn't downbeat, however, and hoped that the City of Culture stint would bring people to the city. Bradford saw off Wrexham, Southampton and Durham to win the 2025 prize, which is administered by the Department for Culture, Media and Sport. It was Andy Burnham – then Labour Culture Secretary – who came up with the idea of a City of Culture, back in 2009. Derry got the nod in 2013, Hull in 2017 and Coventry in 2021. When plotting the itinerary for this book, those three cities were nowhere near my radar, their visitor numbers being safely midtable, suggesting that a stint as a CoC can have a lasting effect. When Hull pitched for the title, I wouldn't be surprised if the city made something of its connection with Philip Larkin, who worked as a librarian in the city for much of his life, and who suggested in one of his poems that 'sunlight destroys the interest of what's happening in the shade', which is a notion I'm very much onboard with. London is banned from applying for CoC status, for the record, which is fair enough seeing as it's hogged the cultural sunlight for the last 800 years, its unjust prominence casting a deep and lasting shadow over supposedly lesser towns and cities. In Sally Wainwright's *The Amazing Mrs Pritchard*, a drama series aired on the BBC in 2006, a disgruntled supermarket manager from the North of England gets randomly elected Prime Minister. One of the first things Mrs Pritchard attempts as PM is to move the whole of Parliament up to Bradford. While I can't say for certain that the people of Bradford would unanimously welcome that particular institution turning up on its doorstep, I am confident they would support the idea behind its transference – that is, the redistribution of jobs, status, energy and investment. It is hardly outrageous to suggest that a dissipation of focus and opportunity is a tad overdue; that some light would be nice in those places accustomed to shadow; and that, well, a bit of levelling up wouldn't go amiss.

Bradford

I had an appointment with an alpaca. There's a farm on the edge of town, up on the moor. Among other animals, the farm is a home for rescued alpacas. Every Saturday lunchtime, the alpacas allow themselves to be promenaded on the moor by humble members of the public. I took a train to Shipley, tramped up to Baildon, then ascended Hope Lane all the way up to the farm. There were ten of us. Pam and Mick were a local pair. They'd had a terrible two years, said Pam. First Mick had a heart attack and now it was his lungs, which is what you get for working in a foundry, and then a smoky nightclub, and then a coal mine. I gave Mick a look – of wry support. 'Mustn't grumble,' he said. 'I could live in Wakefield.'

Danielle arrived with the gang. A posse of two-toed mammals that are more commonly found grazing the level heights of the Andes than the lofty moorland of Yorkshire. The alpacas didn't look put out, mind you. They looked pretty chilled, to be honest. 'They do spit and kick,' warned Danielle. 'And not always in that order.'

I was introduced to Arnie, a long-necked brunette, with a fringe on him like that DJ in Newry. Before being handed the reins, Danielle told me Arnie's story. Turns out some wally bought him off the internet. Thought it would be a laugh. Because alpacas are meant to live in groups, it's fair to say that Arnie didn't exactly take to living in some douchebag's conservatory. Danielle got tipped off, made an intervention, then brought Arnie into the fold, where he's been miserable ever since. No, he hasn't. He's a happy boy. And why wouldn't he be? The worst element of Arnie's schedule these days is having to wander around with the likes of me on a Saturday. The best element of his schedule is visiting the local care home on a Tuesday ...

'Sorry, what?' I said.

'Yeah, they get right into the bedrooms.'

'Are you kidding?'

'No, I promise you.'

'To what end?'

'It's healing.'

'It's not healing if Arnie kicks Gladys in the hip.'

'He wouldn't.'

'Wouldn't he?'

'He knows that Gladys would kick him back.'

Danielle handed me a bag of snacks, which was thoughtful of her. Only after I'd sampled a couple did Danielle go on to say that the snacks were for keeping Arnie in line. Arnie knew where the snacks were, that's for sure. He was nuzzling around my pocket like there was no tomorrow. It wasn't unpleasant, if I'm honest. Also not unpleasant was being out in the sticks. The sweeping Yorkshire vista, the soft squelching underfoot – all was well with the world. That is until Arnie got loose and made a dash for Halifax.

It was a novel experience, and educational too. And it was exercise to boot, meaning we were all getting slightly high on a range of positive hormones. When you get up to things like this, novel things, quirky things, the brain isn't dumb to the fact and rewards you for being weird, for being daft, for being different. It gives you a pat on the back for rubbing its belly – if you know what I mean. Trekking with the alpacas was also a romantic experience, I'm afraid to say. At one point, during a photo break, Danielle asked if I wanted to give Arnie a kiss.

'No, I'm alright.'

'Go on, he loves it.'

'Really?'

'Go on. He'll be sad otherwise.'

'Are you sure? He looks about as keen as me.'

'No, honestly, he loves it. Let me get my camera.'

Nothing against Arnie, but the prospect of kissing him didn't exactly excite me. If he opened wide and really went for it, he'd

Bradford

have my nose off. In the event, it was fine. Quite nice, even. He tried to lick my lips at one point, but I wasn't having that. I mean, I haven't tongued a human for six years, for heaven's sake. I wasn't about to snog an alpaca now, just because he was giving me the eye. Danielle caught our kiss on camera, but said the pic wasn't good enough, and got us to do it again. Four takes it required in the end. I was getting a bit wound up by the end of it.

'Do you want to know something, Ben?' said Danielle, when the shoot was finally through.

'What's that?'

'I only make southerners do that.'

After the alpacas, it was back into town to see a film at a pop-up cinema in the studio of the Alhambra. The film was *Ali and Ava* (2021), written and directed by Clio Barnard, who also did *The Selfish Giant* (2013). I wanted to see the film because it's set in Bradford, and the director is decorated. I liked it. It is a fusion of contrasting parts. A hyperactive Ali, a bruised and reticent Ava. Both of Bradford, but from different backgrounds. Somewhat star-crossed, as Romeo and Juliet, but drawn with sufficient finesse and subtlety to avoid seeming derived or cheap. After the film, I got chatting to a lad called Kamal, who happened to be in it. Not only did Kamal act in the film, he also served as a script consultant. He's done his own writing too: *Bangla Bantams* and *Breaking up with Bradford*, both for Radio 4.

We went across the road to a restaurant – My Lahore, a self-styled British-Asian kitchen that began in Bradford but now has outposts in London and Manchester. I had the spaghetti bolognese, which was spicy and made with mutton instead of beef. It was a welcome hybrid of approaches, which is true of the place as a whole. The restaurant embodies the slow mingling of tastes and instincts that happens with time as places evolve and alter. Because it does take time, doesn't it? Genuine fusion isn't swift. Integration doesn't happen on a sixpence. It takes a while for things to blend in a meaningful way. First there is suspicion, ignorance, hostility. Second there is less suspicion, less ignorance, less hostility. Third there is tolerance, familiarity, and very little hostility. And fourth? Well, we'll see. I'd like to think the next stage is a genuine colour-blindness, an instinct to love thy neighbour no matter their creed, colour, club or whatever. An absolute inability to take sides. Come on, England!

Kamal studied at Cambridge. Did architecture on a scholarship. He was happy at Cambridge. Said he stood out more for being broke than being brown. We shared a cornflake tart with custard for pudding. It was a delight – for Kamal more than me. His experience of the dessert was charged with nostalgia. He used to have it at school. He told me that the school dinner – as an idea, as a provision – was invented in Bradford. Said the first free school meals were had at Green Lane School, just up the road. Told me that the headmaster of that school – and the person who ladled out the stew – was none other than Jonathan Priestley, father of old J.B. I looked down at the remains of our pudding. It looked more appealing in the light of that story.

'Kate and Wills came here a few years ago,' said Kamal.

'Get around, don't they?'

'They had the cornflake tart.'

'Oh yeah?'

'One each, mind you.'

'I suppose they can afford it.'

'Putting Bradford on the map.'

'One tart at a time.'

'Shall we?'

'Let's.'

For the record, Kamal insisted on picking up the tab, which was exceptionally kind of him. The bill was lighter than it might have been, mind you. Kamal got 10% off for having recently completed the pilgrimage to Mecca. I don't think that's why he completed the pilgrimage, but you never know. This is Yorkshire, after all.

The Midland Hotel is a solid Victorian job that's had all sorts in its time – The Beatles, Harold Wilson, George Formby. The famous actor Henry Irving called it a day here in 1905. Came a cropper on the stairway (to heaven). Not the worst place to call it a day. Can't say it was bustling, though. The hotel is Bradford writ small in a way. A lot of charm and pedigree, but currently punching below its weight. It needs a bigger job to do. I'd seen a lot of buildings like this one. Old-school pomp, vintage muscle, frayed edges, a slightly downcast mien. When you add them all up – all these buildings I mean – it's tempting to reach the conclusion that Bradford was built for a certain way of life, and a certain moment in time, both of which have since passed. It's tempting to reach the conclusion that the city can no longer support its frame, that it has shrunk in scope and stature and now its clothes don't fit. The answer isn't to alter the clothes, I don't think, but rather to bolster the body that has to wear them. A bit of extra muscle, some extra vital organs. Bradford needs to put on some weight. Its numbers need to change. The number of people coming to study or sightsee or give something a go – chancers, if you will – needs to jump. It could do with a divine intervention, if I'm honest, of the kind experienced by Wrexham. A random surge in interest and investment. A sudden influx of capita (and capital), a rush of heads, a wave of bums on seats. Maybe Taylor Swift could buy the cricket team and move to Little Germany. I reckon that would do it.[29]

---

[29] The Brit School is heading to Bradford. There'll soon be a northern outpost of the famous performing arts academy, graduates of which include Adele and Amy Winehouse. A step in the right direction.

I turned on my heel and went out to Saint George's Hall, yet another sandstone heavyweight. Completed in 1853, it is surely one of the oldest purpose-built concert halls in the country. They were flooding in that evening. The draw was Brian Cox: telly scientist, Professor of Physics, and presenter of a radio show called *The Infinite Monkey Cage*, whose title relates to the infinite monkey theorem, which holds that a random monkey, given enough time, would eventually bash out the works of Shakespeare. Hope for me yet then.

There were about a thousand in the audience, ready to be told about the universe. There was a lot of good will in the building, that's for sure. Had Brian told us the M606 was blocked I'm sure we all would have gasped. The next two hours were an absolute headfuzz. As Brian big-banged on about such things as stars and solar systems and galaxies and multiverses, I entered a kind of trance, a slightly stupefied state that was intensified by a visual backdrop of deep space astrophotography. Most wondrous of all, however, was when my neighbour (who reckons there are no shops in Bradford but Ilkley is nice), told me that she's the proud owner of a pair of alpacas called Blur and Oasis.

As the applause died down and we all came to our senses, it occurred to me that had someone asked me there and then – a curious usher, perhaps – to paraphrase what Brian had been on about, I would only have been able to muster the following: there's a lot of stuff out there and some of it's really hot. Tarrying in front of the venue, it was great to see and hear a thousand Yorkshire folk heading out under a full moon, saying such things as, 'It's them quarks that get me, Paul,' or, 'I don't care what he said, Mary, if I walked into a black hole I'm quite sure I'd notice.'

That was Saturday night and this was Sunday morning. I walked south through a sparse Bradfordian hinterland. Light industrial, slight residential, all caught and relieved by the sun. I went under a railway bridge and into West Bowling, solid homes on an angle, not a whiff of prefab about them. I dropped into Bowling Old Lane Cricket Club, got talking to the wicketkeeper, who was putting out a cordon of chairs in readiness for a meeting. You want to go right, he said. Then up a snicket. Then follow your nose or ask someone else. It was a well fielded enquiry.

On Manchester Road I confronted an elephant. A white one. A leisure centre of cosmic appearance that has been enjoying a leisurely lifestyle of late – doing sod all. The Richard Dunn Sports Centre is named for the former British, European and Commonwealth boxing champ who challenged Muhammad Ali for the world heavyweight title. The challenge didn't last very long, but then again, not many did. Richard came out of the bout with 10% less face. Throughout his career, Dunn combined boxing with scaffolding to make ends meet. He did the scaffolding for the sports centre that bears his name, abandoned now because it's too expensive to heat. The council built another one up the road, not banking on this one getting listed and becoming untouchable. The council's plans to pull Richard Dunn down and build flats on the land were totally scuppered. So it's doing nothing now. Going nowhere. Strictly dormant. Listed status, I am coming to see, is not always a blessing. Beware what you protect.

I was told all this by a steward who was manning the turnstiles of the Odsal Stadium, home to the Bradford Bulls, a rugby league team that had once been potent and super and practically unbeatable, but was now plodding along in the second division. The team was founded in 1907 and has been playing at Odsal since 1934. Over 100,000 piled in for the 1954 Challenge Cup

Final. The stadium is gorgeous, and romantic somehow, suggesting a site of timeless drama and pathos. It's by no means flash. This is no Wembley. No Murrayfield. No Stadium of Light. Half of it is uncovered: al fresco terraces, curved and steep and evoking ancient Rome somehow. The stadium must have an antique look about it otherwise it wouldn't have been used for a scene in the 2010 film *The King's Speech*, wherein Colin Firth, playing George VI, stutters through an important address.

I know little about rugby league, other than it's a professional offshoot of rugby union, and the teams are comprised of thirteen players instead of fifteen, presumably to economise. Widnes were today's visitors. Nicknamed the Vikings, they are known for going home with the spoils. I was put in the main stand, close to the action. You could hear the bone-crunching tackles, the particle collisions, the corporal punishment, the unsound meetings. A few hundred groaned when Widnes took the lead. There was early wind in the Vikings' sails.

At half-time, I bought something odd – a 'brookie', which is half cookie, half brownie. Eating the mashup, I detected a theme. The spicy spag bol; Ali and Ava; the lady who gave me directions to West Bowling, who was part Tobago and part Tunbridge Wells, and who claimed that the best thing about dual heritage is the right, in the event of indecision, to have double dinners. Fusion. Sharing. Mingling. It was beginning to resound, to emerge as a motif. And a welcome one too. I won't say that conflation is for the good of us all, or that it doesn't have its moments, but I will say that, in my lifetime at least, I've appreciated almost every instance of the stuff I've ever encountered, an exception being that half-cake-half-biscuit thing. Just choose one or the other and be done with it.

The mascots at half-time were also an interesting pairing. A couple of bulls, Bradley and Brenda, the latter got up in a miniskirt. Further entertainment was supplied by a group of cheerleaders, who took to the pitch to share a routine to Shania Twain's 'Man! I Feel Like a Woman!', which was probably what Brenda was thinking. Watching the performance, I was taken back to the cheerleading class I took a couple of years ago in a mistaken attempt to improve my wellbeing.[30] Ten minutes into the second half, the Vikings went further ahead. They were cruising. Set for a smash and grab. I couldn't stand the prospect of Bradford getting hammered, so bailed out with several phases to go. Besides, I was struggling to keep up with what was going on, if I'm honest. The rules were a mystery. I'd understood more at the Cox gig the night before.

I boarded a bus, rode it four miles, then alighted on the other side of town, outside Bradford Grammar. Founded in the 1500s, the school's motto is 'Do this!', which wouldn't have appealed to me as a kid. Alumni include Alastair Campbell, David Hockney, David Miliband and the Brownlee triathletes. The school started admitting girls as early as 1999, so hopefully there'll be some women on that list before long.

Across the road is Lister Park. I enjoyed the crocuses, noted a boating lake, marked the fetching range of trees. It was a proper, old-fashioned, Victorian park, intended to give the suffocating classes a breath of fresh air. In the middle of the park is Cartwright Hall, a public art gallery done in the local stone, splendidly and painstakingly shaped. I headed upstairs, to the permanent exhibition of Hockney stuff. Voted the most influential UK artist of all time in 2011 by thousands of his peers, Hockney is a Bradford boy to the marrow. He did many sketches of Bradford as a teen, and had this to say about the place: 'This big city I live in may be grey

---

[30] Evidence of that mistaken attempt is available on my Instagram grid – @benaitken85.

and black, but there is magic in it if I look at it closely.' Fair enough. After attending the Royal College of Art in London, Hockney did what all proper Yorkshire lads on the brink of maturity are liable to do, which is move to California and enter a vibrant swimming pool phase. He rented an office on Santa Monica Boulevard in West Hollywood, which sounds about as far away from Bradford as it's possible to get.[31]

On the face of it, Hockney isn't one for half measures. When he published a book in 2016, it weighed 35 kilograms, cost £1,750, and came with a lectern. When he had a major retrospective at Tate Britain in 2017, it proved the most popular show in the gallery's history. And when he did a painting of two blokes – one in a pool, the other watching the one in the pool – it sold for £70 million. In short, Hockney is a big deal. And a big Bradfordian deal. The work at Cartwright Hall, and up the road at Salt's Mill, are reason enough to pay the city a visit. For the record, my favourite Hockney painting is *Peter Getting Out of Nick's Pool* (1966), which depicts, in acrylic (and in the buff), Peter getting out of Nick's pool. Hockney is the opposite of Lowry in some respects. Hockney paintings are pretty – and pretty vacant to boot. The work looks great but often leaves me unmoved. The works glitter, and are venerated for doing so, but are they gold? That said, I like Hockney's iPad paintings a lot, several of which are on show at Cartwright Hall. Hockney was the first major artist to exhibit work in this medium. Whether he moves you or not – the guy is clearly a maverick.

---

[31] Not quite. The equatorial circumference of the earth is 40,000km, give or take, and the distance from Bradford to Hollywood is only 8,000km, so in fact there are plenty of places further away from Bradford than Santa Monica Boulevard.

Seeing as we're in the building, I should mention what was going on downstairs. It was a temporary exhibition, the work of a local snapper, portraits of women in uniform, served with accompanying bios. Shamim Chowdhury, foreign correspondent. Tasneem Abdur-Rashid, author. Lamia Radwan, farmer. Dr Aicha Bahji, lecturer in sociology and criminology. Najwa Jawahar, engineer. I watched a group of teenage girls enter the space, go around the room, snapping the snaps, reading the bios, taking their example to heart. The artwork showed people they recognised, doing it all, everything under the sun. You could sense the impact happening in slow-motion. Though I may have been imagining it. There's a chance the girls thought the whole thing was naff.

I continued by bus to Saltaire, named after Titus Salt, a former industrial hotshot, and a big deal locally. At one point, Salt had five mills in the centre of Bradford. With time, Salt grew sick of the smog and smoke and so moved a few miles upriver, where he put up one hell of a mill and a model village for his staff, which would later win UNESCO recognition. I wandered around the village for a respectable period, then went down to the Boathouse Inn for a Yorkshire pudding (and whatever it came with). I had a good view of the river and Roberts Park beyond, where a statue of Salt was just about visible, next to a pair of what appeared to be – no, they couldn't be – *alpacas*. Now just what the fudge was going on here? First it was Danielle taking them to nursing homes. Then it was that lady at St George's Hall with Blur and Oasis. And now here were a couple in the park next to Salt. A word with the barperson lifted the wool from my eyes. In 1836, Titus discovered a batch of alpaca bales in a Liverpool warehouse. He nabbed a sample, took it home, mucked about with it, liked the results, and then went back to Liverpool and bought the lot. He spun alpaca wool thereafter.

After dinner, I had a half in the Caroline Street Social Club, which isn't cut from the same cloth as the rest of the village, being modern and unassuming. As the adults played snooker and chatted, the children and grandchildren, sensing that Monday once again loomed, hid from the future beneath mahogany tables. On my way out, among notices for The Yorkshire Gypsy Swing Collective and a keyboardist called Wesley, I was drawn to a certain pin-up – a call for volunteer bingo callers. If I lived in Bradford – and I fancy I will one day – I'd be all over that.

I went back to Bradford by train, two stops, ten minutes, £3.40. I had one more errand to run – to have a look at Northern Parade, Bradford's quirky quarter. A couple of people had mentioned it and so I thought I'd better stick my head in a few doors. Remembering my encounter with that pig on the brink, I was drawn to Boar and Fable, a cosy craft beer joint, the likes of which are ten-a-penny these days. (And why the hell not? Every town needs an answer to Wetherspoon.) I ordered an IPA called Mango Lassi Heathen, then took a pew and minded my own business. If my neighbours had done likewise, I would have been spared several rounds of slippery nipples. But I also would have been spared a glaring example of Bradfordian hospitality, and one hell of a natter. Seeing me alone, one of the group leant across and asked me to join – a nice way to deal with someone on the edge. I don't like using the word bubbly when describing a person or people (when describing anything, to be honest), but sod it, this trio were bubbly, and kind and funny and discerning as well. They provided a list of their preferred watering holes – Peacocks, Hideout, Night Train, Rabbit Hole – and it read like a sinister to-do list. I asked the group what they loved about Bradford. 'The people,' said Ellen, without hesitation. 'Yes, we're a bit mad, but we're decent really. I wouldn't swap 'em.' We talked about Zayn Malik and Gareth Gates and just what the fuck I thought I was up to taking notes in a pub. When I got them to outline their perfect day in Bradford, it didn't feature alpacas, or rugby league, or David Hockney, or St George's Hall. It didn't feature anything I'd done, in fact. Which means I've got it all to do. And will have to come back to do it.

I took a circuitous route home. Indirect on purpose, knowing the wrong way can be fruitful. I came to a junction, where I stopped at some lights. Across the road was a massive sore thumb of a building. High Point. I looked it up and down. It was modern and dull, almost aggressively so. Built in the seventies, and once a flagship HQ, it has been empty for decades. It was described by the architectural heritage charity Twentieth Century Society as 'the last-gasp of a sort of Heath–Wilsonian regional resurgence', which doesn't sound like something you want to be, even if you're inanimate and made principally of concrete. At the top of the building, an ultimate vision for Bradford was spelt out in unmissable neon: 'City of Dreams', it said. I wanted to photograph the building, to capture this dreamy urban High Point, but how best to frame it? I could wait until the traffic lights turned red, and then juxtapose that colour – with its implications of 'stop' and warning and danger – with the aspirational neon. That would be the cynical move, the negative take, the carefully pessimistic composition. The subtext would be: no chance, forget it, you ain't going nowhere. Alternatively, I could wait for the lights to turn green, with that colour's suggestion of advance, possibility, momentum and progress. That would be the positive take, the optimistic framing – the dream was on, was going ahead, was happening. In the end I took both pictures, walked away, stopped, then came back to snap amber as well.

Back at the hotel, I sat at the bar, ordered a glass of milk and honey, and thought about what it would take for Bradford's dream to come true, for the city's fortunes to turn.

It seems to me that Bradford could do with a thousand people coming every weekend, from Leeds and Manchester and Newcastle and London, filling the flats and hotels, creating demand, spending money. If Bradford is to flourish, it can't be an inside job. The city needs the disposable income and the passing interest of outsiders like me. The frivolous pound. The avocado economy. The Instagram contingent. The footloose crowd. Turning Bradford around involves you turning up – to walk an alpaca, to watch an old film, to read a chapter of Priestley in Terrence's caff. If you do make it up, I'll see you there. And I mean that. I'm going to put myself where my mouth is. (If you know what I mean.) Monthly walking tours. First Saturday of the month. The Wool Exchange. Little Germany. High Point. City Hall. A quick bowl of spicy spag bol, a slippery nipple at Boar & Fable, and then over to Valley Parade to watch Bradford come from behind to beat Leeds 3–1. (OK, maybe not that last one. It could be decades before the clubs are in the same league.)

At risk of sounding dramatic, I'd come now if I were you. Before the crowds turn up. While there's more space, and the locals are happy to see you, and the whole thing is affordable. There might not be a chic boutique hotel on every other corner. There might not be ceviche at every waking hour. Not every shop will be open, and of the shops that are, not all will be flogging bespoke salads and artisanal keepsakes. There will be some things missing, and other things amiss – of that you can be sure. In their place, however, will be novelty and learning and character and whimsy. Travelling in the 'wrong' direction can be fulfilling and formative and rich. It can leave an impression, a trace, a mark. It can plant certain ideas and pose certain notions –that great things can be found on the margins, that sometimes cream gets stuck at the bottom.

Heck, what have you got to lose? (That's the first time I've used the word heck in a professional context.) I mean, you've already been to Munich. You've had a look at Lyon. You've seen Venice four times, for crying out loud. Give Bradford a chance. And bear in mind – seeing as we're talking – that Bradford stands for all those other unsung cities and towns across the land, across the world, that have gone under the radar for ages, some fairly, others less so. So when I say Bradford I also mean Sunderland, and Wrexham, and Wolverhampton, and Limerick. My time in each was measurably excellent, was appreciably sound. 7.6 out of 10 on average, if you're after a stat. (For context, London is 7.1 in my mind, and Paris 6.9.) By banging the drum for the edge and the margin, I'm not saying there's nothing decent at the top or in the centre. I'm not saying that the mainstream is utterly without merit. Not at all. I'm just saying there's also merit in the wings and in the shade. It just needs seeing and believing and framing and sharing.

You might think I'm asking you to come prematurely. You might think such a call to action should appear at the end. But the fact is … I felt it in Bradford. It was in Bradford that my initial hunch – that certain cities were being shortchanged – started to resemble a conviction. Besides, who says you can't peak three chapters early? Get it off your chest while it's there, I say. After all, the three cities to come – Newport, Gibraltar and Dunfermline – could prove objectively unpleasant and scientifically rubbish, and suck all the gusto and optimism from my sails, and I'd forget everything I felt and thought and reckoned in Bradford, about boxes and underdogs and quality and margins, about the wrong direction being a decent way forward, and this book would lose a good chunk of its positivity. So, yeah, I'm calling it early, I'm calling *you* early. Get yourself on a flipping shitty break.

10

Newport

You knows it

The Welsh city of Newport has a baseball team, hosts the World Cup of Pool, is being overrun by people of a certain religious persuasion (with the percentage of atheists jumping from 16 to 41% in the last twenty years), and boasts a School of Art renowned for documentary photography. In my view, the only thing the place has got going against it is the fact that it's up the road from Cardiff.

Newport railway station is shiny and modern and ultra-eco, befitting a historic Victorian heavyweight with an unhealthy coal habit. This is Wales, said a sign on the platform, in case I wanted to turn back. It wouldn't take me long to escape – Newport is just a whisker over the border. It's in a part of Britain liberally decorated with castles. A ring of said was erected by a series of anxious England managers who wanted to get a certain point across to the Welsh – we've got eyes on you, boyo, so do mind your step. It's a demilitarised zone these days. The last proper scrap between the Welsh and the English was in the early

1400s, though there was an anti-tourism movement in the 1970s, when fed-up locals kicked back against vintage English buying holiday homes and then only using them seven hours per annum. Whether they went at the grockles with water pistols, as the locals are doing in Barcelona these days, I can't say.

The lady manning the barriers suggested Rogue Fox for breakfast, just over the bridge and up the hill. On entering the café, I was pleased to discover an eclectic menu handwritten on a length of parchment. (The chef isn't above the humble jacket potato, I'm pleased to report. When you go rogue, there's no need to throw the baby out with the bathwater.) When I asked the young lady behind the counter what she liked to do in Newport, she said (*drum roll please*) another place entirely – Cwmbran, because the parking is decent. When pressed for attractions in Newport that weren't other towns, she said the Passport Office was popular. At this point I ordered mushrooms on toast, just to change the subject. When the shrooms arrived, they came on a tile of sourdough and topped with micro garlic chives, homemade hummus, and a decorative dribble of balsamic. As well they might.

I headed into the belly of the city. Much of the core is quirky Victorian, neither straightforwardly classic nor obviously gothic, talking its own language, speaking its own idiom. Newport had a belle epoque, that much is clear. A period when it splashed the cash on downtown construction. Like Bradford, it was a boomtown in the 1800s, when it made money (and mess) exporting coal and iron that had been mined in the valleys of South Wales. Newport towered over Cardiff at one point, in terms of stature and turnover. As elsewhere, that money changed the face of the town – starting with its façades. Much of the architecture in Newport speaks of its industrial honeymoon.

Westgate Hotel is such a building. It's not receiving guests anymore, but remains deeply significant, being the scene of an almighty hoo-hah back in the day. Where there is work there are workers, and where there are workers there are bosses, and where there are bosses there is unrest. In 1839, Newport saw the last armed uprising in Britain, when a bunch of unhappy toilers gave voice to longstanding peeves. They were called the chartists.

Chartism was a working-class movement that ran for ten years from 1839. The goal was pretty simple: to give more people a say on the nature of their fate. John Frost was the main man in Newport. He was the local delegate. On that fateful day in 1839, Frost had wanted a peaceful march on Westgate Hotel, where a number of prisoners were being held for calling for reform. However, a bunch of professional troublemakers, disguised in cowskins, had other ideas. They whipped things up royally, and so doing gave the army an excuse to fire on the crowd. Twenty were killed. Frost and his fellow leaders were sentenced to be hung, drawn and quartered. The sentence was later reduced to deportation to Australia, where it was felt the rabble could do less damage to the status quo. Nice one.

Standing in remembrance of this dramatic episode in British history is a group of statues, each of them representing an abstract noun connected to the Chartist movement: Energy, Prudence and Union. The whole thing is, I must say, a tiny bit perplexing. I was looking at the memorial presently, trying to work out if there was any set of circumstances in which I could like it, when, out of nowhere, someone tapped me on the arm and put forward a notion.

'Bit weird, innit?'

'Yeah.'

'Don't mind a bit of weird me, though.'

'No?'

'Know the weirdest thing about me?'

'Go on.'

'I know exactly seventeen words of Welsh.'

'How come?'

'Because they're tattooed on my arm.'

(May the record show that I sometimes ask the wrong questions.) 'Which arm?' I said.

'Does it matter?'

'Fair enough. Why did you do it?'

'Not sure. Went to a rave near the docks, came back with the tattoo.'

'What words?'

She pronounced the words – softly, beautifully. It was kind of touching.

'And what do they mean?'

'What, in English?'

'Yeah.'

'Haven't got a clue. I think one means cheese.'

'That is weird.'

'Told you.'

'You from Newport?'

'Yeah. Wouldn't be here if I wasn't, would I?'

'Like it?'

'Honestly?'

'Yeah.'

'Yeah, I do. It's easy to slag off. But, yeah. I do.'

'Anything you'd recommend?'

'Stay off drugs, don't get married, avoid shellfish.'

'I meant in Newport.'

'I know you did. There's a decent Italian at the top of Stow Hill.'

'What's the name?'

'God, now you're asking. I've not been for years. Not since I've been on the streets.'

'What happened?'

'What happened?'

'Yeah.'

'To me, you mean?'

'Yeah.'

'I lost a few things in the same week. Never looked back.'[32]

I went into a place called The Place on Bridge Street, which was established with Levelling Up dosh on the ground floor of a pebbledash lump that was going to waste. They do events, gigs, workshops, run a small café, offer a place to chill – and a spot to keep warm in winter. Hot drinks cost nothing and the password is WELCOME – that says all you need to know. It's been nicely done. Cosy. Inviting. Whatever the Welsh equivalent of *hygge* is. I went in for a nose, ended up with a free coffee and a chat with Fran, who shared the following. 1) Newport is neither this nor that, it's just Newport. 2) His brother got mugged by a one-legged prostitute in Pillgwenlly. 3) Since the M4 toll was scrapped, people have started moving to Newport from Bristol, which has pushed the prices up. 4) Harry Houdini came to Newport once and performed a feat of escapology by getting out of the city alive. And 5) About twenty years ago, they found a medieval ship in the river and it's now on an industrial estate. In sum, it was a nice introduction to the city. Better than googling from afar. It might all be bollocks, of course, but as a means of gathering information, and gaining an impression, it's preferable to eyeballing an online encyclopaedia.

---

[32] You know what's weird? I saw that person the next day, outside the church on Stow Hill. I gave them a fiver and I mentioned our chat and their tattoo, but they didn't have a clue what I was on about. Said they had no such tattoo and wouldn't dream of getting one, not least because they were from Bristol.

I entered a shop on Cambrian Road that appeared to specialise in souvenirs and school uniform. I wasn't after a blazer or plimsolls, but a translation of a sentiment I'd spotted in the window – *Yma o Hyd*, which was plastered all over the flag of Bolivia.

'It means "still here",' explained the shopkeeper.

'Aha. I'm with you. Still here. As in the song. The rallying cry.'

'That's the one.'

'And the Bolivian flag?'

'It's not the Bolivian flag.'

'Lithuania?'

'It's actually no one's flag. Which means there's no intellectual property to consider.'

The song is now a second national anthem. It was penned by Dafydd Iwan, a lifelong nationalist and the former leader of Plaid Cymru, the Welsh version of the Scottish National Party. It's sung at sporting events and got to the top of the iTunes chart. Despite everyone and despite everything, the Welsh are still here. That's it in a nutshell. I, for one, enjoy being reminded that the Welsh are still here, because they're a fair bunch in my book. I can't claim to have met them all, but the Welsh I have met have been unusually sound. With the exception of a man from Swansea who went up the back of me in 2009 and said I should have been looking where he was going. But that's probably a Swansea thing rather than a Wales thing. The DVLA is based in Swansea. They get complacent.

Next up on my opening amble was the recently restored indoor market. They've done a decent job of it, and I wasn't alone in thinking so – the place was bustling. At least forty people were spending too much on lunch. Not much hawking of plums and tomatoes, mind. It's not that kind of market anymore. There's even a plush shower in the upstairs loo. Any instance of change, or act of renovation, is bound to put a few noses out of joint – and a few people out of work – but on balance what's happened here seems to have been very much for the better. It was all local vendors, doing all sorts of stuff. Food, comics, records – out of neat little stalls and units. A business called Rogue Welsh Cakes caught my eye.

'What's a Welsh cake, then?'

'It's basically a condensed scone that's been cooked like a pancake.'

'Any good?'

'You knows it.'

'And what makes them rogue?'

'They deviate from the norm. Like Newport. Have a go.'

I had a go – and then another one. Bought a trio of the most deviant, which I saw off while completing a lap of the market. By the main entrance was a scale model of The Trannie – which is what the locals call the Newport Transporter Bridge. The bridge somehow manages to incorporate a gondola, which is a nice instance of globalisation – bit of Venice in South Wales, don't mind if we do. I was interested to read that the market was reopened by the leader of the council, one Jane Mudd, who was perhaps destined for a job in this city, given the character of its river.[33]

No sooner had I stepped outside to continue my unstructured mooch about town than it started raining cats and dogs. The rain suits Newport. Elevates its appearance. Some cities respond to the sun, but Newport glows in the rain, like Mr Darcy

---

[33] Mud gets a bad press. Not many nice things are said about it. It's only ever something you fall into, or get stuck in, or sling in anger. We wouldn't be here if it wasn't for mud. Don't worry, I'm not asking you to be more appreciative. This is just a note to self.

Newport

being improved after jumping in that lake. When the rain abated, I walked along the high street, which has been pedestrianised for a kilometre or two. Between Griffin and Skinner Streets, I watched a young girl pursuing a pigeon. Because the pigeon knew it had the pace to outwalk the toddler, it didn't bother to demean itself by flying off in fright, resulting in a low-speed pursuit lasting thirty metres or so, at which point the child was called back by an adult.

Soon after, on Commercial Street, I noticed something peculiar. At first I chose to ignore it, to carry on regardless, but then stopped and backtracked, wanting a closer look. It was a faintly ghoulish and perturbing sculpture of a figure covered head-to-toe in a bedsheet. As chance would have it, the sculpture that had caught my attention paid homage to the poet W.H. Davies, a local lad most famous for a couplet imploring the reader, amid the hurly-burly of life, to stop and stare now and again. The poem in question, 'Leisure', was published in 1911, and is a gentle invocation to slow down and smell the roses. It is frequently voted one of the nation's favourite poems, and enjoyed a surge of popularity when it was used in an advert for a chain of leisure centres, institutions that really aren't about observation at all, or at least shouldn't be.

At the time of my visit to Newport, I knew very little about W.H. Davies. Since my visit, I've clued myself up a notch, and it turns out that he was some character. Born in Newport in 1871, Davies grew up in a pub, was charged with shoplifting at the age of thirteen, then spent his twenties travelling back and forth across the Atlantic in cattle ships. During his stateside jaunts, Davies tramped about, did seasonal work, went out on the lash, and lost a leg attempting to jump a ride on a freight train. It was at this point that Davies moved to London, where he did long stints in the dosshouse, composing poems in his head to avoid the mockery of his cellmate. With the 50p that he got a week in benefits, Davies self-published some poems and sent them out to some of the biggest names in London. When he sent George Bernard Shaw some poems, the covering letter went something like this: 'Dear George. These are worth half a crown. If you're in need of them, please send half a crown. If you're not, send them back. Cheers.' Shaw wrote back saying: 'There's no money in poetry. I'll take eight copies. Here's some people you should get in touch with.' By hook or by crook, Davies became a popular poet. A literary celebrity even. A bit of a diamond in the rough, was old William Henry. A bit of gold that didn't exactly glitter. They called him The Supertramp.

I set off down a side street to check out the Barnabas Arts Centre. It was closed, but I got a dose of culture nonetheless. The centre, you see, is surrounded by backstreet murals, 24/7 displays of bright ideas and sharp compositions. One mural carried a notion – 'no mud, no lotus' – suggesting that good things come from troubled conditions. I know it's a twee and slightly saccharine echo of 'no stars without darkness' or 'no pearl without grit' but still, I was taken by the sentiment. It was apt, and fitting, and felt true in this context, in this back-alley gallery, down this dead-end lane, so bursting with life. I've said it before but it bears repeating: we should look anywhere for value, and to anyone for skill, from the highest echelon to the lowest ebb, from among the stars to beyond the pale, from way back when to fresh off the rack. Brilliance – of mind, of mode, of style, of heart – can reside anywhere. By all means give the limelight and mainstream a healthy portion of your esteem and regard, but reserve a morsel for elsewhere, for erstwhile, for out of sight and out of sync and out of line and out of print. We move on.

I came to Newport's famously muddy river – the Usk. In 2002, they found a ship in that mud – the one that Fran mentioned. It was a medieval merchant ship, and was discovered when a team of builders started digging the foundations of a new riverside theatre. The council weren't over the moon. They wanted to take a few pictures of the ship and then rebury it with haste. But that caused a public outcry and the council was forced to get it out for posterity. My gaze followed the mud downriver, as it wound its way to the sea, where it met another of Newport's historic attractions – its infamous Trannie. It's one of only a handful of transporter bridges in the world, which might imply that they're not ever so practical. This one was put up in 1906 to carry 120 people and up to six cars across the Usk in a gondola. You can't call it an oil painting, but it's arresting nonetheless. In the film *Tiger Bay* (1959), the protagonist is shown stepping off the Newport Transporter Bridge – and into Cardiff. *Cardiff.* The cheek! Get your own bleeding transporter bridge, Cardiff!

I walked east on the A48 until I came to the velodrome, which, in essence, is a big bowl for cycling. You ride on the sides of the bowl, often parallel to the floor, rather than perpendicular to it, which is what I prefer. The velodrome is named after Geraint Thomas, a Welsh cyclist who won the Tour de France. The GB Olympic team train here, I'm told, and the facility has produced a lot of talent over the years. It is an incubator of pedallers. You don't have to be tidy or determined to get involved, however, because three times a week you can do a one-hour track cycling taster session. Which is what I was about to do. I was a touch apprehensive. Not least when I heard the news.

'What about the brakes?' I asked.

'Hm?'

'The brakes?'

'There aren't any.'

208   SHITTY BREAKS

'Ah, fantastic. Anything else you need to tell me?'

I had been issued a 'Dolan pre cursa aluminium fixed wheel' – which meant nothing to me. I didn't like the look of it. For a start, the saddle was about half a metre higher than the handles. Given the choice, I'd have it the other way round. My cleats felt like clogs, and because I don't own any cycling shorts, I'd packed some swimming shorts that were miles too small for me. Emerging into the velodrome, I'd never felt so curiously attired. During the briefing, the lingo came out of Cerys, the instructor, like it was meaningful and sensible: hoods and toppers and Côte d'Azur. There were three others in the session, not an ounce of fat on them. They had all the gear – reps from the Republic of Carbon and Lycra.

Getting on and clipping in was hard enough. That took up a third of the session. By the time I was mobile, the others had been whizzing around for ages. I started off on the flat, getting used to the mode, then moved up to the blue band (the Côte d'Azur), which is on a slight tilt, and then to the black band, which is on a slightly steeper tilt, by no means perpendicular to the ground but getting there. It's vital to pedal hard around corners, I was informed later than I would have liked, because if your speed drops then you drop with it, which is the sort of incentive I could do with on a day-to-day basis.

Let me say this: after five minutes on the track it felt like I'd been pedalling for an hour. It was exhausting both physically and emotionally. I wanted to yell. My calves started to spasm, and then my glutes got wind of my calves and followed suit. Soon they were all at it. Even my face muscles were freaking out. I returned to the flat, absolutely shagged, and then, because it's the most natural thing in the world, I abruptly stopped pedalling – which is what you're not supposed to do. It wouldn't be an exaggeration to say that I almost went head over heels. Got a peptalk from Cerys, then got back on track, freshly determined to complete a lap without being overtaken.

Track cycling isn't feel-good at first. It is painful and scary at first and then great afterwards, once you've survived. What track cycling is at first and then afterwards as well is mindful. I'll give it that. You have to concentrate at all times, meaning you can't think of pet concerns, or dwell on perceived imperfections, like not being able to load a dishwasher proficiently. People do 200 laps after work to suppress and stifle and weaken their demons, to squash thoughts of throttling their line-manager. I'm all for it. It's making the world a safer place.

'Kids love it,' said Cerys.

'That's not saying much,' I said.

'Teenagers, too. It's getting more and more popular – should be part of the curriculum.'

'Yeah, I can see that. Once a term, get all the year 11s down here, out of their bubbles and into the bowl.'

'Exactly. You off, then?'

'Yeah, I'll see you later, Cerys. Nice chatting to you. Take care of yourself.'

I gave Cerys a platonic wink, cool as ice. I was halfway across the carpark before I heard her calling after me. Probably wanted my handle.

'What is it, Cerys?'

'Ben. You're still wearing the helmet.'[34]

---

[34] When retelling the above episode, about forgetting my helmet, I allowed myself to get halfway across the carpark before Cerys made me aware of my oversight, when in reality I was just a few paces down the corridor, heading for the exit of the velodrome. It is for this reason, I assume, that certain bookshops have started shelving travel writing under Fiction.

Next up, a spot of rugby. Two breaks in a row! I hear you cry. Thing is, this was Union rather than League, and besides, I couldn't come to Wales and not engage with rugby. It's the national sport – albeit one they pinched from the English. In the 1800s, posh Welsh kids picked it up at posh English schools, took it home, sowed the seeds, and now the game means more in Cardiff than it does in Rugby. Walking to the stadium along Corporation Road, I popped into a betting shop, where there was a nice lady at the helm. Used to work on cruise ships, in the Caribbean, didn't mind it for a stretch but started pining for Newport. It's a mystery why we miss what we do. The lady helped me back the Italian opposition, Zebre Parma, the underdogs, on holiday like me. In the event they got battered. Battered by the Dragons. Or roasted rather, flame grilled. Not that it mattered much. The two teams were essentially competing to avoid coming last. And with no relegation, the stakes weren't exactly high. And you could tell. The atmosphere in the stadium was peaceful and light-hearted, polite even. What's more, the home fans didn't seem entirely sure of themselves. Gwent Dragons? Newport Gwent Dragons? Just Dragons? No one seemed to know for certain. The young ones near me were going for the latter, as well they might. Keeping it simple. Drop the jurisdictions, stick with the mascot. And what is it with Wales and dragons anyway? I put the question to a mother and son who were standing nearby. Between the two of them, they came up with half an answer. It went something like this ...

Many years ago, a king was trying to put up a castle, but it kept falling down. A boy wizard called Merlin discovered the reason: two dragons – one red and the other white – were troubling the castle's foundations by sleeping beneath it in a lake of booze and honey. When the dragons' slumber was disturbed, the pair had an almighty scrap, presumably because they were massively hungover and a bit pissed off that they'd been built upon. The red dragon – *Y Ddraig Goch* – prevailed on points and went on to become a symbol for Welsh struggle, and presumably the king's castle stopped falling down. It's the sort of story that started in The Cock and finished in The Bull, if you catch my drift.

The next hour or so was quite pleasant – stood on the uncovered terrace, a chicken and leek pie in hand, beneath a carpet of stars. I could have nodded off. After the match, it was nice watching one of the home players going along the touchline engaging with his fanbase and posing for selfies – one after another, for absolutely ages, a smile for the kids and a word for the adults, patiently waiting for mum or grandad or auntie Gwen to figure out the zoom, and then putting up with dad insisting on taking ten just in case. Good lad. I wish him all the best, even if he did let their winger off the hook on more than one occasion in the second half.

I followed the crowd out of the stadium and down to the river. It looked lovely, romantic even, like you could set a rom-com here, starring Michael Sheen and Carol Vorderman. You could have a scene wherein the on/off couple have a row, over cheesy chips or the cost of parking, causing one of them to storm off and turn their collar up against the autumn chill and strop along the riverside and cross the new footbridge in a meaningful and ominous huff, before sinking six pints in Potter's, which will only make matters worse of course but by now Carol is beyond caring.

I went into Sainsbury's for a couple of bananas and a bit of advice. I asked the security guard for directions and got far more than I bargained for. 'I won't teach you to suck eggs but it's a fairly complicated route so listen up.' He talked me through the whole two miles, every inch of the Chepstow Road, as though it were part of a key operation. He's had another career, this fella, and it wasn't primary education. Paying heed to the man, I went past The Dodger, past the Art Deco cinema (closed for the time being while police dismantle a cannabis farm), past a tractor parked up on Somerton Place, past a salon called Herr Kutz (whose roots are presumably Germanic), past glimpses of chimney and bridge at the end of humble sloping side streets named for Tennyson and Coleridge and other hard bastards, past every iteration of suburbia that one could imagine (from high-pitched mock Tudor to low pebbledash rows), and then past two men sat at a bus stop sharing a fish supper in silence. By the time I'd passed the Man of Gwent, formerly the Man of the Cardiff–Newport Metropolitan Area, I was completely and utterly spent, the pack on my back weighing more than before. Crossing the M4, whose bittersweet lanes must have accounted for a lot of old Newport, I stopped halfway along, atop the ongoing rush, to enjoy a happy-sad moment recalling 'America', that great song by Simon and Garfunkel wherein everyone's on the hunt for something only no one knows what. That sort of walk – two miles up the Chepstow Road – shouldn't float my boat but it does and I struggle to explain it.

Celtic Manor is an award-winning resort that boasts three golf courses, two hotels, two spas and an International Conference Centre. It hosted the 2010 Ryder Cup (a big deal in the golf world) and the 2014 NATO summit (a big deal in the world). You can do all sorts here: despair, archery, laser tag, fishing – all without having to go anywhere near the city it's a part of. Ideal.[35] Despite its pedigree, I was reluctant to stay at the resort. For

---

[35] I'm being sarcastic.

one, I was running low on funds. For two, I didn't want to give the impression that I was only interested in pampering myself (because I'm not, else I wouldn't have based my travel-writing career up to this point on budget coach holidays, a minimum wage job in Poland, and unpopular cities). And for three, I worried I'd be a bit detached from the centre. But when I saw that rooms were going for a hundred quid, and none of the downtown B&Bs got back to me, I decided that the best course of action all-round would be to stump up, bunk down, and then reckon with the 'problematic' nature of the resort (it being a part of Newport but not wanting anything to do with it) while in situ. To ignore Celtic Manor would be to ignore an elephant in the room, and in my experience, which is admittedly limited, ignoring elephants in the room doesn't tend to pan out well.

Looked at one way, you might say that Celtic Manor got going in the 1930s, when the eponymous manor house was converted into a maternity hospital and started delivering babies. One of these babies was Terry Matthews, who would go on to become a high-tech Welsh-Canadian with an awful lot of money. When Matthews found out that the building he was born in was up for sale, he decided to buy it (and a portion of Wales to boot) with a view to developing a resort. That resort duly opened in 1999.

After checking in, locating my room, and then sleeping for nine hours, I got up, got dressed, and then got a lift to one of the resort's three golf courses – The Roman Road. (So-called, presumably, because none of the holes are doglegs. A dogleg being a technical golfing term meaning a hole that heads off in one direction before turning sharply to the right or left, usually to the frustration of the golfer.) I won't bang on about what followed because that would be the last straw for some readers, but I will say this: a game of golf – no matter the course and no matter the outcome – is, to me, more about the small things that one gets to appreciate along the way than the simple pleasure of getting a ball into a hole, like the sight of mistletoe and daffodils, or the prospect of a pheasant, so unaware of its majesty, holding up play on the fourth. It is for such things that I golf, and anyone tempted to say my round was a good walk spoiled is wrong, because I had a buggy.

When I asked the lad at the clubhouse what I should do with myself that evening, he said that Caerleon was nice, or failing that Cardiff. When I mooted Newport as an alternative he looked at me in a way that suggested he'd never heard of the place. Then, when I asked the guy who gave me a lift back to the hotel where he'd go out for dinner in Newport, he suggested a Nepalese place in Chepstow. I wish I was making this up, I really do. It started to get a bit weird, if I'm honest – as if all the Celtic Manor staff were conspiring to wipe Newport off the map, as though its existence were an embarrassment, or a liability. I must have asked ten people how I might fill a weekend itinerary and not one of them mentioned the city the resort is a part of. Hm.

Here's the thing. If Celtic Manor sent just one guest to Newport for every nine it sends elsewhere, such an injection of bums would still provide a significant boost to the city centre's evening economy, which, admittedly, isn't as vibrant as it could be. Like countless other places, Newport's centre has been hollowed out a touch – it's the donut effect again. When a place starts to get a bit hollow and down on its luck, because shops and flats have been shifted to the perimeter, and people start to say, 'Nah, I wouldn't go there – it's a bit quiet', then it gets even more quiet, at which point people start saying things like, 'Nah, I wouldn't bother – it's dead', which only makes it quieter still. And so on. It's a difficult cycle to reverse. Especially when the parking's free in Cwmbran.

Newport

215

Back at the hotel, I met a statistician in the sauna. (How many times does that happen a week, I wonder?) His name was Mike and he works at the Office for National Statistics, which has a big site in Newport. The ONS is an interesting organisation. It's a part of the State, but independent of Government, meaning it can't be pressured to massage the figures, even if a tricky knot was discovered that the PM considered unpalatable. The ONS measures hundreds of things. With the information it gathers, it is able to paint a picture of the country's evolution, and inform governmental policy. By no means trivial stuff. The current National Statistician (and what a moniker that is) is a bloke called Ian Diamond, who has an approval rating of 102% and unwinds in his spare time by officiating cricket and football matches. Whether Diamond works out of Newport, I can't say. The ONS was meant to move across from London wholesale back in 2006, following the Lyons Review on public sector relocation, but it didn't because the prospect caused a bit of a stir, the top brass in London not liking the idea one jot. By way of compromise, the ONS retained a small office in London to complement the big new one in Newport. Although Mike works in Newport, he's based in Cardiff and doesn't really hang about after work. Which is true of most of the office, he'd wager. I asked him what percentage of Celtic Manor guests visit Newport. He knew where I was coming from.

I took the 73 bus into town, then headed to the cathedral, which is a chunky uphill affair, muscular and flinty – you wouldn't mess with it. St Woolos is the patron. Woolos loved skinny-dipping with his missus in the Usk all year round, I understand. He also nicked someone's cow once and wouldn't give it back until the cow's owner christened Woolos' son. Lad. I wasn't here for Woolos or his church, however. Instead, I was here for the Italian across the road – Vittorio's, which I'd been told about at the rugby. There's a fairly big Italian community in Newport (which is to say a fairly big community of Italians, rather than a community of fairly big Italians), the descendants of miners who came across from Puglia and Tuscany in the nineteenth century to work in the Welsh valleys. Vittorio's is run by third-generation Italian ex-pats, and, on the face of it, they've got their work cut out – the place was teeming.

'Burrata!'

I was sat next to a big birthday party. Long table, bunch of friends, high spirits, the birthday boy in a loud shirt and with balloons tied to his chair. Some bread came as standard. I dipped the bread in this, dabbed it in that, then almost choked on the balsamic. (Does that happen to anyone else?) I caused a bit of a scene, to be honest, but rode it out and then stuck to the breadsticks.

'Polpette!'

Across the room, a couple looked bored. In the way only couples can. Arms crossed, waiting on the mains, taking it in turns to offer a comment every few minutes. *Spare me*, I thought, rather uncharitably. Then I remembered those lines of Betjeman about a similar pairing, seemingly dreary, sat in a café, who the poet reveals to be no lower than the angels. The man was offered cheese. He nodded in agreement. As the cheese was spooned onto his pasta, the man stared at the small bowl of parmesan intensely, as though he'd never seen such a thing. I do the same.

'Capellini!'

The birthday party was getting boisterous. They switched seats to catch up with old friends. In any circle, there's always one or two that we most like to natter with, as there's always one or two that we'd prefer to be spared. Looking at the party, and their expressions, and catching bits of what they were saying and sharing (or not saying and not sharing), it occurred to me, and not for the first time, what a mystery this life is, so pointless

Newport 217

per capita, and yet so vast and vital and thrilling and special that sometimes all you can do is laugh at the thought of it. Still looking at the party, I decided that other people's joy can sometimes have a greater impression than our own, which is altered by the complexity and insistence of our own being.

'Rigatoni!'

I needed an Aperol. Or the bill. Or both. I came in thinking I'd ask about the family, their story, but I didn't feel like it anymore because the whole place was full of them, full of stories I mean, each one mad and magic and utterly unpredicted. I definitely needed the bill.

'Norma!'

A special place, Vittorio's. That's what I'd say. An assessment altered by vino, granted, but you know that line about truth and wine. I settled my tab and then went across to the churchyard. As I was minding my own business, an Easter service kicked out abruptly, choristers suddenly streaming out in ghostly bedsheets. It scared the life out of me. I had a nice view of the city from up there. Appreciating it, I enjoyed a feeling of deep fondness – towards this place, these people, this moment. It had crept up on me. Had emerged behind my back. It was definitely there now, though.

I put my head round the door of a place called Le Pub, an artsy co-op musical-boozer, situated at the top of the high street. Big front terrace, heaving with public-spirited folk, exchanging fifty shades of droll. A gig had just finished, the Burning Firs, and now there was dancing and a DJ in the pub's bit on the side, its groovy adjunct. The manager was Sam Dabb. Bit of a local legend. She got Le Pub back on its feet, and subsequently opened the Corn Exchange opposite, again leveraging community spirit and public support to do so.

It had character, Le Pub, and a genuinely nice vibe: warm, quirky, open, and a tiny bit unhinged. There are artists among us, said a sign. Don't be a dick, said another. I asked the bartender what the local tipple was. She said Trevor Nelson, and made me an example. I took Trevor outside, where I was invited to sit with some others. They were all drinking Trevor Nelsons. I asked about the recipe and the nomenclature, but none of them had a clue. Strange.

Had a decent chat with a local lad who's studying in Bristol but was back for the weekend. Dylan. Would have been a chartist, I reckon. Would have been deported to Australia had he been born in the mid-1800s. Said Newport has been let down by the UK government. Said the city's history and heritage, its docks and its works, and the muck that made a lotus for others elsewhere, should warrant ongoing support and investment but no, the city's been spared, spurned, put out to pasture. 'They used to come here from Cardiff and Bristol! Now we're a designated hub for the chronically disaffected. Clinging on. Too much energy and talent is going elsewhere.' When I pointed out that he too had gone elsewhere, he said he had to for his course, but plans to come back and start a community hub cum think-tank thingamajig, to give people another reason to stay. Good lad.

When Dylan went inside, his seat was taken by a lean gentleman about my age, wearing a white vest and a leather jacket. His name was Benedict Butters, and he told me, calmly and fluently, why he had gained the ability, some years ago now, to kill people should he need to. A wiry, lively, lovely guy, who wanted deep down to feel safe, and knowing he could disable anyone should the need arise brought that feeling of safety. He wanted others to feel safe, too, which is why he did self-defence training, pro bono. He offered me a lesson the following morning.

'The clocks go forward in a minute but dawn is no closer,' I said, not answering the question.

'That's good,' said Butters. 'We'll get an extra hour of rain.'

It was only when he got up to go to the bar that I realised that Butters was wearing, along with his skinny jeans and leather jacket, a pair of leopard print stilettos. Further evidence that there really is nowt as queer as folk.

In the first books I wrote, there was too much beer for some readers' taste. The books were over the limit in terms of alcohol content. On reflection, there was too much beer for my taste too. Passages that detail a person getting sozzled, and then coping with the aftermath, aren't especially interesting, and are rarely original. Such passages are there – in my case at least – because such passages happened, and form part of an honest report of my experience of a place. It's only in later books that I've discovered the fine art of omission. So I won't bang on about my night in Newport, which, after Le Pub and Benedict Butters, saw me round a corner and do karaoke in Cross Keys ('You Sexy Thing' by Hot Chocolate), before sharing cheesy chips with a guy from Barry Island who's been homeless for six years, but I will say this – there is something about being away, about being elsewhere, all eyes and ears, all open mind and open heart, that improves one's chances of getting occasionally pickled. Why should this be so? Put simply, travel is animating, is elevating, is energising. It can be a heady experience, and it can leave you light-headed, and therefore prone to the wayside. It is also unavoidably social (unless you're travelling through a wilderness or in a cupboard). During any period of travel, you will encounter others, be drawn to others, will witness and weigh up and reflect on others, and you will take the result of what you witnessed and weighed and incorporate it into your understanding of the human condition. Of course, one can witness and weigh without alcohol, and without being on the road, but (and call me vulgar and impoverished if you wish) I think there are few things more enjoyable than finding oneself away, among others, after a long day on one's feet learning and looking and roaming and feeling, getting a little bit tipsy. It's an enlivening experience, rich and daft and even, just now and again, profound and moving and character-building. But – and this barely needs saying – it can – and often will – go on too long, past the point where it ceases to be any of the above, not least because Trever Nelson is a slippery customer, who doesn't know when it's time to call it a night. Which is why I am always turning leaves. Calling it a day. Pulling the plug and letting the beer drain away from my life entirely. Which is why I am always going months at a time without touching a drop. Because I'm one of those who gets carried away, and I wish I wasn't, I wish I didn't, because it tarnishes and taints the brilliance of being half-cut, when one feels and thinks and shares in a way that is unconducive to sobriety. I'll leave it at this: I had a blissful few hours in Newport, first at Le Pub and then briefly at Cross Keys, but then it flopped and fizzled out, until I found myself on the forecourt of the hotel at three in the morning, my fondness for Newport knowing no limits, looking for someone to talk to. I know that by painting such a scene I am hardly covering myself in glory; that I am inviting judgment and courting disapproval; that I am opening myself up to charges of idiocy and shortcoming – but so it goes. This book wouldn't be anywhere near complete if it didn't contain such an admission.

I woke up the next morning feeling like a piece of absolute lava bread. I opted to walk back to the station, but by a different route. First I made my way to Caerleon, a former Roman fortress that backs onto the Roman Road golf course just about. At the bottom of Caerleon's high street, I stopped to stare at a sign hinting at the town's Arthurian connections. Then I asked a man opening a shop to spill some more beans. The man said that Geoffrey of Monmouth – a sort of medieval travel writer cum historical fantasist – wrote at length about Arthur and Merlin, and listed their address as more or less where I was standing. The shop the man was opening was called Spirit of Awen. I followed Mark in, fiddled with his stock, then plumped for a piece of Preseli Bluestone, meant to deliver focus and stability.[36]

At the top of Caerleon is a museum dedicated to the Roman legion that was stationed here back in the day. It was free to enter and so I popped in for a mooch. There were displays of coins and buckles and pots, and plenty of information about the Roman invasion of Wales. A centurion's outfit brought Benedict Butters to mind. It was the mix of camp and martial that did it. Around the corner from the museum, meanwhile, are the remains of a Roman amphitheatre. I enjoyed watching a bunch of kids mucking about on the ancient grassy grandstand, with a scattering of cherry trees and a set of rugby posts adding to the frame in the background, and dating it too.

I picked up the riverside path, via a school and a cemetery, two ends of an old story, each, on this morning, equally brilliant in the sun. Also brilliant, when I came to her, was the slowly flowing Usk – or Isca as the Romans had it – broad-shouldered at this stage. I paused at a dogleg in the river, framed by sedge and rush and bracken, where a swathe of field was hosting a roguish parliament of crows. Joggers and cyclists were out for their Easter constitutional. I crossed the M4, picked up my pace, and then dropped it again to consider a butterfly, which had been painted onto the concrete of a bridge, a type of lotus in a type of mud, and another hint that anything might be anywhere.

---

[36] It has delivered neither. Must have picked up the wrong bit.

Back in the urban realm now, I had just enough time for a bite to eat before I needed to catch my train. I entered Cairo Corner, a modest Egyptian café near the indoor market. No sooner had I put a foot in the door than I was being advised by a regular. 'Have the *koshari*,' she said. 'I'm Egyptian so I know what I'm talking about.' When the proprietor said something to her in Arabic, regarding some chickpeas he was trying to get rid of, she snapped at him for being rude and told him to speak English. It was an odd moment: an Egyptian telling an Egyptian – in Wales – to say something about chickpeas in English.

When my food came, she wouldn't let me eat it alone. She insisted I join her and her mum – Dalia and Mona. I enjoyed the food – and for quite a long time. It went on and on. It contained about eleven types of carb – rice, lentils, pasta, chickpeas – and was topped with onions and a spicy tomato sauce.

'You have to come again,' said Mona when I'd finished.

'Here?'

'Here. Newport. Wherever you wish. It can't be avoided.'

As I pondered the Beckettian quality of Mona's last sentence, she ordered something theatrically in Arabic. When the tea came, she sent it my way.

11

Gibraltar

Very strange but very nice

Gibraltar. A parcel of land the size of an Amazon warehouse dominated by a rock at the tip of a peninsula where the sea meets the ocean in view of Morocco. They drive on the right, are invariably bilingual, and get 300 days of sunshine a year. Clearly a British city.

Gibraltar is an oddity – at least to me. Doubtless it doesn't feel odd to the 30-odd thousand people that live there. It might feel a bit odd to the Spanish, given that Gibraltar is attached to Spain like a curious patio while the rest of the UK is effing miles away being polite and rained upon. To give it its official title, Gibraltar is a British Overseas Territory, like the Pitcairn Islands in the South Pacific (population: 48) and the South Sandwich Islands near the South Pole. It is prized less for its beauty or fertility or poetic output and more for its position. And yet, somewhat ironically, when, on the eve of this trip, I asked a bunch of people where it was, most of them didn't know. Not didn't know exactly, but didn't know at all. One person thought it was in

South America. Another near the Faroe Islands. It's not as if Gib is a new kid on the block (or rock rather) – it has been a British outpost since 1713. In fact, it's been British far longer than it was ever Spanish, which is a curious thought.

The official language of Gibraltar is English and the monarch is Charles III. The country is devolved, but in a major way – like Scotland on drugs. It has a UEFA-recognised national football team, and it competes in the Commonwealth Games, albeit with little success, which isn't ever so surprising when you consider that Gibraltar is 3,000 times smaller than Wales and has the same amount of residents as Clapham Junction railway station. The Parliament has 17 members, who must sit simultaneously on front and back benches, and on every select committee. It doesn't have any celebrities, and when the locals natter in English they sound, to my ear, like they come from *everywhere in the UK.* A bit Cornish, a bit Geordie, a bit Welsh, a bit Buckingham Palace. It's not an unpleasant confusion. Gibraltar pitched for city status in 2022, the year Wrexham got the nod. The bid was refused but while digging around in the UK National Archives, researchers discovered that Gibraltar was *already a city*, having been made one by Queen Victoria in 1842. Which is a bit like applying for a promotion, not getting it, then discovering in the process that you were promoted 140 years ago. An odd day at the office.

Prior to my visit, I didn't know an awful lot about the place. I knew about the rock, the monkeys, and the border with Spain, but that was about it. My ignorance owed in part to the fact that Gib doesn't get ever so much media coverage, and when it does pop up in the news, the story tends to be about border issues in the wake of Brexit, killer whales upending yachts, or the national football team losing by a newsworthy amount. Granted, there was a little flurry of travel articles during the Covid pandemic when Gib found itself, more or less alone, on the UK's list of places reckoned to be safe to travel to. Around that time, a Welsh tourist in Gibraltar admitted to the *Guardian*, 'We're here because we couldn't go anywhere else.' A last resort. Right up my street, then.

The girl on the plane told me in no uncertain terms that the local monkeys lack a moral compass. She said it was in their nature to steal, that they're born criminals. 'They took my headphones,' she said in evidence, 'and showed zero remorse.' I hoped the girl was being ironic but she wasn't, she was being deadly serious. She went on to tell me that her mum had a flat in Spain but always nipped across to the Morrisons in Gibraltar for mince, and that when I come out of the airport terminal it's left for Gibraltar and right for the real world.

'You just walk across the runway and you're there.'

'Walk across the runway?'

'Yeah. It's one of the most dangerous in the world.'

'No wonder if people are being invited to walk across it.'

'Not because of that.'

'Then what?'

'Because it's unusually short and there's water at each end,' she said as we began our descent.

In arrivals, a recruitment poster tempted prospective residents with the promise of low taxes, zero crime and fantastic weather. Personally I'd prefer fantastic taxes, low crime and zero weather, but that's just me. Elsewhere, a poster announced that the comedian Sarah Millican would soon be coming to the Rock to do a gig in a cave, which got me worrying about the local arts infrastructure. Before I was out of the airport, I also learned that Gib was twinned with Goole and Ballymena, which was hopefully a case of opposites attracting, rather than birds of a feather flocking together. Time would tell.

When I left the airport the first thing I noticed was a red letterbox like the ones at home. The sight of it made me feel all fuzzy inside. I walked across the runway, making sure to look both ways before I did so. When some clown behind shouted, 'Duck!', I couldn't help but bring my hands to my head and bend my knees a bit. There was a fair number going across. The bulk of Gibraltar's workforce – about 15,000 – comes across from Spain every day, from the town of La Linea, just over the border. Which is why Brexit was a bit of a nuisance. The Gibraltarians might be patriotic and loyal to Britain but they're not daft: 96% voted to stay in Europe. Since leaving the EU, Gibraltar has been in talks with its neighbour regarding how best to keep the threshold fluid. A meaningful agreement is within 'kissing distance', according to Chief Minister Fabian Picardo. Let's hope he's got a big tongue.

On the far side of the runway, a 'Welcome to Gibraltar' sign was busy advertising the city as the 'Cradle of History', which might be overplaying it a touch. That said, it's seen a fair bit of action. First it was the Neanderthals throwing their weight around, then it was the Romans sticking their nose in, then it was the Vandals doing some damage, then it was a North African lad called Tariq popping across to get the Muslim conquest of the Iberian Peninsula going in 711. After a significant spell of Moorish dominance, Gibraltar fell under the Spanish Crown, where it remained for a couple of centuries until 1704, when it was captured by an Anglo-Dutch outfit who were working for an Austrian bloke who fancied a stint as King of Spain. That old chestnut. The territory was formally ceded (in perpetuity) to Britain in 1713, as a way of getting the British to leave the War of the Spanish Succession, which had been triggered when Charles II (of Spain) died without an heir. Now a British naval base, Gib was besieged by the upset Spanish in both 1727 and

1779 – neither intrusion proving a picnic for the locals. During the latter siege, miles and miles of tunnels were dug out of the rock – for shelter and sneaking about in. Gibraltar was of strategic importance during the Battle of Trafalgar and the Crimean War, and its significance was dialled up further with the opening of the Suez Canal – Gib becoming a gateway to the East. It came under attack during the Second World War (you won't be surprised to learn), when the local population was evacuated to England, Morrocco and Jamaica. If not the cradle of history, then certainly a key witness.

I walked along Winston Churchill Avenue until an erection caught my attention: a no-frills block of flats called Referendum House, which presumably remembers the count of 1967, in which the locals turned down the chance to become Spanish, and by some margin. Only 44 people were up for it. In retaliation, Francisco Franco, the Spanish dictator, cut all ties and closed the border – tried to suffocate Gib into submission. These were tough times. The border only reopened in 1982, I understand. There was another referendum in 2002. This time the locals rejected a joint custody arrangement, again emphatically. Evidently, they do not fancy a Spanish yolk, no matter if it comes with British soldiers.

I continued walking until I came to Ocean Village, a fairly modern marina: fancy flats, shiny offices, a five-star floating hotel, chain restaurants like Wagamama and Pizza Express, a casino, bars, PWC and KPMG (here for big margins and low tax). On a whim, I entered Dolphin Adventure, taken by the notion. Inside I chatted to Cherie from Retford. After discussing dolphins for a polite amount of time, things moved onto politics – as they are liable to around here. She said that since Brexit it was no longer easy to escape. Residents who weren't Gibraltarian, like Cherie, couldn't cross the border unless they'd booked a hotel on the other side or had an appointment for a tummy tuck or something. As I write (and as I mentioned), talks are ongoing to remedy this situation, but they're dragging on, and a solution doesn't seem imminent. Playing devil's advocate, I suggested to Cherie that maybe Gib should become Spanish. She pulled a face that gave every impression that she'd rather eat her own kidneys. She reckoned Spain couldn't claim the moral high ground when it had overseas territories of its own – i.e. Ceuta and Melilla, across the water in Africa. She pointed out that Gib had been British far longer than it was ever Spanish (yes, yes, we knew that Cherie), then went on to ask, with a touch of hauteur, whether Spain would be wanting Portugal as well, seeing as it shared a border with that country too. On the evidence presented to me, Cherie was not for turning – or giving an inch. I booked a dolphin adventure for two days later.

Cherie directed me to Casemates Square, an old fortification that is now an easily breached open space in the heart of the old town. Behind the square, residential tiers climbed the side of the rock, like the stages of a cake, and beyond them, stretching as high and wide as I could see, was the rock's tree-covered west flank (olive and pine in the main). I had a nose around the square. There was a Moroccan street food stall. A British copshop. Sandwich boards plugging 'top-notch paella'. A John Lennon mural. A bagpiper belting out tunes on a temporary stage. Roy's Fish and Chips doing a brisk trade. A couple on a bench chatting away, switching between Spanish and English as if there was nothing between them.

Tucked away in a corner of the square was a boozer called The Lord Nelson. A sign above the entrance said I was expected to do my duty. And there was me thinking Gib was duty free. The Wi-Fi password was Victory, and there was Old Speckled Hen on tap – which would have pleased my granddad. My granddad was a Nelson fanatic. Knew the bloke like the back of his hand. When he died a few years ago, I inherited about sixty books on Nelson. So I already knew that after duffing the French at the Battle of Trafalgar in 1805 – episode three of *The Napoleonic Wars* – Nelson was delivered to Gib in a barrel of Bacardi or similar. The local £20 note depicts HMS *Victory* being towed into the waters of Gibraltar.

The pub was decked out in Nelson memorabilia. Even the menu paid homage to the man. I ordered the Nelson Club Sandwich, and when it came it was as high as a flagship. A hole had been cut in the top deck of toast – creating a kind of sunroof for a bright orange yolk. A skewer ran through the middle of the structure, suggesting a mast. It was a work of art, to be honest. An upshot of the sandwich's design, however, was that I ended up with egg on my face – it shot out the sunroof each time I took a bite. Ordinarily I'd steer clear of somewhere called The Lord Nelson on continental Europe, but Gibraltar has a genuine connection with the man, meaning the pub cannot be accused of unimaginative jingoism. Just as I was getting a sense of my whereabouts, a text came through welcoming me to Spain. *Que?*

I went looking for my digs – a hostel close to the centre – only to find a lot of other things instead. A notice encouraging people, from March onwards, to dial 999 in an emergency (surely the emergency services aren't a new thing around here?); flashy newbuilds that looked like cruise ships; a brutal, curving block, Soviet in style and peppered with aircon; a seagull feasting on the head of a fish; cannons and bastions and barracks and curtains, befitting a city steeped in skirmish.

Having seen all that, I would like to say this: travelling is about listening as much as seeing. But we prioritise the eyes, don't we? Must see this and that and the other. Gotta get the snaps, the shots, the footage. We are led astray by our peepers. This is all to say that I just had an enjoyable conversation with the receptionist at Mackintosh Hall, where I dropped in for a nose (though really an eyeful) of its charming courtyard and its collection of paintings by local artist Monica Popham (who was recently crowned Landscape Artist of the Year). What the receptionist said was far more interesting and noteworthy than how he appeared (a bloke in his fifties leaning back in a swivel chair). It was surreal but vivid, abstract but clear. It was like a Dalí painting – in that I recognised all the bits but not the arrangement. It began when I asked a fairly open question about Gib and what he thought of the place. Here's an approximation of what I heard. By all means take a picture.

'1992 was a good year. "Rhythm is a Dancer". What a tune. Squaddies and their families, dancing in Main Street. Loved it. Pack of Royal Crown cost 37p, and it was 70p a pint, and I'm not on about milk. Every day of my life was the same: up at 11, bit of breakfast, Eastern Beach by 12, off we go. Mum went to London in the sixties. She wasn't alone. When Franco closed the border, thousands left. It was the Great British Dream back then. Guildford was the land of milk and honey. I met Mussolini's cousin once. Nice bloke. I don't mind a holiday but they're not as good as a Friday night after a week at work – do you know what I mean? Things used to be either simple or hard. Black or white. None of this everything being grey. And the grass was *actually* greener. That's the thing. But that was then and this is now. Things change. I've changed. You've changed. You try not changing. I used to finish at five and now it's half past. Case in point. Angry Friar tonight. Two and a half pints. No more, no less. And then another two and a half at The Trafalgar. I know it's a Monday but sometimes Mondays feel like Fridays, don't they? It'll be alright in the end. No one's keeping score. I used to work at Gatwick. *Massive* runway. Couldn't stand it. That's how it goes, though. Would you like a map, by the way? Toilets are down there on the left.' While I was spending a penny, a text came through welcoming me to Gibraltar.

I was checked in at the hostel by Addie, the Moroccan godson of the previous owner. I paid 50 quid for two nights in a six-bed dorm. I'd wanted to stay at a hotel but my budget couldn't handle it. Not going to lie, I struggle with dorms. As a rule of thumb I like every single person I meet – until they fall asleep, at which point I go off most of them. I remember staying in a hostel in Newcastle a few years ago. All was quiet in the dorm with only one person left to come in. They came back at two in the morning, got into bed, and then started eating a kebab while listening to a podcast.

I got talking to a Belgian in the hostel garden. We shared a rotisserie chicken from Morrisons while discussing why people bother going anywhere. I mentioned Geoff Dyer, and what he said about us being here to go somewhere else, and shared my idea of travel as a sweet spot, being social, educational, novel, energising, unwinding, unpredictable, multi-faceted and so on. She looked at me and then at the sky. And then at me again. 'Personally, I travel because I inherited a lot of money and it's better than going to work.'

I dumped my backpack, returned to the main square, resisted the opportunity to have my photo taken inside a red telephone box, picked up Main Street, erred left at Venture Inn, then climbed the Castle Steps, turning often to take in the escalating scene, of the bay and Spain and all the refuelling ships. It was a fair way to go – orange trees, red shutters, pink faces. The palette of the place, in that light, at that time, was nothing short of enchanting.

And so too was the small talk I struck up with folk on their doorsteps, watering plants and seeing to washing. No two accents were the same, hinting at a people drawn from many corners – Italy, Malta, Spain, Scotland, Morocco. Melting pot doesn't get close to it. Down the years, that variety of influence and style has gone into the language – both Spanish and English are spoken here in a manner entirely Gibraltarian. Llanito is the local mash-up. The national vernacular. Llanito is also a demonym – a name for the people. Ask any of them whether they feel Spanish or British and they will likely wave you away for being insolent or dumb, for they are neither, they are Gibraltarian, they are Llanito. British by extension, by default – so much is admitted – but essentially they are of this place and of nowhere else besides. *Vale?* Got it?

I passed an ancient Moorish castle and then entered the nature reserve that dominates the uppermost region of the rock (and is free to enter in the evening). I paused at a viewpoint, and in the still-pleasant heat, pondered the ships at bay, the dockyard below, the tennis courts and rooftops, the running track of Victoria Stadium, the low Spanish hills, the pristine outline of a famous hotel, and a sign that explained how a certain Elizabeth had peered from this spot back in 1954. There's more to see now. And less sea as well, for Gibraltar is reclaiming land all the time.

I saw my first Barbary macaque – and then my second, my third, and my fourth. I was eyeing up a frame, a tracery of trees lit from behind, when a monkey strolled across my viewfinder, settled on the old stone wall, then turned to me, as if having been invited to pose. I was initially wary of the monkeys, having been warned of their crime-loving nature, but they got up to nothing more scandalous than checking each other for ticks. (As they did so, it looked like they were searching through a suitcase, on the brink of a trip, checking whether they'd packed their flipflops or goggles.) One stared up at the Union Jack in what appeared to be reverence, before abruptly launching, not into song, but into an olive tree. Another lounged on the roof of a Peugeot. Paul Theroux, the venerable American travel writer, in his book *The Pillars of Hercules* (1995), compared the monkeys unflatteringly to tourists, mean and antsy, but I found them to be insouciant and coy, lazing about on full show, before discreetly sloping off into their shrubby netherworld, whenever they had occasion. Another thing Theroux wrote is that no monkey corpse or skeleton has ever been found on the rock, hinting at a secret mortuary deep in the limestone, and stirring thoughts of mysterious burial rites. Spend more than a day in Gib and you will hear it said or see it written that while there are monkeys on the rock, Gibraltar will remain British. Which might be why Churchill was so perturbed when news got to him that monkey numbers were tumbling in the wake of the Second World War. He ordered something to be done about it – and at the double! A hundred were drafted from across the water, and the day was saved.

I continued up and around and across the west slope of the rock, beyond batteries and gun placements, boltholes and bastions, before negotiating a new addition to the rock's infrastructure – the Windsor Suspension Bridge, which dangles excitingly (if you enjoy terror and jeopardy) 200 metres above *terra firma*. The view was good – but then you'd expect it to be, wouldn't you? A good view being Gibraltar's *raison d'être*, its USP. If you couldn't see much from up here, Gib would never have cut it as a lookout. I had been given a list, by the well-endowed Belgian. Things to look out for when up high. I couldn't be sure how serious the list was, for it read like a bloated haiku, a haiku that had lost the plot. 'Olive and pine; monkeys and candytuft; churches, mosques, temples and synagogues; Molly Bloom in the botanical garden; and the Cathedral of St Mary the Crowned (built in 1462)'.

Gibraltar

I had a feeling as I walked – as I went, as I climbed – and the feeling was that while travel is unquestionably an educating activity, it is also extremely good at exposing one's ignorance. As I tramped the west flank of that longstanding crag, I knew nothing of the trees or the flowers, or the stone or the stories, and each instance of unknowing was a gentle, not unpleasant rebuke. While I travel for knowledge, I also travel to be reminded of how little I know. They are two sides of a similar coin, I suppose. It is both slightly sad and slightly wonderful to think that even if I dedicated myself totally to the intake of info, to the study of this and that (and the other as well), I'd die knowing next to nothing. Do we learn for the sake of knowing? Or do we learn because it is pleasing to do so, and pleasing to share what it is that we've learned? They say that walking is the handmaiden of thought, and so it proved as I scarpered happily south towards northernmost Africa and the Strait of Gibraltar, the latter's earlier blue having turned purple with the coming of dusk.

I found the Mediterranean Steps, which, I'd been told, would take me from here up to the top just about. Cor blimey, what a climb! Round and upwards for over an hour I went, panting and puffing and perspiring for fun – and this was in the shade and in spring! Sod doing it under the sun and in summer. I kept an eye out for funnel web spiders, and geckos and kestrels and all manner else, but to be honest, there was little time or energy or headspace for spotting, so heavy was the going, so dominating was the serial act of climbing those steps. It was proving a reductive incline – all I could think about was my huffing. I rested at an old battery, no longer charged, where I could see the eastern beaches, and a coppice of freshly baked towers, and the Spanish coast going north and then east. The colour of the water, the quality of it, was arresting. So icy smooth in places, in patches, like you could skim a stone as far as Malta.

Recovered, I continued onwards and upwards, zigzagging through the hot shadows, up the rough, rocky path, which was initially laid not with sport in mind but war. Once a military exercise, now a feel-good ascent, locals racing up on a daily basis, to stay lean and lithe and comparatively attractive. The rock was present even when absent, its great shadow filling half the vista as I looked out to the Med. When we got to the top (I was part of a chain by this point, puffing along), I got a text on my phone: 'Welcome to Morocco.'

I surveyed the scene: three countries, two continents, and a lot of unseen drama at the bottom of the sea. Before the Suez Canal opened in 1875, this was the only way out. If you wanted to sail a boat from Lebanon to India, you'd have to come this way. For the ancient Greeks, this was the end of civilisation, the final frontier. How did the Brits choose to decorate such an important eminence? With the mother of all guns. Big enough to make any cannon blush. They also put up a tower, so that Cadiz could be monitored. But when the tower was finished, and they climbed to the top for a look, they came to see that Cadiz couldn't be seen. The tower is known as O'Hara's Folly.

Speaking of folly – if I loitered much longer, basking at the summit, I'd end up descending in the dark, so I turned for home. My comedown took me past St Michael's Cave, the ancient auditorium where that comedian, Sarah Millican, is due. I took a short cut along Martin's Path, down to sea level, overtaking a West Ham fan on the phone, who was telling someone to be nice to their sister, even if it killed them. Back on tarmac now, I continued to spiral downwards as the final sun fell on Europa Road. Soon I was beneath the Rock Hotel, that pristine block of vanilla, straight out of LA, its title typography the essence of Art Deco. A pang of accommodation envy. I know the grass isn't always greener, but on this occasion it most certainly would be.

I popped in for a nose. Illustrious guests were on show. Framed faces, hung up to impress, including Diana and Churchill and the former manager of Reading. It was a rum gallery. Got me thinking about who and how we vaunt, who and how we value and venerate. Seems like you've got to either marry a prince or end up the boss. I won't knock the hotel, though. It had a certain mystique, a certain class. Something quietly iconic about it.

Opposite the hotel are the Alameda Botanic Gardens, where I found Molly Bloom, looking as odd and perturbing as the novel that issued her. All manner of flora (including some of that candytuft) was arranged across the site's undulating square mile, while the front steps remembered Elizabeth Regina in a mosaic of tiles (big points in Scrabble). I wandered on until I reached Queensway Quay, where I admired the super yachts for roughly a second, then entered Casa Pepe on a whim. The restaurant had an eclectic interior – antlers and sickles and facsimile hams – and had the feel of being candlelit without actually being so. I ate a boneless John Dory with sliced spuds and Padrón peppers – very good indeed. For pudding, I ordered a digestif, which I took for a walk around the restaurant. I enjoyed the snaps of Pepe with various boxers and former rugby captains. No sign of the Reading boss, unfortunately, who must have got held up at the hotel. My waiter proudly showed me a stuffed owl (not on the menu). When Pedro invited me to consider more taxidermy, I feigned fatigue and slung my hook.

King's Bastion is quite something. I found it just along from the quay. Once a bulwark, and then a power station, it's now a multi-storey pleasure centre. There's a bowling alley on the ground floor, a gym above that, and an ice rink above that. A stack of fun, if you're still into enjoyment. I wandered through, just for the hell of it, briefly joining in with a game of staff football. I exited via a tunnel, which is adorned with stories and images of the Great Siege of 1779. The siege lasted three years, in which time Gib got absolutely wrecked. Most of the town had to be rebuilt in the aftermath. They got an Italian in to do it. The result is a pleasing concoction – architecturally speaking. Some bits are rightly defensive and martial. Other bits bring upper crust London to mind, with their Georgian manner and stucco faces. While other bits give humble Andalusian vibes. Walking around Gib, you could be in Genoa or Chelsea or even the Algarve. It's nice feeling all over the place.

I came to Irish Town, a modest lattice of pedestrianised lanes, dead at this hour. The office of *Panorama*, a daily paper, had pulled its neck in for the day, while a beloved café called Sacarello, marshalled by an Italian family for over a century, was getting twenty winks. Café Roxy, just up the lane and around the corner, is cut from a different cloth. It was busy with nighthawks and cab drivers. I went in for a shot of decaf in an unflattering ambience. At first, I thought the bloke at the counter had got the wrong end of the stick and had called me 'ayatollah', which I understand is a kind of Islamic bossman, but on reflection I realised that what he'd said was a coming together of hiya, alright and ola. In any case, it was decent enough coffee and a nice crowd. One guy moved his copy of *Panorama* so that I understood that I was welcome at his table. When I remarked that Gib appeared a bit quiet that evening, he got a touch defensive. He said that Gib's nightlife was appropriate to a place of 30,000 residents, spread out across the foothills of a Jurassic outcrop. 'It's different during the day. Everyone comes during the day. From the cruise ships, from across Spain. At night it's just us. Unless you go to Ocean Village ...'

What nightlife there is in Gibraltar, can be found at Ocean Village, and what nightlife there is at Ocean Village – namely Bruno's and Hendrix – can seem a trifle unhinged. Outside the latter, I watched younger Gibraltarians – Giblets, if you will – letting off some serious steam, alongside a mixed bag of yachty types, who were pushing the boat out as far as it would go. Hendrix isn't a big place, but it sure crams them in, kippers in a fishtank going berserk, pressed up to the plate-glass windows, bellowing along to 'New York, New York'. A more sensitive being would have got a half decent poem out of it all.

It was the job of a broad geezer on the door to let the fish out for air. He told me that at last orders the crowd tumbles into the casino for more grog. I went across, ahead of the curve, and was given a free bet for simply turning up. I backed the underdog in an American dead rubber, then took a tipple out onto the terrace, where I closed my eyes and listened to the blend of automated disaster and accidental delight. The gambling inside was just the tip of the iceberg: a staggering 25% of Gibraltar's turnover comes from betting done elsewhere – at home, on the move, abroad, online. A lad called Victor Chandler came over pre-internet and started taking bets on the phone. It went from there. If people in Hull and Harwich and Hammersmith stopped fluttering online, Gibraltar would be skint.

It felt like I was trying to sleep on the Pyrenees. I got up in the small hours to investigate – and, yep, the middle section of my bed frame was being propped up with something uncomfortable. I switched to another bed – much better – and returned my attention to the yelps and groans and outright snores issuing from every corner of the dorm. (The Belgian sounded like a mid-coital fox.) When eventually the room fell silent and sleep became a genuine possibility rather than a pipedream, a fly the size of Kentucky arrived on the scene, apparently determined to land on my nose. It has been said, by Bertrand Russell I believe, that lacking things we want is indispensable to happiness, so in theory I ought to have been cock-a-hoop that I didn't get any sleep and nearly lost my mind.

I went out for a Sunday morning stroll. It was quiet out and about. I'd chanced on a window wherein the locals were at prayer and the tourists were at bay. Main Street is mainly attractive, I decided as I ambled along it, full of bright shutters and iron balconies and lots of pastel faces. The courthouse at the southern end of Main Street is such a lovely building that it made me want to offend, while the neighbouring boozer, The Angry Friar, seemed full of people who might well have done so. A shop called Florida, a branch of M&S, the Consulate of Belgium – all things considered, it was a diverting meander.

Also diverting was a notice on City Mill Lane concerning something called a whirligig, an old-fashioned means of punishment that used to be deployed hereabouts. A whirligig, I understand, was a revolving cage used to spin some sense into whoever was reckoned short of the stuff. Very irresponsible indeed. Imagine the queue. Just along from City Mill Lane was the cathedral, which was erected in 1462, just after Spain had nabbed Gib off the Moors. It's a good-looking church – elegant, humble, not too proud or flash. I popped my head round the door and enjoyed the sight of a kid not giving two hoots for the sermon. He was crawling beneath the pews, plucking hairs out of legs, too down to earth for the bishop's lofty ideas. It was busy inside. Over 70% of Llanitos are Roman Catholic, and about 70% of that 70% clearly attend The Cathedral of St Mary the Crowned every Sunday morning. The other 30% were probably still in Hendrix, gaining material for Confession.

By now Main Street was flooded, church having kicked out and a cruise ship having pulled in. At a bakery on the square,

I had a bit of Gibraltar Pudding, which is like bread pudding but with a croissant ceiling and lots of embedded fruit. From my sunlit table, I watched a lady writing postcards in the shade of an orange tree, her silver hair never left alone by the steady easterly breeze. A girl sat down next to me and we started chatting. She was a recent graduate of the local uni, which opened in 2015. (Up until then, Gib was in the habit of paying its school leavers to attend university in the UK.) I asked about life in Gib.

'Weirdest place in the world,' she said.

'Oh yeah?'

'I'm not from here. I'm from Luton. But I've been here for five years and I promise you it's weird.'

'More weird than Luton?'

'Way more weird. But it's great. I like the weirdness.'

'I'm curious – does Gibraltar have celebrities?'

'No, but everyone's been on the local news. I was on for graduating. My mate was on for being Dutch.'

'You get to go on telly for being Dutch?'

'Yep. That's Gibraltar for you.'

'What else do you like about the place?'

'It's safe. That's massive. There's basically no crime. My boyfriend is a police officer and wishes he had more to do.'

'I've got a spare few hours. What would you do if you were me?'

'A lap.'

'Of what?'

'Of Gibraltar. It will take you about four hours. If you leave now and go clockwise, the sun will follow you around. Finish at Camp Bay. There's a lovely restaurant called The Dolphin. Then – what day is it? Sunday? Then go to Hendrix.'

I kicked off my lap by heading back to Referendum House, crossing Winston Churchill, then following Devil's Tower Road all the way down to Eastern Beach, which, although big and sandy, lacked character. It had a nice little beach bar, mind you – Bella Vita. I took a pew at the bar and ordered some squid. Lightly battered, fresh off the boat, doused in lemon, cheap as chips – *muchos gracias*. A guy called Jim, perched on the neighbouring stool, was good enough to give me his life story. Over the course of an hour, Jim spilt some rather broad beans – infidelity, private detectives, ultimatums – and some half-baked ones too, at one point urging me to live each day like it was *nearly* my last. Jim left me with the impression that there are a disproportionate number of 'big characters' in Gibraltar – exiles, fugitives, lovable rogues – which is no bad thing. Jim lives on a boat near Casa Pepe, should you be after him.[37]

I left Jim to it and resumed my circumlocution. I rounded the corner (Gibraltar's right shoulder) and came to beach number two – Catalan Bay. It was half the size of Eastern but had twice the appeal and personality. I loved the stacks of jaunty seaside dwellings, pink and apple and peachy tones, the type a kid might imagine when asked to draw a village by the sea in the sun. I had a quick chat with the lifeguard. He knew he'd landed a good gig – looked like a Chesire cat up there on his perch, surveying the bay's even keel. Harrison. Born and bred in Gib. Said that when he grows up he plans either to move to Madrid and pursue journalism or stay put and teach paddleboarding. (He's 32.) Said that his favourite thing about Gibraltar is his nan (who isn't easily incorporated into a visitor experience), and that his least favourite thing – and in admitting this he came across as a

---

[37] Of course his name wasn't Jim and his boat is nowhere near Casa Pepe. It's John and it's outside Bruno's.

bit unsympathetic – was when someone starts panicking in the water and he dashes out only to find that all that's happened is they've dropped their phone.

On Harrison's advice, I popped into the Catalan Bay Social Club, where I found a table of lads nursing small beers and gassing in Llanito. I was invited to sit next to a Leeds fan. Apparently the affliction is rife in Gibraltar, and the incidence rate is climbing.

'What made you do it?'

'I was young. Impressionable. All my mates were doing it.'

'You know that's not a good reason, right?'

'I know, I know …'

'Anyway. Got any recommendations?'

'What like?'

'Somewhere to eat, have a drink, have a natter.'

'Spain's good. Nah, I'm kidding, erm … I'll tell you what, have a look at Charlie's.'

'Charlie's?'

'Yeah, or Bianca's.'

'OK.'

'Trevor's is good, mind.'

'Trevor's?'

'And Alan's isn't bad either.'

'You taking the piss?'

'Yeah. But only the last two. Charlie's and Bianca's are legit. They're good.'[38]

I rounded the rock's southern tip and came to Europa Point. I could see Tangiers across the water, and Ceuta too, that bit of Spain overseas. Most impressive of all was a mosque, standing

---

[38] They may well be good. I didn't investigate. Because I didn't trust that they existed.

244   SHITTY BREAKS

tall and proud and polished, in finest cricket whites, its principal tower slim and crowned with a telling half-moon. The mosque was dressed for the occasion – for a game of cricket was in train on the nearby oval. I got an ice cream from an old-fashioned van, wandered down to the lighthouse, spared a thought for all the ships that were wrecked off these shores, then watched a googly evade the keeper and run down to fine leg for four. On reflection, it was quite the assembly of things: ice cream van, mosque, Morocco, cricket, lighthouse, Med – hints of Africa and Spain and Britain and India, knitted gently together, without fuss or fanfare, at the southern extremity of Gib. I had another 99.[39]

Back on the west side of the rock now, I moved on to Camp Bay, a youthful hotspot – cages and courts for a variety of sports, skins versus skins in the comfortable sunshine. A less sandy stretch of shoreline. More a pebble dash down to the water. One boy, more restless than the rest, pulled long wheelies on the concrete boulevard, spoiling his trick by doing it on loop. I overheard something that offered a lesson on Gibraltar's Gen Zed: 'Chicos, what you feeling? English or Spanish?' The chico in question was wearing a Morocco top and speaking of tunes.

My lap all but up, the sun all but down, I came to Rosia Bay, where Nelson shipped up that time, half-cut in a barrel. On Rosia Road, I looked through the window of the Gibraltar Broadcasting Corporation, hoping to spot someone Dutch under the spotlight. The things that came next were familiar, and welcome for being so – cemetery, courthouse, parliament, Florida. I had dinner at Vinopolis on John Mackintosh Square. Tomato

---

[39] In 1920s Scotland, a bloke called Stefano opened an ice cream shop at 99 Portobello High Street. He got into the habit of adorning his ice creams with half a Cadbury Flake. He named the resultant concoction after the shop's address. Don't say I never tell you anything.

Gibraltar

salad and aubergine mousse, then cheese ice cream with walnuts and balsamic. The latter dish shouldn't have worked but somehow it did: elements that shouldn't align had been carefully resolved into a kind of tangy sorbet with lumps. Very strange but very nice. Like Gibraltar.

Had a much better night's sleep, thank you for asking. Chiefly because I had the dorm to myself. The Belgian had left for Lisbon. The Canadian for Seville. And the guy from London for a silent retreat among the olive groves of Ronda. I went to The Waves for breakfast, by the marina. The owner was a lovable eccentric, a French lady not afraid to call *un chat un chat*. (The French speak frankly to cats rather than spades.) The café is as the owner wishes, not as the owner thinks the customer might wish it. A small, idiomatic place, that doubles as a convenience store. To a Brahms concerto, I ordered this and she brought me that, knowing what was good for me. When it got to a bit that she particularly liked, she turned the volume up and closed her eyes.

It was time for my Dolphin Adventure. About six or seven of us donned buoyancy aids then clambered aboard. Leaving the marina, we slid by yachts of all shapes and sizes, chunky albino seagoing creatures, then a swathe of lime-green apartments with rooftop sombreros – it could have been Miami. As we cruised out to a good spot in the bay, we were told a few things. We were told that the common dolphin can dive to 200 metres, stay there for five minutes, and likes oily fish; that the striped dolphin can dive to 700 metres, stay there for ten minutes, and much prefers squid; and that a bottlenosed dolphin called Billy was recently adopted by a pod of common dolphins, which is a bit like a Capulet taking in a Montague.

By this point I'd heard enough about dolphins and fancied clocking a few. I'd been told I stood a good chance. There's a resident pod of 150 who pop up most days, and there's another 2,000 who come across in peak season – flipping second-homers. On cue, a pair appeared, coy and cresting, tame and twisting, intermittently breaking the calm, dimpled bay. They looked too good to be true. Then a couple of babies started backflipping, and then six in a row shot off for Morocco. I was fully persuaded: dolphins are graceful and endearing mammals, deserving of the acclaim and good will that comes their way. (I mean, I'm sure they can be fantastically unkind to other marine life, but we'll overlook that.)

It was good to see the rock from this angle, in profile as it were. I could see the snow-white mosque, Camp Bay and the Rock Hotel, and a party of monkeys up on Windsor Suspension Bridge, coming up with fresh villainy, the intractable thugs. It was easier from this angle to envisage the rock's internal tunnels, which have played such a crucial role in the story of this land – its batterings, its victories, its persistence, its punishment. Clambering around the vessel for snaps, I ticked myself off for chasing evidence, for letting the tail wag the dog, for letting a future souvenir spoil the thing it would remember. Pulling into the marina, our adventure at an end, I spotted the skipper's tattoo. He lowered his forearm and showed me the text. *Little Hand says it's time to rock and roll.*

'What's that about?'

'It's from *Point Break.*'

'Don't know it.'

'It's a film.'

'Decent?'

'No. Well … yes and no. It's objectively average but subjectively wonderful, if you know what I mean.'

'I can think of places like that.'

'So can I actually. Now, would you mind moving out of the way. I've got to sling this ...'

Treading water until due at the airport, I thought about what my perfect day in Gib might look like. I would have slept well and alone, for a start. I would breakfast at The Waves, and then I would earn my lunch by running to Catalan Bay, where I would take a quick dip and then have a snifter in the social club, before heading back on myself for squid at Bella Vita, ideally minus Jim. At roughly five o'clock, I'd climb the Mediterranean Steps, pausing often to smell the flowers and admire the sea and read a text message that said 'Welcome to Portugal!' I would descend to Camp Bay, where I would watch the people bask and bathe and turn a kind of gold. The Dolphin would be open so I'd go there for a large cold lager. Nelson would rock up, and so would my granddad, and so would the skipper of the dolphin boat, who would be pleased to see me and show me his new tattoo, a line from *Home Alone* or *Aladdin*. There being sod all else to do in the evening, I'd go up to Saint Michael's cave for a gig, an evening with Palin or Portillo or Perkins, and then I'd walk home in the penultimate sun, across Windsor Bridge and down Castle Steps, stopping for a knees-up at the Angry Friar or Hendrix, where I'd get sufficiently pickled on Old Speckled Hen, before being put in a barrel and pushed out to sea. I'd wash up in Morocco, where I'd be asked some questions by a GBC reporter, and doubtless the local authorities too.

12

Dunfermline

The somewhat loveliness of anything and anywhere

The recently crowned city of Dunfermline sits at the west end of the ancient Kingdom of Fife, an east-side peninsula in the south of Scotland, the filling between two slices of firth – the Tay and the Forth. The first thing that struck me about the city upon arriving at the station and having an initial wander around was that it in no way resembled Gibraltar (where I left my flipflops, incidentally). The second thing that struck me was the sight of a peacock called Angus standing guard outside a bakery on the high street. And the third thing that struck me was the number of buildings named after someone called Andrew Carnegie, who, I would quickly come to learn, was an unthinkably rich industrialist who grew up in Dunfermline (or Dunfy for short) before moving to the States and becoming absolutely minted. There is a Carnegie Hall, a Carnegie Library, a Carnegie Birthplace Museum, a Carnegie Leisure Centre, and even a Carnegie Pole Dancing Society. It was to the latter institution that I presently set off.

When I arrived at the address and came to understand that the guy who'd told me about the Pole Dancing Soc (who'd been washing his car on Comely Park Lane) had clearly been winding me up, I went to the museum instead. On my way to said institution, it became clearer and clearer – until it was blindingly obvious – that once upon a time Dunfermline must have been really rather flush. Like Bradford, Dunfermline was a big player in the fabric field, linen in particular. At the start of its textile adventure, back in the eighteenth century, a spy had been sent across to Edinburgh to pick up some industrial intel. By posing as a simpleton, who didn't know a bobbin from his backside, a certain James Black got into a damask factory and memorised the tricks of the trade. It took him nine years, mind you, suggesting that James might have discovered one or two things in the capital beside the tricks of the trade, namely the pubs of Princes Street.

Before entering a museum, it's always a good idea to line one's stomach, and so I popped into a butcher's on the high street, thinking I'd pick up a sausage roll or similar. I ended up staying in there for over twenty minutes, so engaging were the items on display. Lorne Sausage Block looked formidable – like you could dam rivers with the stuff. Dunfy Pie – which is filled with haggis, black pudding and square sausage rondels, and topped with a removable lid – wouldn't look out of place in an episode of *Grand Designs*. And the Breakfast Slice is a sort of patty that contains, well, just about everything really. Bryan was at the helm. He told me that the arrival of three Tescos and two Asdas had given him plenty of sleepless nights, but he'd risen to the challenge and was now doing 150 products and offering a better service than the big boys. I bought a Dunfy Pie, which I experimented with at the summit of a recently installed public artwork, just across from Bryan's shop. It was hard to decide which structure was more beguiling – the pie or the weird 6ft viewing platform erected with Arts Council funding. It was like someone had started building a staircase (on a patch of green space next to the high street), realised it was going nowhere, and then stopped. The pie was good, though.

The Carnegie Birthplace Museum comprises the seventeenth-century cottage that Andrew arrived and grew up in plus an Edwardian extension that houses a permanent exhibition of artefacts and intel relating to the rags-to-riches boy-done-good. Over the course of an hour, I learnt all about how Dunfermline's most famous son went from being skint and Scottish to unthinkably rich and a tiny bit American. It's some story. Allow me to present a nutshell version.

Born in 1835, Andrew Carnegie was the son of a humble weaver – the heir to a loom, if you will. Though poor, he wasn't uneducated. At eight years old, he started going to a school that had been gifted to Dunfermline by a Scottish philanthropist, and got a general education off his Uncle George, who, among other things, introduced young Andrew to the fundamentals of business. (It is said that when Andrew was asked by his teacher for a quotation from the Bible, he answered that if you took care of the pence, the pounds would take care of themselves.) The Carnegie family were thrown a major curveball when the power loom put a lid on the cottage industry that employed Andrew's father. The family had little choice but to up sticks and move to the US, where young Andrew got a job as a bobbin boy, changing the spools of thread in a cotton mill in Pittsburgh, 72 hours a week for just over a dollar. Andrew's next job was as a messenger boy at a telegraph company. Able to translate morse code by ear, Andrew's amazing proficiency caught the attention of his superiors, and eventually got him a job minding a section of the Pennsylvania railroad. Aged 20, Carnegie was tipped to buy shares in a company that, at the time, was hardly

Dunfermline

more than a boy and a wheelbarrow, but that would go on to become American Express. Over the subsequent decades, he'd continue to make canny acquisitions at opportune moments. He got into steel and coal and oil and iron at just the right time, and struck gold with each. When Carnegie sold his steel empire to JP Morgan for $400 million in 1901 (equivalent to $6.5 billion in today's money), he became the richest man in the world. Did he put his feet up at this point and bask in his riches? No chance. Believing that a man who dies rich dies disgraced, Carnegie set about giving away every penny he had – a course of behaviour that still gives his descendants nightmares.

I stepped out of the museum and returned to Dunfermline's Historic Quarter, which is by no means a misnomer. Dunfy was the HQ of Scotland for hundreds of years up until 1437. It was King Malcolm III that established Dunfermline as the capital, when he started working from home in the town about a thousand years ago. Malcolm III was married to an Anglo-Hungarian called Margaret. Born in Hungary, Maragret was the daughter of Edward the Exile – an Englishman abroad. When Margaret was twelve, the family decided to leave Hungary and chance their arm back in England. They got back to Blighty just in time for the Norman invasion of 1066, which was less than ideal. Fearing for their health, the family legged it to Northumbria, meaning to cut their losses and catch a ship to Europe – Mykonos or Ibiza or Sardinia, somewhere nice. In the event they got shipwrecked in Scotland, and then taken under the wing of Malcolm III. Little is known of what Margaret made of Dunfermline, or made of Malcolm, for that matter, but let's assume she didn't mind either. Margaret died just shy of her fiftieth birthday, a few days after her husband and son had perished in battle. She had a fairly busy afterlife. She was enshrined in the local abbey, canonised for being a generally good egg, and then had her head removed and delivered to Mary Queen of Scots, to help the latter give birth. (No comment.) Margaret's head then somehow found its way to France, where it was lost during the Revolution, hardly a surprise given what was going on at the time. If a head was ever going to go missing, it was then and there.

I was staring up at the aforementioned abbey now. Margaret wasn't alone in being laid to rest here – between 1093 and 1420 eighteen royals were buried on the site. Evidently, this was *the* place to be seen dead. Stylistically, the abbey has a split personality – beautifully so – on account of the changing fashions and various extensions. As it stands, the abbey is a pleasant confusion of modes – fifty shades of church if you will. Next door to the abbey are the remains of a palace. It was here, in 1295, that pen was put to paper on the Auld Alliance – a deal that saw Scotland buddy up with France against England. Interestingly, the alliance has never been officially squashed or revoked, which bodes ill for contemporary England, which could, at any moment, be the subject of a pincer operation featuring Ally McCoist and Marine Le Pen.

King Charles I was born in Dunfermline Palace, and so was his older sister, Princess Elizabeth, without whom we wouldn't have our current Harry and Wills, for it was Princess Elizabeth's grandson – a German called George – that got the England job when no other royal Protestants could be located, and it was this George that gave us all the subsequent Georges, including the father of Queen Elizabeth II. Another royal Charlie was in Dunfermline recently, for the record. Charles III came up to officially turn the town into a city. From the footage I've seen, the monarch got a better reception than the leader of the Scottish National Party. Following the King's visit, there was a nice piece in *The Times* about the city. It was a positive article – gave Dunfy some love – but interestingly, and perhaps revealingly, six of the seven photos used to illustrate the piece (stock shots from the shared media store cupboard) were of other places, which is a bit like illustrating an article about cheese with pictures of ham.

I was due some refreshment and found some at Abbot's House, which is a peach of a building in more senses than one. It is one of the few survivors of the great fire of 1624, when three quarters of Dunfermline got burnt to the ground. A café called Prost is housed within. I ordered some lunch and then headed out to the garden. There had been frost that morning, and snow was in the offing, but it was nonetheless sufficiently warm to sit outside – in view of the abbey and surrounded by flowers. My sandwich – turkey with Swiss cheese and spicy mayo – did not fit the genius loci, but so be it. One isn't obligated to eat haggis at every waking moment. When in Rome, do as the Romans – and here the Romans eat turkey and Swiss cheese.

To pass the time, a nearby three-year-old was collecting stones in a poo bag, and then making little towers of them, cairns if you will, while wearing a jumper that said: VISUALISE THE LIFE YOU WISH TO LIVE. When I tried to do as the jumper demanded, the attempt precipitated a minor existential crisis that forced me to abandon my sandwich. When it was time to go and see grandma, the child asked if she could take a flower with her. The mum said that she could. The child wanted a rather humdrum thing. The mum suggested something nicer, a tulip perhaps, but the child's untrained urge – yet to be taught what's winning and worthy – held firm.

When they left, and I was alone, and the waiter had been out to check I was alright and if I wanted another (I did as it happened), and a family had passed by in the throes of an in-joke, and I'd overheard a bloke, tattooed to the hilt, chatting softly on the blower about a cousin who'd gone AWOL, I had a bit of a feeling, if I'm honest. It went a bit like this.

254   SHITTY BREAKS

When you go around a country, and you don't have the telly on, or the radio on, or the apps pinging away, and you just attend and regard and sense and appreciate what's immediately about you at any given moment, and when, with time, those given moments have totted up to hours and days and weeks of sensing and attending, and you come away from it all with a distinct and deep impression that the country you've been travelling in is overwhelmingly warm and kind and tolerant – well, it's nice, a nice thing to feel, a nice impression to form, notwithstanding the fact that every place has its drawbacks and dipsticks, as sure as eggs is eggs. It's a shame, perhaps, that the drawbacks and dipsticks can so dominate the common sense of a place – be that England, be that Britain, be that wherever. We shouldn't let them. Bad news must be given its due – but no more. Right now it's given its due and then some, at the expense of everything else just about. We must find, I feel, more time and space to tell and share better stories about ourselves. Why, if there was a focus on the positive, it could just plant some ideas, or sow some seeds, or have a knock-on effect, or, failing that, simply provide a bit of reassurance that, beyond and above and beneath and beside all the sound and the fury, the world is overwhelmingly comprised of decent people just doing what they can and while they can do it.

It was time to unload. Time to get to the hotel. Abbot Street, New Row, East Port – each lined with longstanding classics, cut from old silver sandstone. I passed a vegan restaurant, a Masonic lodge, a notorious late-night music venue called PJ's – and the obligatory closed-down Debenhams. The Alhambra Theatre made me look twice. It has a memorable face. You can't miss it – it's made-up with neon. It's been around for a hundred years, and has worn several hats in that time. It was a cinema for a stretch, then a bingo hall for forty years, at which point it was tragically repurposed – back into a theatre. It's putting on some decent stuff – and John Bishop.

Nearing the hotel, I lost my way. I asked for directions and got escorted instead. I repaid the man's kindness with some top-drawer small talk. He used to work on the oil rigs. Retired now. Nothing to do, all day to do it in.

'My cousin was a writer. You might have heard of him. Iain Banks.'

'*Wasp Factory?*'

'That's the one.'

'Loved that book. How's he doing?'

Iain Banks was born in Dunfy, to an ice skater and an officer. He spent his childhood writing novels, which gives an idea of how much there was going on in the area back in the sixties. *The Wasp Factory* was a breakthrough hit in 1984. Banks wrote twenty-odd novels all up, and even won *Celebrity Mastermind*. His specialist subject was malt whisky and the distilleries of Scotland. His final novel, *The Quarry*, was published the month of his death.

'Ah. Shit. Sorry. Didn't know that.'

'Nae bother.'

Bob explained how, back in 2013, Iain had been diagnosed with liver cancer and given months to live. 'We were in Venice. Three weeks before he died. We had a meal in St Mark's Square. Iain ordered the liver for his main course. We had to laugh.' He pulled out a newspaper clipping from his wallet, notice of an upcoming exhibition in Stirling based on Iain's work. It was touching to know that Bob still collected any mention of Iain – a proud cousin. Bob delivered me to the hotel. To the front door just about. 'I got married here,' he said, a touch ruefully. 'Where does it go, eh?' He wished me luck, then went on his way. It was a brief encounter to cherish, and one that wouldn't have happened had I known where I was going.

Garvock House Hotel is a standalone Victorian job. The solemnity of its grey exterior is undone by its lush wraparound garden and a fluttering Saltire. There was a giant deckchair in the front garden. I sat in it for a while and admired a beautiful acer tree, which took me back to the one in my old landlady's garden. She quizzed me about trees one day, and got upset when I didn't know what a conifer was called. I said there weren't any trees in my garden growing up. She replied that there weren't any Egyptians in hers but she still managed to learn a thing or two about them. Ah, Winnie. I do hope you're resting in peace. (Rather than running around heaven trying to keep everything in order.) A couple called Barbara and Nick joined me in the deck chair. I asked what they were up to and they said they were visiting Edinburgh. When I gave them a confused look, they explained that they were staying in Dunfermline because Edinburgh was too expensive. When I said (with tongue in cheek) that they were barking up the wrong tree, and gave them a low-down on the local history, they looked at me as though I was making it all up.

I was checked in by Pamela Fernandes, who, with her Portuguese husband, had opened the hotel thirty years ago. She agreed that Edinburgh was pricing people out, which wasn't bad news for her necessarily, though she'd prefer it if the people coming her way were coming her way to have a butcher's at Dunfy, rather than to nip back to well-trodden Edinburgh. City status was turning the dial for Dunfermline, Pamela reckoned, as she led me through to the dining room. You just wait and see, she warned, simultaneously setting down a breadbasket and cor-recting a tablecloth.

I'm getting better at eating alone in hotel dining rooms, but still can't claim to be nailing it. I fiddle with cutlery, poke the bread roll, look at the wall again – that sort of thing. It's always a bit of a relief when the food arrives. My haggis bonbons came decorated with a Drambuie reduction (naturally), and weren't bad at all. One thing I like about haggis is that it tastes how it sounds somehow. A bit fierce, a bit moody, a bit intense, like a rebuke or a swear-word, but ultimately satisfying. I'd happily make it a regular thing. Irn-Bru on the other hand, which I paired with my bonbons, can stay in Scotland. Bubble-gum nonsense, disguised as something fiery and Gaelic. Snake oil, basically. Rui Fernandes brought me some literature to consider as I waited for my cheese – the favourite recipes of a group of ex-Dunfermline football players, Sir Alex Ferguson among them. I was amused to discover that Fergie was proposing seabass alongside fettuccine and ratatouille, which sounded like a plausible midfield.

It was a fine Saturday morning. I set off for Pittencrief Park, or The Glen as the locals call it. I entered through the Nether Vett (or south gate). It was enchanting at once. A bending path amid thick vegetation. A babbling brook – auld and lang. A waterfall. A witch's grotto. Bits of the ruined palace visible through the trees. It had a fairytale quality – romantic, I guess. Having the quality or feel of a *story*. Also apparent from the park was the tower of the abbey. Around its four sides, the name of King Robert the Bruce was spelt out, each letter a chip off the old block. Robert is buried in the abbey – not a bad outcome for an Essex boy with Norman roots. Robert de Brus was a sixth-generation immigrant, albeit one with posh lineage and a claim to the Scottish throne. When Bob became monarch, in 1306, the job description was essentially to get England to piss off and leave Scotland alone. This Robert did, though not without fuss and bother. There were lots of early losses and setbacks – recall that incident in a cave or barn when Robert, on the run after an unsuccessful bout of argy-bargy with the English, watched a spider struggling its arse off and instead of helping the spider got up and went home with renewed determination to win Scotland's freedom, the selfish git. Got his reward at the Battle of Bannockburn in 1314 – when he absolutely thrashed the English. No mention of that spider when speaking to the press after.

I'd arrived just in time for the start of Parkrun, which takes place (against all good sense) all over the world at 9am every Saturday. It was quite the sight: a swarm of joggers, up to their ears in skin-tight clobber, pink and lime and turquoise, with a few dogs getting in the way, unnerved by the carry-on, the sound of a hundred soles bounding by. Half a dozen were pegging it, a hundred were puffing along at a decent lick, and the rest were clearly just here for the cappuccino afterwards. I chatted to one of the volunteers who help facilitate the run. She said it was the best way to start a weekend. I was tempted to argue back, and propose a number of alternatives, but didn't want to rain on her parade.

I sought out the peacocks. The volunteer had recommended them. Had said they roam around the park, giving it all that, flashing their tail feathers at anything with a pulse. Had said the peacocks had even been awarded the Freedom of the City, and that one takes it a bit far – up to the high street in fact, where it stands outside the bakery looking like butter wouldn't melt in its mouth. (So I wasn't imagining it!) I found the aviary, and there watched Louis unfurl his seductive display feathers, turning himself into a giant fan, one part peacock, four parts chat-up line. As gestures go, it's right up there. I'd take the bait. If I was a peahen, I mean. I asked one of the people looking after the peacocks why Louis wasn't out and about with the others. Her answer was a sad story. Louis doesn't roam anymore because he was recently

Dunfermline

traumatised. He got attacked by two kids (who need to find better ways to amuse themselves, and sharpish). The kids all but left Louis for dead, and now it's a case of once bitten twice shy. Poor thing, stuck in the aviary while his mates, innocent of violence, unschooled in the crap that some people are capable of, happily bowled about town. I started having second thoughts about that thought I'd had about travelling up and down the country and not seeing anything cruel or out of line.

Near the aviary, I spotted a little kid all upset and with his head in his hands. What now? I thought. After that feelgood outburst a few pages ago, all I was getting was dipsticks and distress. I was getting taught a lesson: that the world is full of woe and nastiness and don't you think otherwise. Nope, hang on, the kid was actually counting down from fifty. (He found his mate behind a wheelie bin, for the record.)

I moved on to the Peace Pole, which has pride of place in the middle of the glen. It was quite an aggressive looking pole given what it stands for. If you wanted to impale a unicorn, this is what you'd do it with. It was planted to remember the visit of the Dalai Lama, said another Parkrun volunteer.

'I met him,' she said.

'Who?'

'The Dalai Lama.'

'And how was he?'

'He was alright.'

The volunteer told me that the park was voted the best in Scotland. I could believe it. This all used to be private land, explained the volunteer, until Andrew Carnegie bought it for the people in the early 1900s. Speaking of the devil, here he was now, the man himself, up on his pedestal, looking tough and gifted and not a little bit pleased with himself. It made a lovely picture, with the surrounding cherry trees and the city's towers and spires beyond. When I got a little closer the view wasn't so fetching. All the money in the world and you still can't stop the pigeons crapping on your head.

Café Wynd is a decent place. Nordic vibes, succulent pots, affogato on the menu, a daily soup and bread for a fiver, a sandwich called The Belter – it was right up my cup of tea. I was taken by a painting by an eight-year-old called Katherine, which had a charmingly apocalyptic quality, and then by a poster in the toilet that displayed the '50 Shades of Scotland', from fudge and kipper and ginger and heather, to drizzle and whisky and Irn-Bru and oatcake. Just when I thought it might be time to actually order something, rather than perv on the décor, Dr Who entered the building – albeit under the arm of a customer, and on the cover of *Radio Times*. (The new Dr Who – Ncuti Gatwa – grew up in Dunfermline, after his parents fled the civil war in Rwanda.) I ordered the chilli and coconut hot chocolate, drank it outside weighing up the Saturday action. It was busy enough in town, all things considered. It wouldn't take much of an injection for the place to be pretty damn lively, in fact – just a fraction of the visitors that its illustrious neighbour is getting would do the job. As it stands, Dunfermline is punching below its weight. It's got more history per square foot than it knows what to do with; it's compact and good-looking; and it's bordered by a range of off-kilter diversions, such as motor racing, waterskiing and, as we shall imminently see, hovercrafting.

I took a taxi out to Craigluscar Farm, a couple of miles northwest of the centre, where I was met by John and Graham, who have been up here working this land since *auld lang syne*. Only now they also do clay pigeon shooting and archery and hovercrafting and mini Highland Games for stag parties based in Edinburgh. Not being a member of such a party, I had to watch from the sidelines, like a weird loner who really wants some mates. The stag party spotted me staring, and instead of calling me out on my nosey behaviour, invited me to join them. It was fun. We tossed a mini caber. We threw a haggis at a bottle of whisky. We a launched a welly. In short, we did all the stuff that made the Highland lifestyle the envy of the world. They were a nice bunch of lads, really friendly given the circumstances – i.e. that I might well have been a weirdo and most of them were alarmingly hungover. The stag was Callum. I asked what he was hoping for from marriage. 'Don't mind,' he said, which I felt was a refreshingly honest answer.

When the stag party had had its fun, it was time for me to have a go on an F2 hovercraft, which had the look of a bathtub that had bred with a hairdryer. John revved one up and then gave me a demo, zigzagging up and down a well-groomed field as if it were as easy as buttering toast. It looked like he was mowing the lawn in a massive hurry. I was issued some earplugs, a helmet, and a fair bit of advice. Stay on your knees, lean into corners, steer before you need to turn, don't fall out, accelerate *into* the corner, and so on. Rehearsing the information, I kept on getting things muddled – turn into your knees, steer before you lean, accelerate as you fall out … In the event, hovercrafting was no easier than it looked. It was tricky and awkward but exhilarating nonetheless. It was also *knackering*. I was only behind the wheel for fifteen minutes, but it felt like I'd done an hour's circuit training. I'm not used to being on my knees or leaning, to say nothing of doing both while hovering above the earth. It took it out of me. When my thighs started wobbling, and then my whole lower body got the shakes, I knew it was time to pull into the pits. The six-lap record for the circuit John has laid out is two minutes and ten seconds. It took me a quarter of an hour.

I had planned to walk back into town, but my thighs were still wobbling and John kindly offered to give me a lift. He dropped me at Jack 'O' Bryan's, a reputable restaurant next to the strapping main gates of the Glen. Titular Jack is one of the top 30 chefs under 30, according to someone. It's a novel eatery, with one leg in Scotland and the other in South America, which is no mean feat. All the food was good but the best was saved to last. For pudding, I splurged on four homemade chocolates. (Jack is a chocolatier first and foremost – and you can tell.) The chocs came in a wooden box, were served on a bed of chocolate nibs, and were a rum quartet flavour-wise: pornstar martini, cherry cognac, apple pie, and peanut butter and jelly – certainly the most unusual and good-looking foursome I've ever seen on a bed. In the end, the apple pie choccy was the winner. Its case tasted like Caramac, the vintage caramel-flavoured chocolate bar that was discontinued in 2023, while the filling was a small bomb of sweet and salty apple. In short, it was lush. I tried to keep it in my mouth as long as possible – which drew some looks.

Ah, that post-dinner feeling. Deep breath, bit of a stretch, and then a carefree, unhurried wander. The downhill views to the lights of the Alhambra. The elegant peaks of the new bridge over the Forth. The dark, mountainous clouds. The sight of the city's tower silhouetted against the night-blue sky, its clock face blank and moon-like. I tarried a while by the mercat (market) cross. It was here, back in the days before web, press and gram, that you came to proclaim and announce and brag and gossip. Bring the tradition back, I say. Imagine if every tweet or update or post or story or brain-fart issued on social media had to be bellowed from this cross. That would nip a lot of accounts in the bud. Including my own.

I resisted the temptation to head back to the gaff and watch *Outlander* from start to finish, and instead headed up to the old fire station, which is now a multipurpose arts hub, with a bar and a café and a dozen studios upstairs, as well as a regular calendar of gigs and talks and shindigs and so on. I was lucky enough to chat with the founding director, Ian. Over a brew, Ian told me how he got a band of creatives together, mooted the old fire station as a potential HQ, then ran into a council-shaped barricade. He persisted and persisted and finally secured the investment that allowed the project to get up and running. It's been ten years now, and in that time Fire Station Creative has grown into a respected arts venue, both locally and nationally. They run Soul and Motown nights twice a month, which sell out within hours, and there's live music every weekend. They also do film screenings, exhibitions, workshops. Ian gets no funding; his income comes from the café and the studios upstairs, which he rents out to potters and painters, sculptors and snappers, who, when no one's looking, slide down the pole when they fancy a cuppa. One of the studios is rented by an initiative called Falling Up – a father and son duo who take people who are struggling in some way and introduce them to the world of art (to make matters worse, presumably). Before I left him to it, I asked Ian about that weird viewing platform cum artwork at the top of which I'd eaten that peculiar pie. Ian shook his head, still coming to terms with the thing. According to Ian, the council got a chunk of cash from Tesco when the company planted a supermarket the size of Falkirk at the top of town – about £100,000. Following some eye-bogglingly expensive consultation with a firm from Brighton about how to best spend the money, it was decided that an artist from Glasgow should be invited to install some steps at considerable expense, the better to see the roof tiles of Bryan's shop. Ah, the world.

I hadn't come to chew the fat with Ian. I'd come to see (and hear) an illustrious artist. Sandy Moffat has been a major influence. Not on me, but on Scottish painting. He helped to lead a revival of Scottish folk culture – poetry, music, old stories – and also to launch what became the Edinburgh Fringe. All the while, Sandy was painting portraits of key people in the Scottish folk scene – Hugh MacDiarmid and Hamish Henderson not the least of them. One of his paintings, *Poets' Pub*, hangs in the Scottish National Portrait Gallery.

Sandy was at FSC that evening to present a series of films about his work that had been made over the years. In the first of those programmes, made for the BBC, Sandy is shown painting his mate, a poet. That's about it. That's the extent of it. And yet the film was oddly mesmerising. During the short question-and-answer session that followed, someone asked if Sandy was still at it. 'All the time,' he answered. 'I go down to the studio first thing in the morning, never meaning to paint, and now I've got all these pyjama bottoms splattered with paint.' Nice. Someone else asked about Sandy's preferred working environment. It's a question often asked of artists, I've noticed, as though what radio station they listen to or tea they drink were more important and fascinating than the particulars of the work they produce. Anyway, Sandy Moffat agrees with Cézanne – no interruptions! 'I pray that the phone won't ring,' said Sandy. And here's me praying that it will.

That's what distinguishes true artists, I feel; what separates them from the pretenders. Their work is never a chore. They have no wish to be elsewhere. But maybe it's easier for a painter to be 'in the zone' than a writer … I raised my hand, a question having come to me. The hand was noted. 'Sandy,' I said, 'Can you imagine a sort of interactive canvas that, at the dab of a brush, could open a little window to somewhere else entirely, revealing football scores and email accounts and whatnot? And do you think that, if such a canvas became mainstream, the painter would be down in the bog with the rest of us, always distracted and never in the zone?' Sandy gave a small laugh, which told me that he could indeed imagine such a canvas, and could also imagine coping just fine in the face of it.

Given Dunfermline's royal connections, I went next to The Monarch, an unassuming backstreet pub with an upstairs function room. The function tonight? A self-styled post-punk two-piece called Model Worker. The lead singer, a lad called Lewis, a mid-twenties union rep, put in one hell of a shift. Must have burnt a thousand calories. Shirt off, up on the tables – an egalitarian display, giving us all a turn in the front row. I liked the music. It was sort of unignorable. Sort of unwilling to negotiate – take it or leave it. I was getting The Cure vibes, and The Sex Pistols when they were in a good mood. After the set, I got chatting with a bloke who moved to Dunfermline from Miami about six years ago. Must be the only person in human history to have made such a decision and stuck with it. 'I love it here,' he said. 'Apart from the weather which sucks. But you know what? It makes me appreciate the sun more. I've got a better relationship with good weather now, and that's all down to Dunfermline.' He told me about the city's musical heritage – Big Country, Barbara Dickson, Nazareth – and said that the front man of Big Country, Stuart Adamson, was the true King of Dunfermline and worth looking into. Then he introduced me to a guy called Billy. Full of beans was Billy. Ran an annual gig at PJ's down the road, to remember his mate Leroy whose heart gave out 29 years ago. Billy reckoned that city status had been good for Dunfermline, because now the place was expecting more of itself. But Dunfermline folk would never be full of themselves – 'We're all Tam's bairns, around here,' he said, meaning (I think) that we're all the same in the end, that we're all just passing through.

On my way out, I ran into the post-punk frontman, young Lewis, who was sat behind a table selling merch. Sound lad. Sold me a t-shirt that was never going to fit in a million years.

'It symbolises your support,' he said. 'Symbols should fit,' I said. I asked Lewis what his perfect day in Dunfermline would look like.

'My perfect day?'

'Yeah.'

'A walk in the park, a bike ride to Alloa, a pint at The Commercial, a gig at PJ's, and then a spicy haggis supper from Sauro's in Abbeyview.'

'A spicy what?'

'A spicy haggis supper. It's legendary Brown sauce and vinegar. You'll be wanting to take one back in your suitcase.'

Back at the hotel, I looked into a couple of the musicians mentioned by the guy from Miami. I started with Barbara Dickson. A local lass, up there with Scotland's bestselling musical artists. Had a hit in 1980 with 'January, February'. I don't imagine it was easy getting a hit out of a song with a chorus that went 'January, February, I don't understand', but she managed it. The music video is great, by the way. In it, Barbara, wearing a white suit and black bowtie, basically walks her massive hair around an abandoned Italian restaurant for five minutes, all the while struggling to understand the start of the year. Stuart Adamson, meanwhile, was a different kettle of fish. The driving force behind Skids in the first instance and Big Country in the second, Adamson was once described by the great John Peel as the 'new Jimi Hendrix', while Edge from U2 reckoned Adamson wrote the songs U2 wanted to but couldn't – which is to say good ones, I suppose. 'In a Big Country' was a massive hit on both sides of the Atlantic. The song contains the lyric: 'I'm not expecting to grow flowers in the desert. But I can live and breathe and see the sun in wintertime.' That's lovely. I can drink to that.

Adamson struggled with success, I was sad to learn, and the pressure that came with it, finding solace in familiar places. In his early forties, he moved to the US, started drinking again after a decade off the sauce, checked into a Best Western in Hawaii, and then hung himself. He was cremated in Dunfermline. There's a commemorative bench in Pittencrieff Park. I think I saw it. But it meant nothing at the time. I would have taken a pew, and paid my dues, if only I'd known.

There were a couple more things I wanted to do before it was time to sling my hook. The first of them was the library on Abbot Street, which was the first of the 3,000 that Andrew Carnegie would ultimately bankroll. The building is getting stronger as it ages: the initial sandstone element having been wedded to a fancy new extension. I headed to the latter, which houses, over two floors, a rum collection of odds and ends pertaining to the city and its story. There was a car with three wheels, reputedly the only vehicle ever produced in Dunfermline. There was a wedding dress cut from the same cloth as the late Queen's. There was a film about Nazareth and Barbara Dickson and Skids and so on. There were oral accounts of what it was like to work down a coal mine. And – a touch inexplicably – an example of a typical nineties kitchen.

 I went across to the art gallery, which is in the original library building. The paintings were a varied and diverting bunch, including one of a scaffolder, another of some blokes playing dominoes in the pub, and another still of a single, graceful wave. There was also a Lowry painting – one of only two or three in Scottish hands, and a happy reminder of Sunderland, where my journey began. The painting was called *An Old Street*. It was another example of the artist looking where others didn't, and celebrating what others weren't, and seeing what others couldn't. I started with Lowry and I'm tempted to finish with him – on that note of seeing beauty and brilliance and depth and significance in all sorts of places – but had made up my mind to try this bloody haggis supper that was meant to be legendary.

I went past Nether Vett and Andrew's humble cottage, and then up Hospital Hill, pausing at a tennis and bridge club to watch a fella double fault and then have the temerity to blame the ball. (You can't say the Scottish don't have a good sense of humour. Bono did a gig in Glasgow once. He made the crowd go silent, then began slowly clapping his hands above his head. 'Every time I clap my hands,' he said emotionally, 'a child in Africa dies.' A woman in the front row shouted back: 'Then stop doing it, ya evil bastard!') I went past The Olive Tree restaurant, which is also the Scottish headquarters of Zoroastrianism, and then Beyond Val-U-Blinds, whose wilful misspelling I shall never understand. I picked up Aberdour Road, and then moved onto Tay Terrace and into Abbeyview, where I found the chippy without fuss, its tricolour front revealing Italian roots. While in line, I sized up what they were frying – which was anything, by the look of it. A handwritten note, on a fluorescent cardboard star, said that I could bring anything I wanted and get it battered for 20p. The girl behind the fryer said she experiments all the time, with M&Ms and biscuits and tomatoes and cabbage. 'It's trial and error,' she said philosophically (and no doubt honestly). I did what I came here to do – ordered the spicy haggis supper, the chip shop's bestseller by far. When it appeared, I added brown sauce and vinegar, as per the received wisdom. It looked a monstrosity, if I'm frank. I asked the girl where she'd go to eat such a meal. She whipped a phone out of her pinny and showed me her favourite spot on the map. It was a bench by a duck pond, about two miles away.

With my supper under my arm and my hands in my pockets, I walked out of Abbeyview in the direction of the pond. I picked up a main road, cut through Dunfermline's Eastern Expansion Area, passed the crematorium, skirted a suburb called Touch, and went over a number of roundabouts – all in search of a pond. To tell the truth, it was my kind of assignment, my kind of travel – i.e. the type unlikely to be endorsed in a travel section or guidebook, and with good reason, no doubt. I reflected on the strange genealogy that had brought me here. A butcher suggested a pub which yielded a punk who said a chippy, where I was told to walk out of town to a bench by a duck pond because the view of the bridges at dusk was a belter. Now that's an algorithm.

As I walked unreasonably away from the centre, away from the railway station where I was due in two hours, I thought of the things that made me like Dunfermline. Here's a selection in no particular order. Learning that Robert the Bruce was actually an Essex Boy. The deep, ubiquitous views of the Forth and its bridges, which add a touch of romance and drama to most corners of the city. The tall grey spire of the old linen exchange (a middle finger to the surrounding area), and the barman at The Yeoman who dealt with someone needing the loo as though they were a long lost pal. That apple pie chocolate. That topless union rep. That brief encounter with Robert Banks, cousin of Iain. That beautiful park, that staggering philanthropist, that *amount of history*. And tipping the balance in the other direction? Learning that the Dalai Lama was only alright was a bit of a blow, if I'm honest, and a place called The Creepy Wee Pub was a bit too creepy for my liking. Other than that? Nah. I've got nothing.

Now, who was it that said that it's better to travel hopefully than it is to arrive? Stevenson? Defoe? In any case, the sentiment suddenly felt appropriate when I found the pond and unclothed my supper and discovered that the scran was average and the view no better than the ones you can get in town. But I was happy nonetheless. Because I got here, because I went, because going is the main thing in the end. At that moment – give or take a few seconds – a cloud formed above the twinkly bridge in the distance that resembled, if looked at in a certain way, a ginormous peacock. (Looked at another way the cloud resembled Russia, but we won't dwell on that.) I thought briefly of Louis in the park, and then less briefly of Louis MacNeice, and those lines of his about life being various and heady and incorrigible and thick. And because this was a journey about the gentle complexity and somewhat loveliness of anything and anywhere, that felt, and feels still, like a half-decent note to finish on.

But I didn't want a note that was half-decent. I wanted a note that was decent, or three-quarters so. And so I finished the haggis and walked on towards the bridge, thinking I'd just carry on to Edinburgh on foot, where I'd be able to intercept my train. I came to the middle of the three bridges: rail to my left, road to my right, and this one for bikes and buses and pedestrians. It opened sixty years ago, is about a mile long, and was first traversed by the Queen. I leant over the edge and peered down on North Queensferry. It looked like a toy village, with its muddy bay and its horseshoe of pubs and houses. Tiny binmen were doing their rounds, with the rail bridge beyond, a line of crimson dinosaurs, sloping off to Edinburgh. It was beautiful. The ensemble, I mean. All of those things together. It was the scale and the colours and the mix of modesty and grandeur, all happening at once, so unexpected, so unintended. It was perhaps the most beautiful thing I'd seen on my journey. There were workers beneath me, down on a lower rung, keeping the bridge crossable in highly visible tunics. I didn't see them at first. I was too on top of them to notice. You need the right amount of distance to see something, I fancy. The right amount of space.

Ways of going surrounded me – train, boat, bike, plane, foot. To be able to go anywhere freely is a privilege. It is a privilege that affords all manner of things – quiet education, gentle edification, accidental perspective, useful humiliation, steady wonderment, and regular reminders that people are good, and that places are too, even the ones that rest in the shadows. A sperm whale came this way once. Swam upstream under the bridges. Was severely off-track and paid the highest price. Poor Moby should have stuck to the North Sea rather than following his nose. I guess it doesn't always pay to go in the wrong direction.

Halfway across the bridge, I was tempted to take the opportunity to reflect on my journey, and perhaps plate up an overview, something about value and quality and decency turning up where you least expect them, but I really couldn't be arsed, so instead just peered down at the river until a common seagull, well positioned up in the rafters, made a deposit on my shoulder. A man on a bike with heavy panniers pulled over.

'That was unfortunate,' he said.

'I thought it was meant to be lucky?'

'Nonsense. That's just putting a positive spin on crap.'

'Where you off to?'

'Anywhere.'

'Seriously?'

'Yeah. It's the best place to go. Why are you laughing?'

'I was just thinking something similar, that's all.'

'Well, keep it to yourself,' he said with a wink. 'We don't want everyone going anywhere.'

I'm not going to stand here (sit here?) and say that you absolutely must drop all your plans and dash to Dunfermline at once. Instead, what I'm going to do is humbly encourage you to consider including the city in any future plans you may have that involve Edinburgh. I'm also, for that matter, going to encourage you to consider adding Sunderland to a Newcastle trip, Bradford to a weekend in Leeds, Wolverhampton to a break in Birmingham, Preston to a session in Manchester, and so on. Dunfermline and Sunderland and Preston etc. are no better or worse than their more illustrious neighbours, but they are different and other and inescapably unique and utterly deserving of more love and attention than they're currently getting. It's also worth adding that there's a dividend to be enjoyed in defying the norm and giving the underdog a chance. It will be cheaper, for a start, and everything will come as a surprise (because you won't have seen it plastered all over the mediascape), and you'll be doing something modest to spread the love and give over-touristed spots some breathing space. It would be, if only slightly, a more sustainable and democratic type of travel. That may sound a bit fluffy and high-minded, but I don't care, because it happens to be true – or somewhat true (as far as I can tell). What's more – and this, of course, is of utmost importance – *you'll have a good time*. In the places above. And if you don't, by all means get in touch and I'll make it up to you. I'll bake you a stottie, or a pink slice, or some Gibraltar Pudding. That's my covenant. In the event of you having a genuinely and indisputably shit city break – in Wrexham or Newry or Preston or Chelmsford – get in touch and I'll send you a Dunfy Pie, or some jellied eels, or some loose-leaf Limerick tea, or some orange chips, or a framed picture of Ryan Reynolds – something to remind you of the place you didn't enjoy, by way of apology.

It won't be Venice. It won't be New York. It won't be a City of Dreams. It won't be a nirvana or Eden or paradise. It won't be unblemished or spotless or beyond reproach – and it will be more interesting for not being those things. The Japanese think vases are more beautiful after they've been smashed and glued back together again. Leonard Cohen says the crack is how the light gets in. John Legend reckons imperfections can make something more perfect (which sounds conceptually impossible but still). I know that I'm looking at the glass and calling it half full, and I know that the glass I'm calling half full is rose-tinted too, but I'm glad and unapologetic about the fact. You don't need me to tell you the world isn't ideal, that people aren't perfect, that places fall short and falter and so on, because thousands of others are telling you that. That's old – and daily – news. I could be called a clown a hundred times – by people back from Bradford feeling cheated, or back from Newport feeling conned – and I'd still hold fast to the conviction that *anywhere* – like anyone – can be interesting and nourishing and enjoyable if approached in the right fashion. (With the exception of Reading, which, I'm sorry, just can't.)

I'd like to end on the title. Were the trips I went on shitty breaks? No chance. There's no such thing. Not in my book anyway.

Acknowledgements

For their support and advice and company and assistance, I would like to thank the following people. Ellen Conlon, Ed Wilson, Connor Stait, Steve Burdett, Elle-Jay Christodoulou, Amelia Kemmer, Matt Boxell, Nick Hayward, Steven Tucker, Glenda Young, Iain Rowan, Susannah Aynsley, Raimy Greenland, Joel Jackson, Ian Fegan, Tom Hicks, Mohammed and Sitab Kahn, Tom Marlow, Penny and Frannie, Patricia Roberts, Etta Austin, Eleanor Purcell, Mary Kelly, Emma Foote, Ken Abraham, Cathal Fegan, Pól Ó Conghaile, Ger Lawlor, Sinead, Sophie Neal, Carys Underwood, Rosie Burke, Thomas Cheetham, Leah Snelus, Lisa Brankin, everyone at YMCA Milton Keynes, Lee Farran, Jane Harris, Paul Williams, Donald Mackenzie, Gillian McCracken, Pamela and Rui Fernandes, John Graham, Lewis Akers, and Ian Moir.